STRATEGIC STUDIES INSTITUTE

The Strategic Studies Institute (SSI) is part of the U.S. Army War College and is the strategic-level study agent for issues related to national security and military strategy with emphasis on geostrategic analysis.

The mission of SSI is to use independent analysis to conduct strategic studies that develop policy recommendations on:

- Strategy, planning, and policy for joint and combined employment of military forces;

- Regional strategic appraisals;

- The nature of land warfare;

- Matters affecting the Army's future;

- The concepts, philosophy, and theory of strategy; and,

- Other issues of importance to the leadership of the Army.

Studies produced by civilian and military analysts concern topics having strategic implications for the Army, the Department of Defense, and the larger national security community.

In addition to its studies, SSI publishes special reports on topics of special or immediate interest. These include edited proceedings of conferences and topically oriented roundtables, expanded trip reports, and quick-reaction responses to senior Army leaders.

The Institute provides a valuable analytical capability within the Army to address strategic and other issues in support of Army participation in national security policy formulation.

i

Strategic Studies Institute
and
U.S. Army War College Press

STEPPING UP:
BURDEN SHARING BY NATO'S
NEWEST MEMBERS

Joel R. Hillison

November 2014

*****

Comments pertaining to this report are invited and should be forwarded to: Director, Strategic Studies Institute and U.S. Army War College Press, U.S. Army War College, 47 Ashburn Drive, Carlisle, PA 17013-5010.

*****

All Strategic Studies Institute (SSI) and U.S. Army War College (USAWC) Press publications may be downloaded free of charge from the SSI website. Hard copies of this report may also be obtained free of charge while supplies last by placing an order on the SSI website. SSI publications may be quoted or reprinted in part or in full with permission and appropriate credit given to the U.S. Army Strategic Studies Institute and U.S. Army War College Press, U.S. Army War College, Carlisle, PA. Contact SSI by visiting our website at the following address: *www.StrategicStudiesInstitute.army.mil.*

*****

The Strategic Studies Institute and U.S. Army War College Press publishes a monthly email newsletter to update the national security community on the research of our analysts, recent and forthcoming publications, and upcoming conferences sponsored by the Institute. Each newsletter also provides a strategic commentary by one of our research analysts. If you are interested in receiving this newsletter, please subscribe on the SSI website at *www.StrategicStudiesInstitute.army.mil/newsletter.*

*****

There are countless people to whom gratitude is due for the successful completion of this book. I owe a special thanks to Dr. Jamie Shea for his keen insights on NATO and for agreeing to write the forward for this book. I would like to thank everyone at NATO Headquarters and SHAPE for their assistance with my research including Colonels Michael Klingele and Jeff Shivnen; Steve Mirr, Heather Wagner, Caroline Brady, Susan Vranckx, Dorothy Nevins and Dominique Vanmarsnille. I am thankful to the entire Political Science faculty and staff at Temple University.

I especially thank Professors Mark Pollack, Orfeo Fioretos and Kevin Arceneaux. My colleagues at the United States Army War College and National Defense University were also instrumental in the completion of this project. I am especially grateful to Dr. Clayton Chun, Professor Jeffrey Groh, Professor Chris Bolan, Professor Kevin Weddle, and Dr. Sherwood McGinnis. I would also like to thank Colonels Charles Van Bebber, Josef Kopecky, Krzysztof Mitrega, Vasile Roman, and Indrek Sirel, Lieutenant Colonel Dave Barsness and Dr. Antulio Echevarria II. Thanks to the great United States Army War College Library, especially Diane, Kathy, Nancy, and Jeanette. John Wheatley and Laurie Echevarria also provided essential editorial feedback. Last, but not least, my loving wife, Stacie, who died in 2012. Any success I have, I owe to her.

ISBN 1-58487-649-2

CONTENTS

LIST OF FIGURES

Figure

LIST OF TABLES

FOREWORD

Burden sharing is back. Indeed many observers of the North Atlantic Treaty Organization (NATO) Alliance would claim that it never went away. This is because, from its inception in 1949, NATO has never been an alliance of equals. The United States has always made the overwhelmingly larger contribution, not only for the defense of Europe under Article 5 of the NATO Treaty, but also in the numerous operations that the Alliance has carried out beyond Europe since the end of the Cold War. At one stage in the late-1950s, the United States had nearly 400,000 troops and 7,000 nuclear weapons deployed in Western Europe. It also maintained large stocks of pre-positioned equipment and sent thousands of more troops back to Europe every year for reinforcement and exercises. The European allies may well have provided the basing facilities and indeed the battleground for any U.S.-Soviet conflict; but the U.S. willingness to keep one-third of its Army permanently in Europe certainly allowed the Europeans to have their security on the cheap, and to invest massively less in defense than if they had needed to contain the Soviet Union on their own. Naturally, the United States was not happy with this state of affairs and constantly tried to push the Europeans to increase their defense budgets (for instance, in advocating the 3 percent of the gross domestic product [GDP] benchmark) and commit to periodic capability improvement programs. Congress also became involved, notably through the Mansfield Amendments of the 1970s which threatened to withdraw U.S. troops from

Europe if the United States was not adequately compensated through offsets or U.S. equipment purchases or other European burden sharing efforts. As Europe became more prosperous and an economic competitor to the United States, these pressures naturally became more intense.

Yet throughout the Cold War, there were good reasons for the European allies not to take burden sharing too seriously and therefore not to respond to these congressional pressures with any great sense of urgency. The containment of the Soviet Union was a vital U.S. security interest. Fighting in Europe made more sense than moving directly to U.S.-Soviet nuclear exchanges; and the United States recognized that healthy European economies and welfare states were even more important in discrediting and ultimately defeating communism than healthy European defense budgets. As long as the United States needed NATO, as much if not more than the Europeans, it could legitimately complain about European "free riding," but there was not much that it could do about it without endangering its own strategic foothold in Europe. This said, the Europeans, still at this time, spent (by today's standards) considerable sums on defense and maintained less well-equipped but still large territorial armies and reserve forces. They also contributed to international peace and stability in many nonmilitary ways, such as international development aid reconstruction funds, funding for the United Nations (UN) and UN peacekeeping. They tried to argue in Washington that this should also be taken into account in any objective calculation of fair burden sharing. Throughout the Cold War, these arguments and counterarguments dragged on inconclusively, but as long as the Soviet Union stationed 30 divisions in Central and Eastern Europe, not much actually changed on the ground.

Today's burden sharing debate in NATO, by contrast, takes place in a totally different environment and with none of the old certainties. NATO's task since the fall of the Berlin Wall has been as much to fight as to defend. Instead of hunkering down in Europe waiting to be attacked, the Alliance has had to deploy forces in faraway places, such as Afghanistan, Libya, Iraq, the Gulf of Aden, that were never on its radar screen during the Cold War. On the one hand, this has eased the burden sharing debate in some aspects. The Europeans have also shed blood and have largely stayed the course in operations such as International Security Assistance Force (ISAF) in Afghanistan and Kosovo Forces (KFOR) that have gone on longer than World Wars I and II combined. They may have been only able to sustain small contingents in the field, but after prolonged combat experience in Afghanistan, these forces are arguably more battle-hardened, better equipped, versatile, and therefore more useful to the United States than the larger but mainly static European armies of just 2 decades ago. Indeed one of NATO's key challenges after Afghanistan will be to preserve the connectivity, interoperability, and battle readiness that it has so painfully acquired during ISAF.

Moreover, many European contributions to Afghanistan have been made more out of a sense of loyalty and duty to the United States than because the European countries in question perceive an imminent threat to their security from this region. At the same time, the Europeans have been more prepared to take the lead, whether collectively as Europeans, individually, or under the auspices of the European Union (EU) Common Security and Defence Policy. They were the first into the Balkans in the 1990s and, more recently, into Libya and Mali. They are also operating the largest anti-piracy mission in the Gulf of Aden. Admittedly, these missions have needed U.S. back up, especially in air transport, in-flight refuelling, and intelligence, surveillance, and target acquisition capabilities, as well as precision guided munitions. In Libya, U.S. back-up ("leading from behind") went as far as 75 percent of the key enablers needed, making the United States once more the indispensable nation. But at least those European missions have fostered a greater sense of solidarity and responsibility sharing among the Europeans, even if the nonparticipation of some in Mali and Libya demonstrates that this process has still a long way to go.

Yet, on the other hand, NATO's operations out of area have also revived and exacerbated the transatlantic burden sharing debate. This has to do in part with different rules of engagement and operational caveats that exasperated Americans so much that at one moment some joked that ISAF stood for "I Saw Americans Fight." But the real reason is that the Europeans have tried to do these missions on the cheap while continuing to cut their defense budgets in response to the financial crisis and the gaping holes in welfare state budgets at home. Whereas the United States almost doubled its defense spending after 2001 in response to the September 11, 2001 (9/11) attacks, and has so far spent nearly U.S.$2 trillion on the wars in Iraq and Afghanistan, the Europeans have cut their defense spending since 2008 by between 10 to 15 percent. This is not likely to be a short-term phenomenon but rather a long-term decline. For instance, Britain's Royal Air Force now has just a quarter of the combat aircraft it had in the 1970s. The Royal Navy has 19 destroyers and frigates, compared to 69 in 1977. The British Army is reducing from 102,000 to 82,000 soldiers.

This is the smallest number since the Napoleonic wars. In 1990, Britain had 27 submarines (excluding those that carried ballistic missiles), and France had 17. But today, the two countries have only seven and six, respectively. Yet Britain and France traditionally have been the two European countries that take defense most seriously and devote the highest percent of their GDPs to it. Notwithstanding the sharp cuts, the United Kingdom (UK) still has the fourth largest military budget in the world, and France has demonstrated in Mali that it is still willing and able to take on a significant military intervention, largely using its own troops and capabilities. The UK is, for the time being, one of only two NATO countries to meet the NATO target of spending 2 percent of GDP on defense — the other being Greece. Yet if the UK and France are now feeling the strain, the situation is even more serious in other European countries that are now reducing budgets from a much lower baseline. Where just a few years ago most European members of NATO spent between 1.5 to 2 percent of GDP on defense, five are now under the 1 percent mark, including large countries like Spain. Moreover, much European military spending goes on pensions or salaries rather than modernization. Only five NATO member states meet the benchmark of 20 percent of defense budgets to be devoted to equipment and modernization. Today, 17 NATO member states have militaries with fewer than 40,000 troops, and five have less than 10,000.

It is this freefall in European military budgets which is now worrying the United States, particularly at a time when the United States is increasingly focused on the Asia-Pacific region and expects the Europeans to shoulder more responsibility for security in the broader European neighborhood including the Balkans, North Africa, and the Middle East. Former U.S. Secretary of Defense Leon Panetta has announced that henceforth the United States wishes to have 60 percent of its naval assets in the Asian Pacific rather than the current 50 percent. Moreover, the United States has withdrawn two combat brigades from Europe and a number of air squadrons. Additionally, while European defense spending has gone down by roughly 20 percent over the past decade, Chinese defense spending has risen by almost 200 percent. Last year, for the first time in many centuries, Asian nations spent more on military forces than the Europeans. This shift in the geopolitical center of gravity in the world is taking place at a time when the U.S. defense budget, having been more or less a protected fiefdom since 9/11, is now also having to cope with austerity. The Pentagon is already having to absorb nearly half a trillion dollars in defense cuts as part of the budget cutting process and, at the time of this writing, may have imposed on it, under the so-called sequestration procedure, a similar amount over the next decade. Therefore, unsurprisingly, U.S. worries about the credibility of the Europeans as serious allies and concerns that they use their shrinking defense budget more wisely and productively, have become more and more vocal. In June 2011, U.S. Defense Secretary Robert Gates used his valedictory speech in Brussels, Belgium, to issue a sharp rebuke to the European allies for their neglect of their defenses in a still unpredictable world. He even prophesized "a dim, if not dismal future" for NATO if the Europeans did not make a serious effort to reverse the trend. Gates' speech, departing from the usual diplomatic formulas, certainly came across as a wake-up call to the Europeans. Whatever the ultimate outcome, transatlantic burden sharing is at least now being taken more seriously in European capitals, even if not with quite the same sense of urgency as in Washington.

As this debate goes forward, three essential questions will need to find answers. First, as the United States pivots to the Asia-Pacific and has to contemplate cuts in force readiness and equipment purchases in order to come within the new budgetary ceilings, how much capability will it be prepared to devote to NATO and Europe's security in its neighborhood? Will the United States always step in and bail out the Europeans in order to maintain NATO's credibility; or is it prepared to see the Europeans fail in a mission in order to ram home the message that they need to stand on their own feet and be able to conduct at least a Libya or a Mali or a Bosnia-Kosovo type of intervention? Should the United States push the Europeans to acquire major enablers, such as air transport and in-flight refuelling aircraft, satellites and drones, and precision strike missiles or state of the art cyber capabilities; or, in order to avoid duplication, should it instead try to arrange a division of labor with the Europeans whereby they commit to procure certain collective capabilities on the understanding that the United States will be prepared to supply the others?

Second, how can the Europeans be motivated to take defense more seriously and to be prepared to pool their assets and specialize in their roles and responsibilities? Over the last decade, there have been hundreds of seminars on the need for the Europeans to integrate their defense efforts and stop duplicating. But not much has happened. Today, 95 percent of European military units are still nationally owned and organized, and 75 percent of European defense contracts are limited to the home nation.

Europe still produces four different types of jet fighters, has three times more military shipyards than the United States, has over 13 different armored vehicle programs, and still wastes billions of Euros every year because each European country has different certification systems and standards for military equipment. The financial crisis, although a massive threat to European military capabilities, is also an opportunity for Europe to overcome at last national parochialisms and put its defense house in order. But at a time when governments are keen to protect jobs in the defense industries, will there be the political will to move ahead?

A related question concerns intra-European burden sharing. As defense budgets go down, this has become as much a European as a transatlantic issue. For instance, France, the UK, and Germany together account for over 60 percent of European defense budgets even though the EU will soon have 28 member states. The UK and France also account for nearly 60 percent of research and development efforts and deployable rapid response forces. There is also the issue of political burden sharing among Europeans. France has felt rather left on its own during its Mali operation, even if the EU is now deploying a training mission in support of the Mali Army and the projected African stabilization force. Many European allies also stayed on the sidelines during NATO's Libya operation, although this was, to some degree, offset by the involvement of NATO's partners, such as Sweden. Clearly if Europeans are to stand on their own feet, the willingness and capacity of all the EU member states (22 of which are also NATO members) to collectively shoulder the burden of missions that they all claim to support politically will be crucial. But how can this be achieved?

The final question concerns the institutional capacity of both NATO and the EU to influence the defense spending and procurement decisions of their members in the future. At a time of budgetary stringency, it is even more important that allies spend their resources on the key military requirements identified by their senior commanders and address the shortfalls that have been well highlighted after the Libyan and Afghan operations, especially in areas such as intelligence and surveillance, logistics, transport, medical evacuation, precision targeting and better coordination of national and international force structures and headquarters. Both NATO and the EU are starting to address these issues with initiatives such as NATO's Smart Defence and Connected Forces Initiative and the EU's Pooling and Sharing. If these succeed, they will certainly allow the Europeans to acquire considerably more bang for their defense Euros. But there is still a long way to go before a culture of multinational cooperation and mutual transparency regarding defense plans are embedded in these institutions. The Europeans will also have to stop trying to solve the tension between declining defense budgets and the need to preserve hard-core defense capabilities within a purely national context and accept that maintaining a full spectrum of forces will only be possible in the future at a European level. This is going to require a further pooling of sovereignty which is still difficult for many European countries to accept.

These observations underscore that burden sharing is now back center stage in the transatlantic Alliance, and the way this issue is resolved will largely determine NATO's future and the future of the transatlantic relationship. The financial crisis is both a threat and a political opportunity. But success will require constant political attention and leadership at the highest levels. Success will also require a sober, objective, and realistic approach to the issue of burden sharing beyond the traditional arguments and counterarguments about who is right and wrong, and what is fair or unfair, derived from rather different cultures and perspectives.

So never before has there been so great a need for an analysis of burden sharing that genuinely demystifies this topic and puts it in the broader strategic context beyond the world of emotion and political point-scoring. Colonel Joel Hillison has done all those concerned with the health of NATO and the transatlantic partnership a major service by producing this well-researched, comprehensive, and, above all, objective analysis of the burden sharing issue today. Hillison has brought to this task a rigorous intellectual methodology but also a sophisticated sense of politics on both sides of the Atlantic. This has given him, in my judgment, a compelling sense of realism as to what needs to be done, can be done and, most importantly of all, how it can be achieved. Hillison's clear aim is to try to ensure that the new debate on burden sharing produces more light than heat and does not lead only to a new sense of frustration and futility. This would be the worst outcome for the Alliance. But the great merit of his research, based also on extensive interviews with key civilian and military experts in both Brussels and Washington, is to identify the key issues and constructively suggest where the solutions could be found, both in the short term and in coming decades. In short, Hillison has made the issue comprehensive not only to fellow specialists, but above all to the policymakers who have to move these issues forward. So it is my heartfelt wish that they will also read this well-presented and documented study and turn its analysis and sensible recommendations into action.

JAMIE SHEA
Deputy Assistant Secretary General
Emerging Security Challenges Division
NATO

PREFACE

I wrote this book to address the lacuna in the burden sharing literature regarding new member countries in the North Atlantic Treaty Organization (NATO). While working at the Supreme Headquarters Allied Powers Europe (SHAPE) during the first wave of post-Cold War enlargement, I personally witnessed the pride and eagerness with which new NATO members entered the Alliance. The puzzle was whether this enthusiasm translated into concrete contributions to the Alliance.

My research differs from existing literature in that it addresses the varied aspects of burden sharing in NATO and expands the scope of research from a dichotomous United States and Europe analysis to an examination of burden sharing within Europe (specifically focused on new members). It takes a more comprehensive view of burden sharing to include defense expenditures and more importantly, contributions to NATO missions. On the heels of several rounds of expansion and the winding down of NATO operations in Afghanistan, this book contributes to the literature on burden sharing and provides essential information on the effects of enlargement. These findings should inform decisionmakers about the behavior of new NATO members and help them to make appropriate decisions in regards to further expansion.

The main contribution of this work is that it specifically examines the burden sharing behavior of new NATO members and the impact of enlargement on NATO burden sharing. This inquiry is intrinsically important because burden sharing concerns have been salient and recurring issues for the NATO Alliance since its inception. The United States, as the leader of the Alliance, has frequently complained about the low level defense expenditures of its allies. In addition, some NATO members have repeatedly come under criticism for not providing adequate forces and for imposing restrictions on forces committed to the recent NATO mission in Afghanistan. The costs and benefits of NATO's enlargement have also been a topic of discussion in policy circles since the dissolution of the Soviet Union. If new members are relatively more likely to share burdens than existing members, this finding would partially allay fears concerning the detrimental effects of expansion on Alliance cohesion and capability.

The book will appeal to those interested in security studies or NATO, including scholars, university students, and security practitioners. It also contributes to the literature about alliances and collective action. Finally, it will be of interest to foreign policy practitioners and those interested in the European region.

Joel R. Hillison

CHAPTER 1

INTRODUCTION

> The burden-sharing issue will continue to dog the Alliance either until we can successfully redistribute the burden or reduce it. . . .
>
> Jim Moody
> *Shifting into Neutral*[1]

In August 2003, the North Atlantic Treaty Organization (NATO) took control of the International Security Assistance Force (ISAF) mission in Afghanistan. At the time, many European allies were disgruntled with the United States over the war in Iraq. Some allies also felt snubbed by the U.S. decision to act unilaterally in Afghanistan in the aftermath of the terrorist attacks on September 11, 2001. Yet, 12 years later, the Alliance was still involved in the NATO mission in Afghanistan. All 28 NATO allies persevered in the face of intensified fighting in Afghanistan and growing domestic political and fiscal pressures. Given the physical and psychological separation of the ISAF mission from Europe, it is an interesting puzzle why NATO members continued to contribute to the mission in Afghanistan. Assuming that states act rationally, there were significant incentives for NATO members to "free ride" on the United States, meaning they should have let the United States bear the burdens of this operation by itself. Yet NATO members, as diverse as Poland and Albania, continued to contribute to the mission in Afghanistan even though it was increasingly difficult to articulate their national interests in Afghanistan to a skeptical domestic audience. In fact, many new NATO members made substantial contributions at a significant economic and political cost. This book examines

1

this puzzle by analyzing the burden sharing behavior of NATO members, especially new NATO members.

The notion of fairness is a fundamental feature of human interaction. States, as collectives, also value fairness, or equity in relation to other states and institutions such as alliances. This is also true of NATO. Soon after the creation of NATO, the United States began pushing its European allies to increase their contributions and begin "pulling their weight."[2] The 1950 Communist invasion of South Korea was a catalyst for this effort. In a 1956 article on the economic aspects of the NATO Alliance, Lincoln Gordon identified equity of effort as one of the major cooperation issues confronting the Alliance.[3] In this case, equity of effort referred to how the Alliance members were going to distribute the costs of defense given their ability to contribute. Equity of effort and the ability-to-contribute continue to frame burden sharing discussions today. While the norms have remained constant, changes in the post-Cold War balance of power have placed additional stress on burden sharing within NATO.

NATO was founded in response to the growing threat posed by the Soviet Union in the aftermath of World War II. The 1949 Washington Treaty, which founded NATO, linked the destiny of all members together in *de facto* resistance to the Soviet Union. In the preamble of that treaty, it stated that NATO members were "resolved to unite their efforts for (the) collective defence and for the preservation of peace and security."[4] The threat of a common enemy allowed NATO members to overcome many obstacles to cooperation and burden sharing. In fact, NATO endured numerous crises in its more than 65 years of existence, many directly related to burden sharing concerns.[5] Yet, the fall of the Soviet Union placed additional stress on the

Alliance by removing the original threat which had led to its formation in the first place.[6]

> Factors such as politically risky missions overseas, the lack of a common threat perception, and more generally a larger and less homogeneous group of member-states than during the Cold War have arguably added to the challenge of securing a 'fair' sharing of the alliance's burdens.[7]

Most recently, the war in Afghanistan, operations in Libya, and the global economic crisis have resurfaced issues about burden sharing between the United States and NATO. Many U.S. public officials and pundits argued that NATO was not doing its fair share to support operations in Afghanistan or Libya. Often these arguments lacked precision and did not acknowledge the subjective nature of "equity." They also tended to portray NATO as a monolithic entity contraposed to the United States. In reality, there are a broad range of national interests, capabilities, domestic institutions, history, and cultures within NATO. These differences not only impact a nation's ability to contribute to the Alliance, but also its perception of burden sharing.

A common definition of burden sharing is "the distribution of costs and risks among members of a group in the process of accomplishing a common goal."[8] While this definition of burden sharing is precise, the application of burden sharing to an organization such as NATO is more nuanced. The first hurdle is how to identify and quantify costs, which can be either monetary or nonmonetary. Monetary costs, such as contributions to NATO's common fund and expenditures in national defense budgets are easily measured. A normative assessment of the equity of those contributions is less easily defined, especially since some military expenses provide purely private benefits. The measurement of nonmonetary costs, such as troop commitments, basing rights, provision of facilities, and over-flight rights are less easily quantified and thus even more contentious. The related notion of risk is also subjective and malleable. The political and security risks of committing military forces to NATO operations are a real concern within the Alliance, especially in light of out of area operations and the increased potential for casualties in peacekeeping and counterinsurgency missions.

The other component of burden sharing, common goals, is somewhat easier to tackle. This component implies that all members agree upon the collective aims of NATO. Since NATO relies on a consensus decisionmaking procedure, in which every nation has a veto on NATO decisions, it is reasonable to argue that approved Alliance missions represent common goals. If we assume that states are self-interested and act rationally, it is also reasonable to suggest that all states benefit, to some extent, from these common goals. It is the assumption that NATO provides a common or public good that has made burden sharing a collective action problem in much of the literature about NATO.

COLLECTIVE ACTION PROBLEMS

Most scholars studying issues of burden sharing have relied on the theory of collective action to inform their analysis.[9] Collective action theory looks at how actors behave in pursuit of a common goal. Perhaps the most famous work on collective action is *The Logic of Collective Action* by Mancur Olson.[10] In the absence of effective mechanisms to enforce commitments, this work suggests that rational incentives would encourage members of alliances, such as NATO, to free-ride on large members such as the United States. Subsequently, much of the collective action literature focuses on a comparison between the United States and Europe, especially the largest European allies. Olson also suggests that the level of **free-riding** would depend upon the relative size of the members and the absolute number of members. It is surprising that little analysis has focused on the issues of burden sharing within Europe, especially between the larger and smaller European allies. It is also odd that there has been a paucity of research on the impact of enlargement on burden sharing in NATO.

The collective action literature suggests that free-riding behavior is likely to increase as organizations increase their membership. Article 10 of the NATO treaty provides modalities for new members to join the Alliance.[11] During the Cold War, NATO expanded from 12 original members to 16 members over a 40 plus-year period. After the fall of the Soviet Union, NATO expanded from 16 members in 1998 to 28 members by 2009. While all members face incentives to free-ride, these incentives increase as the size of the organization increases. In the absence of a commonly identified threat, the rational incentives to **free-ride** are even more pronounced.

A salient characteristic of NATO enlargement is that all of the new members are smaller than either the United States or the Big Four European members, (Germany, the United Kingdom (UK), France, and Italy). The logic of collective action suggests that larger, more powerful states bear a greater proportion of the costs in producing a public good.[12] Therefore, the new members would be expected to free-ride in relative contributions to the Alliance. However, free-riding by smaller states has not been the case. Something other than collective action theory is required to explain this phenomenon. As expected, the capability and willingness to share burdens varies from the largest European NATO members (in terms of population and geography) to the smallest. Likewise, burden sharing, as a percentage of the gross domestic product (GDP), varies based on the level of national economic output. However, the sharing of risks, as measured by military commitments to NATO operations, less closely follows the collective action model. When national interests more closely aligned with Alliance-wide goals, NATO members were more willing to increase their contributions.

This analysis of burden sharing behavior also revealed that new NATO members demonstrate a greater willingness to bear the burdens of the Alliance than older members, all things being equal. Consequently, free-riding behavior increased with the length of membership in NATO. When states' reputations were on the line, they were more willing to share the burdens of the Alliance.[13] In addition, though many of these new members still view Russia as a potential threat and thus favor a greater focus on territorial defense, their level of military spending was not correlated to Russian military spending. These same nations also contributed their best equipped and most combat ready units to NATO missions in such places as Afghanistan.

These phenomena can be attributed to two explanations. First, new members are concerned with establishing a good reputation, not only within the Alliance, but also with the leader of the Alliance, the United States. By providing troops to NATO missions, new members demonstrate their ability to make credible commitments. By demonstrating their loyalty to the United States and the NATO Alliance, they hope to compensate for their historic fear of abandonment. The other explanation is that NATO has invested a great deal of effort into socializing new members and partners on Alliance norms of burden sharing. Thus, it is not surprising that new members explain troop contributions in terms of appropriate behavior for Alliance members, rather than in terms of rational, self-interest.

Finally, this book examines burden sharing behavior in the aftermath of NATO enlargement. The logic of collective action suggests that free-riding behavior should have increased due to the increase in the number of members. However, the actual record is mixed. Even though NATO expanded its scope and membership significantly, all NATO members are contributing, to some extent, to the various on-going Alliance missions. In explaining this result, this work provides a contribution to the extensive literature on burden sharing.

RESEARCH DESIGN

Since burden sharing is ultimately a subjective assessment, this book uses mixed methods, both qualitative and quantitative, and multiple measures to examine burden sharing. The multi-method design increases the accuracy of the findings and better explains the dynamic nature of burden sharing. The quantitative analysis helps to identify what happened. The other methods help to explain why.

Some measures of burden sharing, such as military expenditures, lend themselves to quantitative

7

analysis. NATO monitors and publishes the military expenditures of its members. Quantitative analysis can also help measure the contribution of member states to NATO operations. However, the case study method is better suited to explain these contributions. Case studies allow for the systematic analysis of the background, environment, and nature of contributions to various NATO missions. The case studies are framed around the basic questions discussed in the previous section. They span the period before and after both waves of NATO enlargement. The case studies not only describe the context in which burden sharing occurs, they also distinguish between capability and willingness to share burdens. Finally, this book uses interviews with key NATO officials to examine why and how burden sharing decisions are made, and to distinguish between the various components of burden sharing behavior.

This book consists of six chapters. Chapter 2, "Measuring Burden Sharing" establishes the theoretical foundation for this book in greater detail. It develops a statistical model to test the hypothesis that large states will share greater relative proportion of burdens than small states when looking at military expenditures. This hypothesis is directly derived from the logic of collective action already discussed. The model of demand for military expenditures, as a percentage of GDP, is applied to the late-Cold War period (1975-91) and the post-Cold War period (1992-2009). In the post-Cold War period, the model also tests whether new members or old members of NATO share a greater relative proportion of burdens. This analysis gives some insight into how burden sharing behavior of new members changed after membership in NATO. This chapter also compares the burden sharing behavior of similarly-sized NATO members to examine the robustness of the results. The chapter concludes by testing whether NATO enlargement increased free-riding behavior.

Chapter 3, "Sharing Risks," takes a different approach to the question of burden sharing. This chapter examines troop contributions to various NATO missions from 1999 to 2010. During this time frame, there were three waves of NATO enlargement. This chapter analyzes burden sharing behavior during NATO missions and examines the "public-ness" of the benefits derived from the contributions to these missions. Contributions of member states to NATO operations are analyzed during four NATO missions: one humanitarian, two peacekeeping, and one stability and reconstruction. The chapter concludes with a preliminary examination of NATO operations in Libya in 2011. These NATO missions suggest that contributions increase when members pursue private benefits, including credibility. They also suggest that the socialization of NATO burden sharing norms mitigate the incentives to free-ride.

In Chapter 4, "Understanding Burden Sharing Behavior," interviews with NATO elites are analyzed. The first part of the chapter discusses some possible explanations for the burden sharing behavior examined in the previous chapters. The logic of collective action assumes that states are rational, egoistic actors and that decisions are always made on a cost-benefit basis. However, there are other plausible theoretical explanations for burden sharing behavior. This chapter takes a closer look at these explanations to better understand the logic(s) behind burden sharing behavior. Finally, the chapter analyzes the distinction between limited capability and the lack of political will in burden sharing behavior.

Chapter 5, "Case Studies in Burden Sharing Behavior," examines several new NATO members using the case study method. Greater focus is given to the context of individual national contributions to understand fully the burden sharing preferences of new members. The case studies examine the unique capacity, threats, domestic constraints, and geographic positions of selected new member countries.[14] This analysis provides further insights into the effect of socialization of NATO burden sharing norms on burden sharing behavior.

Chapter 6, "Conclusions and the Way Forward," places this book in the broader literature on burden sharing. It begins with a summary of the findings in this project and then reviews the results by individual hypothesis. It also identifies some future policy considerations for NATO and the United States, including ways to address some of the issues identified in this book. Finally, the chapter lays out an agenda for future research on NATO burden sharing.

WHY STUDY BURDEN SHARING IN NATO?

This inquiry is intrinsically important because burden sharing concerns have been salient and recurring issues for the NATO Alliance since its inception. Recently, NATO members have come under criticism for not providing adequate forces and for imposing restrictions on forces committed to the NATO mission in Afghanistan. The provision of forces in support of NATO missions directly relates to the fairness or equity of effort debate. The costs and benefits of NATO enlargement have also been a topic of discussion in policy circles since the dissolution of the Soviet Union. If new members are relatively more likely to share burdens than existing members, this finding would partially allay fears concerning the detrimental effects of expansion on Alliance cohesion and capability.

The addition of new members, the end of the Cold War, and the expansion of NATO's role into peacekeeping/enforcement operations represent a departure from the assumptions made during previous studies in the collective action literature. This research differs from existing literature in that it addresses these varied aspects of burden sharing in NATO and expands the scope of research from a dichotomous analysis of the United States and Europe to an examination of burden sharing within Europe itself. On the heels of the last round of expansions in 2009, the unveiling of a new *NATO Strategic Concept* in 2010, the conclusion of NATO operations in Libya, and the drawdown of NATO forces in Afghanistan, this project contributes to the literature on burden sharing and provides essential information on the contributions of new NATO members and the overall effects of enlargement. These findings should inform decisionmakers about the behavior of NATO members and help them to make appropriate decisions in regards to further expansion and the validity of *NATO's Strategic Concept*.

ENDNOTES - CHAPTER 1

1. Jim Moody, "The Congress of the United States," Christopher Coker, ed., *Shifting Into Neutral: Burden Sharing in the Western Alliance in the 1990s*, London, UK: Brassey's, 1990, p. 52.

2. Simon Duke, *The Burdensharing Debate*, New York: Saint Martin's Press, 1993, p. 33.

3. Lincoln Gordon, "Economic Aspects of Coalition Diplomacy—The NATO Experience," *International Organization*, Vol. 10, 1956.

4. NATO Public Diplomacy Division, *NATO Handbook*, Brussels, Belgium: NATO, 2004, available from *www.nato.int/cps/en/natolive/official_texts_17120.htm*.

5. For a summary of the literature on the demise of NATO and a discussion on why NATO survives these recurrent crises, see Wallace J. Thies, "Why NATO Endures," Washington, DC: Catholic University of America, June 2009.

6. John J. Mearsheimer, "Why We Will Soon Miss the Cold War," Richard K. Betts, ed., *Conflict After the Cold War*, New York: Pearson Longman, 2009, p. 22.

7. Ida M. Oma, "Explaining State's Burden-Sharing Behavior within NATO," *Cooperation and Conflict*, Vol. 47, No. 4, 2012, p. 563.

8. Peter K. Forster, and Stephen J. Cimbala, *The US, NATO and Military Burden-Sharing*, New York: Frank Cass, 2005, p. 164.

9. See, for example, Mancur Olson, Jr., and Richard Zeckhauser, "An Economic Theory of Alliances," Santa Monica, CA: RAND Corporation, 1966; John R. Oneal and Mark A. Elrod, "NATO Burden Sharing and the Forces of Change," *International Studies Quarterly*, Vol. 33, 1989, pp. 435-456; John R. Oneal, "The Theory of Collective Action and Burden Sharing in NATO," *International Organization*, Vol. 44, No. 3, 1990, pp. 379-402; Todd Sandler, "Impurity of Defense: An Application to the Economics of Alliances," *Kyklos*, Vol. 30, 1977, pp. 443–460; Todd Sandler, "NATO Burden Sharing: Rules or Reality?" in Christian Schmidt and Frank Blackaby, eds., Peace, Defence and Economic Analysis, London, UK: Macmillian, 1999, pp. 363-383; Todd Sandler, "The Economic Theory of Alliances: A Survey," *Journal of Conflict Resolution*, September 1993; Todd Sandler and John F. Forbes, "Burden Sharing, Strategy, and the Design of NATO," *Economic Inquiry*, Vol. 18, 1980, pp. 425-444; Keith Hartley and Todd Sandler, *The Political Economy of NATO: Past, Present, and Into the 21st Century*, London, UK: Cambridge University Press, 1990; and James C. Murdoch and Todd Sandler, "Nash-Cournot or Lindahl Behavior? An Empirical Test for the NATO Allies," *The Quarterly Journal of Economics*, Vol. 105, No. 4, 1990, pp. 875-894.

10. Mancur Olson, Jr., *The Logic of Collective Action: Public Goods and the Theory of Groups.*, Rev. Ed., New York: Schocken Books, 1971.

11. *The North Atlantic Treaty*, Washington, DC: NATO, April 4, 1949, available from *www.nato.int/cps/en/natolive/official_texts_17120.htm*.

12. *Ibid*.

13. Robert Jervis, *The Logic of Images in International Relations.* Princeton, NJ: Princeton University Press, 1970. See also Anne E. Sartori, "The Might of the Pen: A Reputational Theory of Communication in International Disputes," *Internatioal Organization*, Vol. 56, 2002; and Robert O. Keohane, "Accountability in World Politics," *Scandinavian Political Studies*, Vol. 29, June 2006.

14. See also Duke, p. 1.

CHAPTER 2

MEASURING BURDEN SHARING:
DURING AND AFTER THE COLD WAR

ANALYSIS OF MILITARY EXPENDITURES

> The problem is not just underfunding of NATO. Since the end of the Cold War, NATO and national defense budgets have fallen consistently — even with unprecedented operations outside NATO's territory over the past 5 years. Just 5 of 28 allies achieve the defense-spending target of 2 percent of GDP.
>
> Robert Gates, Secretary of Defense,
> NATO Strategic Concept Seminar,
> February 23, 2010[1]

This chapter analyzes one of the most studied and widely disputed measures of burden sharing: military expenditures. This measure of burden sharing relates directly to the "equity of effort" norms mentioned in Chapter 1. Beginning with Mancur Olson and Richard Zeckhauser's ground breaking study of collective action, burden sharing has been examined using military expenditures as a percentage of gross domestic product (GDP).[2] This ratio is what Simon Duke refers to as "the input measure." Military spending continues to be a good proxy for burden sharing since North Atlantic Treaty Organization (NATO) defense spending still targets to improve contributions to collective defense capabilities.

Analysis begins with the input measure, analyzing defense spending as a form of burden sharing behavior. Using a statistical model, several hypotheses, developed mostly from the collective action literature, are tested in both the late-Cold War period and the period thereafter. The chapter also looks at force structure contributions before and after the Cold War. Finally, it examines whether new or old members of NATO share a greater relative proportion of burdens in the Alliance and whether or not new member burden sharing declined after being accepted into NATO.

In the examination of the late-Cold War period, the statistical model explains over 79 percent of the variance in defense expenditures and confirms several predictions of burden sharing behavior. Large states, as measured by the size of population, share a greater relative proportion of burden than small states, as predicted by the logic of collective action. In addition, among non-U.S. NATO members, military expenditures as a percentage of GDP decrease as the size of GDP income increases. Another interesting finding concerns the relationship between perceived threat and burden sharing. Though U.S. and Soviet military expenditures were correlated, it appears that Soviet expenditures follow changes in U.S. military expenditures as a percentage of GDP. Not surprising, non-U.S. NATO expenditures are strongly correlated to changes in Soviet military expenditures during the portion of the late-Cold War period examined. As Soviet military expenditures increased, so too did non-U.S. NATO military expenditures as a percentage of GDP. This result is statistically significant and reinforces the characterization of the Soviet Union as a threat during this period. This finding conforms to Stephen Walt's theory of balancing against threat and Peter Forster and Stephen Cimbala's assertion that burden sharing is a function of perceived threat.[3] Finally, the U.S. NATO military manpower was generally balanced between the United States and its allies; the United

States contributed a greater relative proportion of aircraft and naval vessels. The disparity is greatest when looking at the most public of these forces, strategic nuclear weapons. However, that imbalance was deliberate and in the interest of the United States.

During the post-Cold War period, the lack of a unifying threat should have increased the collective action problems within NATO. During the post-Cold War period, defense expenditures of NATO members were no longer sensitive to changes in Russian military expenditures. As with the Cold War period, states with the largest GDP, on average, shared a greater relative proportion of burdens than small states. The findings were less conclusive when using population and area as measures of size. The findings also support the conjecture that new NATO members burden share at a greater rate than old NATO members. On average, as the length of membership in NATO increased, military expenditures decreased. Additionally, while new member burden sharing declined after accession into NATO, it did so at a lesser rate than older members, suggesting that incentives to contribute to the Alliance go beyond conditionality of membership.

The enlargement of NATO should have generated increasing incentives to free-ride during this period. The logic of collective action states that as the size of a group grows, it is more difficult to provide public goods without coercion or selective rewards.[4] During this period, the size of NATO increased from 16 members to 28 members. The increased membership and lack of formal rewards or sanctioning mechanisms within NATO should have exacerbated collective action problems. However, the results were mixed. Before looking at these results in detail, it is instructive to review the theoretical underpinnings of the study of burden sharing.

COLLECTIVE ACTION—WHY SIZE MATTERS

Extensive literature on NATO burden sharing stretches back to the late-1960s.[5] This literature was largely based on the theories of "collective action" developed by Olson. In *The Logic of Collective Action*, Olson examined the difficulty of maintaining cooperation within groups pursuing common interests.[6] He also demonstrated why actors who share a common interest are willing to bear the costs of establishing and supporting organizations that foster cooperation and provide a public good. First, he acknowledged that actors have both individual and common interests in certain goods. Provision of any level of a good will depend upon the marginal cost and benefit provided by each additional unit of the good produced. The logic is somewhat different for public goods.

The notion of a public good is central to Olson's logic. A public good is any item or service that has two distinct qualities: nonexcludability and nonrival consumption. Nonexcludability means that those who do not contribute to the provision of a particular good or service cannot feasibly be kept from benefiting from it. For example, once a levee is built to prevent flooding, everyone in that flood plain benefits whether or not they contributed to the levy being built. Nonrival consumption refers to the consumption of a good or service by one actor that does not diminish the amount available to others. Using one of Olson's examples, the number of people watching a parade on television does not diminish the entertainment value provided to each. Thus a good or service that has both nonexcludability and nonrival consumption is characterized as a public good.

The North Atlantic Treaty outlines the commitment of signatory states to contribute to the collective security of the Alliance. Article 5 of the NATO treaty states that an attack against any member is regarded as an attack against all members. This security guarantee was initially established as a deterrent against Soviet aggression and has been considered a public good within the Alliance. While nonmembers are excluded from the guarantees of Article 5, all member states benefit from the security provided by NATO regardless of their individual contributions (nonexcludability). In addition, the deterrence provided to one state does not diminish the deterrence value of the Alliance to another member, meeting the conditions of nonrival consumption. Thus, the NATO security guarantee has the characteristics of a public good.

Ideally, the costs of providing a public good would be borne either in proportion to the amount of benefit received or the ability to pay. However, the nature of a public good makes this problematic since noncontributors cannot be excluded. This often leads to suboptimal levels of public good provisions and an inequitable distribution of costs or burdens of providing the good. This phenomenon is known as the free-rider problem. A free-rider is an actor that does not bear an equitable share of the burden to provide a collective good, such as deterrence.

Olson used these factors to make predictions about the provision of public goods. First, he showed that the larger the group, the more suboptimal the level of public goods supplied. Therefore as membership increases, free-rider problems should also increase.[7] These problems should have increased after the demise of the Soviet Union as NATO membership increased and the traditional threat diminished.[8]

Second, Olson demonstrated that the willingness to bear the burden of providing public goods would be a function of the relative benefit the actor received in relation to the advantage received by the group. Thus, larger states would tend to profit more from a public good and would be willing to bear a greater proportion of the costs. In Olson's own words:

> Once a smaller member has the amount of the collective good he gets free from the largest member, he has more than he would have purchased for himself, and has no incentive to obtain any of the collective good at his own expense.[9]

This phenomenon results in what he called the exploitation of the great by the small. Olson suggested that burden sharing in NATO and the United Nations (UN) were examples of this tendency. In support of this hypothesis, he noted that there was:

> a significant positive correlation [between gross national product (GNP) and defense budgets as a percentage of GNP] indicating that large nations in NATO bear a disproportionate share of the burden of the common defense.[10]

Initially, the characteristics of the NATO Alliance seemed to fit the assumptions of the logic of collective action. Over time, however, the relationship between burden sharing and national income weakened. In fact, it was not statistically significant from the mid-1960s to the mid-1970s. John Oneal and Mark Elrod related a declining statistical significance between GDP and defense expenditures in NATO since 1968 with declining hegemonic power.[11] Since the results no longer conformed to the predictions of collective action theory, they suggested that something else was going on in NATO.

Private Goods and Hegemonic Stability within NATO.

Oneal and Elrod suggested that the more recent empirical trends could be explained by certain NATO nations pursuing private goods. Unlike public goods, private goods are excludable and rival. Oneal and Elrod suggested that countries increased their defense expenditures in pursuit of purely private goods. For example, struggles between Greece and Turkey revolved around conflicts in the Aegean Sea and Cyprus. Defense expenditures, in support of this conflict, supported the pursuit of particular state interests that were excludable and rival to other members of the Alliance and thus, private goods. Similarly, Portugal's military involvement during the 1960s and 1970s in Angola and Mozambique had the characteristics of private goods. In both cases, the pursuit of private goods was correlated to increased military expenditures, thereby masking the incidence of free-riding within NATO.[12] Consequently, Oneal and Elrod excluded data from these countries during the periods they were pursuing these secondary security interests. Once these countries were excluded from the analysis, the data suggested the prevalence of free-riding. This finding reinforced Olson's theory of exploitation of the strong by the weak. Oneal and Elrod also suggested that the declining association between economic size (GDP) and defense burden reflected increased interdependence and cooperation within NATO. Oneal and Elrod attributed this increased coordination to more frequent contacts and cooperation within European organizations.[13]

21

Oneal and Elrod built upon Olson's concept of a uniquely privileged group. "A group is said to be uniquely privileged when there is one member very much larger than the others who can profitably provide the good acting alone."[14] As a uniquely privileged group, NATO members would therefore have even stronger incentives to free-ride on the United States. Conversely, as the relative U.S. power declines, so too should free-riding behavior. As the United States becomes less economically dominant, it will be less willing to bear a disproportionate share of the defense burden. The rationale is that as its relative economic position weakens, the United States will receive less relative benefit from NATO and have a diminishing capacity to bear the costs. Therefore, rising European economies would be expected to increase their proportion of the defense burden to compensate for the U.S. decline and to protect their own increasing economic growth. This theory does not imply that NATO states would collectively provide an optimal amount of security, only that the distribution of costs would adjust to this new balance of economic power.

An Alternative Explanation — The Joint Product Model.

James Murdoch and Todd Sandler challenged Oneal and Elrod's hypothesis concerning the effect of declining hegemonic power on defense expenditures of NATO allies. Murdoch and Sandler claimed that between 1979 and 1987, the U.S. share of NATO's GDP increased slightly (2.16 percent), while its share of NATO's military expenditures rose by 11.9 percent.[15] They suggested that this result was inconsistent with the declining hegemony argument.[16]

More recent data supports the Murdoch and Sandler argument. Using expenditure data reported by NATO and GDP figures obtained from the International Monetary fund, Figure 2-1 presents U.S. defense expenditure and economic data in relation to NATO from 1975 until 2009. This figure suggests that changes in ratio of U.S. to NATO defense expenditures were positively correlated with changes in the ratio of U.S. to NATO GDP between 1975 and 2000. The U.S. share of NATO GDP decreased 13 percent from 1975 to 1980, while its share of NATO military expenditures only decreased 5 percent. From 1980 to 1985, the U.S. share of NATO GDP increased 24 percent, while its share of NATO military expenditures increased only 18 percent. This data supports Murdoch and Sandler's arguments counter the hegemonic decline theory. However, there is an even greater divergence after 2000. While the U.S. share of NATO military expenditures increased between 2000 and 2009, the U.S. share of NATO GDP continued to decline.

These results support the findings of Murdoch and Sandler. Murdoch and Sandler inferred from earlier patterns that U.S. military expenditures were better explained by the joint product model. According to this model, military expenditures usually included a mix of public and private benefits. For example, conventional forces could provide a public good (deterrence), or they could be committed to the defense of one country and thus unavailable for use elsewhere (therefore, rival).

Murdoch and Sandler suggested that earlier studies may have distorted burden sharing analyses by counting all Alliance expenditures as public goods. They further explained that when the U.S. pursued private or imperfect public goods, other allies had to compensate for Alliance shortfalls. Murdoch and Sandler attributed the spike in the relative U.S. military expenditures in 1985 to a new flexible response strategy and a shift in U.S. spending toward more public goods (strategic weapons) under President Ronald Reagan (see Figure 2-1). Both of these changes increased the public security goods provided by the United States, thereby increasing the opportunity for free-riding among NATO allies. More recently, from 2000 to 2009, the U.S. share of NATO GDP decreased by 8 percent, while its share of NATO military expenditures increased by 2 percent (see Figure 2-1). This suggests that the United States might have been pursuing private benefits during this period (e.g., Iraq War). This explanation is examined in greater detail later in the chapter. Building on these theoretical insights, this chapter puts forth some hypotheses about burden sharing within the context of NATO expansion.

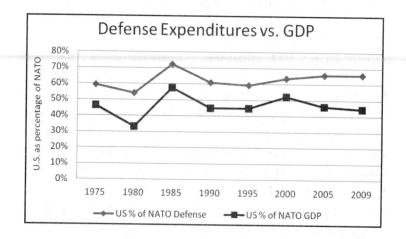

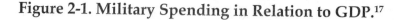

Figure 2-1. Military Spending in Relation to GDP.[17]

COLLECTIVE ACTION, CREDIBILITY, AND SOCIALIZATION

According to the logic of collective action, larger states receive a greater relative benefit from an alliance than smaller states. Because they have more land, people, and wealth to protect, larger countries are willing and able to spend more to receive the public goods of the alliance (security) than economically smaller or less populous states. Conversely, the amount of public goods (security) provided by the larger states satisfies most of the demand for smaller states. Therefore, these smaller states maximize their utility by free-riding or contributing less to the alliance than would be optimal for the collective.

H1: Large states should, on average, share a greater relative proportion of burdens than smaller states.

But size is not the only determinant of burden sharing in NATO. States of similar size contribute to NATO in varying degrees. During the late-Cold War period, potential new member states had feared abandonment by the West and a strong desire to rejoin Europe by entering into multilateral institutions, such as NATO and the European Union (EU). Therefore, new member states had a strong desire to demonstrate their reliability to their fellow NATO members. These states feared that free-riding would weaken their credibility and might result in an exclusion from the security guarantees of NATO and membership in the EU. This concern for establishing credibility and demonstrating capability resulted in stronger incentives to share burdens within NATO, despite outside constraints such as relatively less developed economies.

As Celeste Wallander and Robert Keohane suggest, "having a reputation for keeping commitments can be an asset."[18]

However, there are equally compelling arguments that new member states are willing to bear the burdens of membership for noninstrumental reasons: persuasion and socialization. Alexandria Ghiecu, in her article, "Security Institutions as Agents of Socialization: NATO and the New Europe," demonstrated how the novel environment in the aftermath of the fall of the Soviet Union enabled NATO to persuade aspiring members to change their behavior.[19] In Jeffrey Checkel's study of the EU, he noted that socialization could change the logic of how states act.[20] All new NATO members underwent an extensive socialization process that started with their membership in the Partnership for Peace Program (PfP) beginning in 1994. This sociological literature suggests that burden sharing can be taught and internalized through a prolonged and intense partnership and accession screening process. While burden sharing may have begun as a rational response to conditionality and a concern for establishing credibility, it became internalized over time, leading to continued burden sharing behavior based on identity as a NATO member.

H2: New member states should, on average, share a greater relative proportion of burdens (defense expenditures as a percentage of GDP and contributions to NATO missions) than older members of the Alliance, controlling for size and threat.

There is also theoretical evidence to suggest that new member burden sharing should decline after membership. Judith Kelley, in a study of East European countries after the fall of the Soviet Union, demonstrated that membership conditionality was highly correlated with desired policy outcomes.[21] This finding was collaborated in a study on defense reform in Bosnia and Herzegovina published in 2010 by Gülnur Aybet.[22] Given these findings, once a state has gained membership, NATO loses its leverage over new members. Thus, the new member would be expected to shirk their responsibilities and free-ride. If conditionality is the major impetus for burden sharing decisions, there should be a decline in burden sharing of new member states (compared to older members) after formal accession into NATO. This leads to the following corollary hypothesis.

H3: New member states should, on average, bear a declining relative proportion of burdens after accession into NATO.

Another explanation for levels of military expenditures comes from the realist school of international relations, which explains state behavior within NATO by focusing on power and threat. Most realists would suggest that NATO norms and socialization had little, if any, effect on an individual members' military expenditures. Rather, they suggest that states balance against either power or threats, such as Soviet Union (Russia). Therefore, Russian military expenditures have been used as a common measure of threat in studies of burden sharing within NATO.[23] In these studies, military expenditures were seen as a measurable proxy for determining aggregate military power.

A most promising challenge to this methodology comes from Walt's concept of balance of threat.[24] In this theory, threat is a function of four characteristics of the potential enemy: aggregate power, offensive power, offensive intent, and geographic proximity.[25] Therefore, increases in Russian (Soviet) military expenditures could be seen as threatening both because their effect on military power and as a possible signal of intent.

It also follows that the effect of Soviet military expenditures should be conditioned by the distance between states. In other words, countries closer to Russia or the Soviet Union would be more susceptible to actual or perceived threatening behavior. Of Walt's four characteristics, the only threat variable that definitely varies by country is the proximity to the Soviet Union.[26] Thus, Poland's threat perception of Russia will always be higher than Spain's, all things being equal. Using Walt's characteristics as a proxy measure for threat, it is possible to account for threat effects on burden sharing by examining Soviet military expenditures as conditioned by proximity to the Soviet Union (Russia).

H4: The defense expenditures of NATO members, as a percentage of GDP, should increase as states are physically closer to Russia, or as Russian military expenditures increase.

See Table 2-1 for a hypotheses on burden sharing.

		Theoretical basis
1-1:	Large states will share greater relative proportion of burdens than small states	Logic of Collective Action
1-2:	New members will share greater relative burdens than old members	Rational Choice and Sociological
1-3:	New member burden sharing declines after accession into NATO.	Rational Choice
1-4:	The defense expenditures of NATO members should increase as states are physically closer to Russia, or as Russian military expenditures increase.	Realism

Table 2-1. Hypotheses on Burden Sharing.

A MODEL FOR TESTING BURDEN SHARING HYPOTHESES

The statistical model used in this book builds on the public good demand function in Sandler and Hartley's 1999 book, *The Political Economy of NATO*. In this study, Sandler and Hartley revised their earlier demand function for defense by adding a variable representing a change in military doctrine. The formula for that demand function is listed below:

DEF = f (INCOME, PRICE, SPILLINS, THREAT, STRATEGIC).[27]

In their demand function, DEF, the dependent variable, represents real military expenditures. INCOME represents a measure of real national income, such as gross domestic product. PRICE represents the relative price of defense goods in relationship to non-defense goods. The other two independent variables directly address incentives for free-riding behavior: SPILLINS and THREAT. SPILLINS measure the impact of other allied spending on defense expenditures, in terms of real military expenditures. THREAT represents the defense outlays of the Alliance's main enemy (the Union of Soviet Socialist Republics [USSR]). Finally, a STRATEGIC variable was added to account for changes in military doctrines. This was an addition to their earlier model found in *The Economics of Defense* published in 1995.

This project modifies the demand function identified by Sandler and Hartley. Their model is adjusted to better analyze the NATO burden sharing issue among new members and to reflect actual NATO norms of burden sharing. The resultant model of burden sharing used in this project is indicated in the equation below:[28]

$$\%GDP_{it} = \beta_0 + \beta_1(Gdpchg_{it}) + \beta_2(DVLag_{it-1}) + \beta_3(Spillover_{it}) + \beta_4(Threat_{it}) + \Lambda_5(NATO) + \Lambda_6(EU) + \beta_7(Age) + \sum_{j=1}^{k} \gamma_i \, Country_i + e_{it}$$

In this model, $\%GDP_{it}$ is the dependent variable representing percentage of military expenditures to GDP.[29] This project uses percentage of military expenditures to gross domestic product ($\%GDP_{it}$) instead of real defense expenditures (DEF). Percentage of military expenditures to GDP is the standard used by NATO and member states to evaluate contributions to the Alliance.[30] Using military expenditures as a percentage of GDP also helps control for income effects by including national income in the denominator of the dependent variable. Therefore, there is no need to maintain an independent variable for INCOME in the base equation. Subscript i represents a specific country and t denotes time. The other variables in the model are:

1. $Gdpchg_{it}$ is a variable representing economic growth, or the change in GDP from time t-1 to t for country i.[31] This measures the impact of changes to the denominator of the dependent variable (GDP) on burden sharing as a percentage of GDP.

2. $\%DVLag_{it-1}$ is a 1-year lag of the dependent variable (the percentage of military expenditures to GDP) in time t-1. [32]

3. $Spillover_{it}$ is a variable representing the average percentage of military expenditures to GDP of other NATO allies. This measure checks for benefits received from other members' spending.

4. $Threat_{it}$ is used to control for the independent role of threat in influencing military expenditures.[33]

5. $NATO_{it}$ is a dummy variable to control for the effect of membership in NATO.

6. EU_{it} is a dummy variable to control for the effect of membership in the EU on burden sharing.

7. Age_{it} is one of the main independent variables of interest in this model. It is used to measure the influence of the length of membership on burden sharing behavior. It represents the number of years a country has been a member of NATO.

8. $Country_i$ is a dummy variable to account for fixed, country specific effects that are consistent over time (e.g. size).[34]

In this chapter, the model is used to analyze data on NATO members from 1975 to 1991.[35] The year 1975 was selected as the start point for the first panel for several reasons: it was the first year after Greece, Portugal, and Spain transitioned from dictatorships to democratic governments, it was the last year of U.S. involvement in Vietnam and finally, 1975 was the year that the Conference on Security and Cooperation in Europe (CSCE) signed the Final Act, known as the Helsinki Accords.[36] Among other things, the participants in this accord agreed to greater cooperation in the peaceful settlement of disputes and to respect the sovereignty of national borders. This agreement began a series of "voluntary confidence and security-building measures" that helped to reduce tensions between NATO countries and the Warsaw Pact.[37] It was also during this period that Spain was admitted into NATO; the first enlargement of the Alliance since 1955.

The year 1991 was selected as the end date since that was the year that the Soviet Union collapsed and the Boris Yeltsin government seized power. During 1991, the Baltic States claimed and won their independence. The model is run with the United States included in the data set and without U.S. data. Since the United States is by far the largest and most powerful member of the Alliance, inclusion in the data set may skew the results.

Testing the Logic of Collective Action: 1975-91.

The first interesting result from the model is that defense expenditures, as a percentage of GDP, are only weakly related to economic growth during this period. This relationship is only statistically significant when the United States is included in the data set.[38] Given the enduring threat represented by the Soviet Union during this period, it is not surprising that the demand for military expenditures was impervious to annual fluctuations in economic growth.

As expected, there is a statistically significant relationship (at the .001 level) between military expenditures as a percentage of GDP and the 1-year lag of the dependent variable, *dvlag*.[39] For every 1 percent increase in prior year military expenditures (as a percentage of GDP), current military expenditures (as a percentage of GDP) increased on average, 0.566 percent including the United States and 0.321 percent without the United States. These results were very robust. In fact, much of the explanatory power of the model appears to come from the lagged dependent variable. This finding is not surprising since military spending is relatively inelastic. Much military spending goes toward multiyear procurement contracts and nondiscretionary personnel costs.

There is also a great deal of bureaucratic inertia in military budgeting. In an earlier study on burden sharing, Benjamin Goldsmith found that prior year spending had "a powerful effect, making large changes less likely than incremental ones."[40] Thus, the model confirms that military expenditures are highly path dependent.

The model also supported the assertion that there is a relationship between allied spending and defense expenditure levels. The variable for spillover is positive for both data sets and statistically significant (at the .001 level) when the United States is included. On average, military expenditures (as a percentage of GDP) increased by 0.401 percent for every 1 percent increase in the military expenditures (as a percentage of GDP) in other NATO states.[41] This finding contradicts expectations of free-riding behavior in our fourth hypothesis. A possible explanation is that NATO allies' defense contributions were complementary versus substitutable during this period; therefore, security goods provided by allied countries complement, but do not replace the individual states' requirements for military expenditures.[42] One indicator of this phenomenon was the increasing specialization within the Alliance during this period. This evidence supports the conjecture made by Hartley and Sandler about the importance of spillover.[43]

As expected, there is a positive relationship between **threat** and levels of military expenditures, as a percentage of GDP. With the United States in the data base, the effect of threat is very small and is not statistically significant.[44] More importantly, there appears to be a positive relationship between threat and levels of military expenditures (as a percentage of GDP) when the U.S. data is excluded. These results were statistically significant at the .001 level and very robust.[45] As the value of the **threat** variable increased, the level of military expenditures (as a percentage of GDP) also increased. This result supports the realist predictions of H4; states which are closer in distance to the Soviet Union will have a higher level of military expenditure, as a percentage of GDP. NATO military spending will also increase when the Soviet Union increases military expenditures. This finding was not the case when the United States was included in the database.

If we further analyze the relationship between Soviet military expenditures versus U.S. and non-U.S. NATO military expenditures, the effect is not uniform. U.S. military expenditures, as a percentage of GDP, are positively and moderately correlated with Soviet military expenditures, with a correlation coefficient of 0.56. You can see this relationship graphically for the United States and the Soviet Union in Figure 2-2.

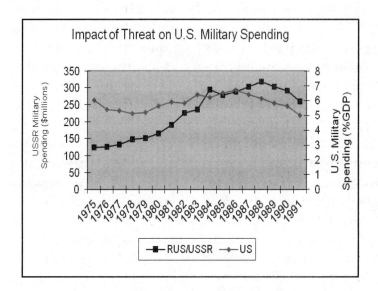

Figure 2-2. Impact of Threat on the United States in the Late-Cold War Period.[46]

In fact, it appears as if increases in U.S. military expenditures, as a percentage of GDP, in 1979 preceded increases at the rate of Soviet military expenditures in 1981 and that decreases in U.S. military expenditures, as a percentage of GDP, in 1986 preceded decreases in Soviet military expenditures in 1989. This information suggests that the Soviet Union reacted to U.S. expenditures as a percentage of GDP, not the other way around. In fact, changes in U.S. defense military expenditures, as a percentage of GDP, explain approximately 31 percent of the variance in Soviet military expenditures during this period.

It is also interesting that non-U.S. NATO military expenditures are strongly correlated with Soviet military expenditures, with a correlation coefficient of 0.81. This result means that Soviet military expenditures explain 66 percent of the variance in non-U.S. NATO defense military expenditures, as a percentage of GDP; which is a much stronger relationship than between the Soviet Union and U.S. defense expenditures. Therefore, NATO allies appear to be responsive to changes in Soviet military expenditures during this period. You can see this relationship graphically for the non-U.S. members of NATO in Figure 2-3. As Soviet expenditures increased from 1980 to 1989, during the Soviet war in Afghanistan, non-U.S. NATO expenditures continued to rise, albeit only gradually.

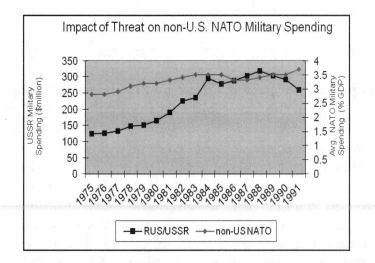

Figure 2-3. Impact of Threat on Non-U.S. NATO Expenditures in the Late-Cold War Period.[48]

CONTROLLING FOR INSTITUTIONAL INCENTIVES: NATO AND THE EU

The next two variables controlled, for institutional incentives and disincentives, to burden share within NATO. A dichotomous variable was added to the model to account for whether or not a state is a member of NATO. Theoretically, NATO membership should yield rational incentives to free-ride, since the allies are committed to defend each other under Article 5 of the Washington Treaty, regardless of whether or not that country was meeting its commitments to defense expenditures. In this model, membership in NATO was positively related to defense expenditures, as a percentage of GDP, but was only statistically significant when the United States was excluded from the data. Even these findings were not robust when checked with other statistical methods. [49]

A dichotomous variable was also added to account for whether or not the state was a member of the EU. A major achievement of the European community during this period was the Single Europe Act of 1986, which sought to improve integration of European countries and develop an internal European market, free of trade barriers. There were also three new EU members during this period: Greece (1981), Spain (1986), and Portugal (1986). Like NATO, EU membership entailed rational incentives to lower military expenditures in order to be competitive in the European economic market. Thus, funding for economic development competed for fiscal resources with military spending. These incentives would suggest that, on average, members in the EU would have lower levels of military expenditures as a percentage of GDP than nonmembers. However, none of the results were statistically significant.

The most interesting finding concerns length of membership in NATO. The membership variable, *age*, is positive and statistically significant at the .001 level.[50] When the United States is excluded, *age* is negative and statistically significant. These results are very robust.[51] In fact, the level of military expenditures decreases, on average, between .042 percent for every year that country has been a member of NATO. The findings suggest that the longer a member stayed in NATO, the more prone it was to free-riding behavior. See Table 2-2.

Independent variables	PCSE I	PCSE II	
ECONOMIC: GROWTH	-.018* (.011)	-.005 (.008)	
DV LAG:	.566*** (.071)	.321*** (.065)	
SPILLOVER:	.401*** (.124)	.151 (.155)	
THREAT:	-.001 (.003)	.0005*** (.0001)	
NATO:	.098 (.130)	.275* (.165)	
EU:	-.217 (.185)	.037 (.147)	
MEMBER AGE:	.016*** (.005)	-.042*** (.012)	I - database includes U.S. data II - database excludes U.S. data

* P < .05
** P < .01
*** P < .001

Table 2-2. Testing the Burden Sharing Model, 1975-91.[52]

A modification was made to test the first hypothesis, concerning the "systematic tendency for 'exploitation' of the great by the small."[53] This tendency means that large states will share a greater relative proportion of burdens than small states, H1. This idea is rather intuitive since larger, wealthier allies have more to gain from the Alliance and therefore should be more willing and able to pay their share of the defense burdens. Many studies have merely defined larger states by the size of their GDP. However, other factors influence a country's demand for security. Using concepts from economics, the other factors of production, land (area), and labor (population), should also be good proxy measures of relative gain from military expenditures.[54] The geographic size of the country should also relate to the demand for defense expenditures. The more land and coastline a country has to defend, the greater its demand for military expenditures. Therefore, three different independent variables measuring size were used to test the exploitation hypothesis: *gdpcat*, *popcat*, and *areacat*.[55]

The ordinal variable, gdpcat, accounts for the absolute size of the economy in constant U.S. dollars (billons).[56] An ordinal variable, popcat, accounts for population size. The four categories used were: very small (under $7 million), small (between $7 and $20 million), medium (greater than $20 but less than $50 million), and large ($50 million or greater). A final variable is used to account for absolute size of a country, measured in square kilometers, areacat. These values were generated by taking the log of the area of the country.[57]

Using the Vector Decomposition method to account for the effects of time invariant variables (see

Table 2-3), all three measures of size (GDP, population, and area) are positive.[58] Both population and area are statistically significant. These findings are consistent with the expectations of exploitation of the large by the small, as suggested by our first hypothesis, and with the results in Table 2-3.

Independent variables	Vector Decomp I	Vector Decomp II
Economy:	.009	-.074***
(gdpcat)	(.027)	(.027)
Population:	.122***	.213***
(popcat)	(.028)	(.032)
Area:	.088***	-.029
(areacat)	(.023)	(.025)

Vector Decomposition I - database includes U.S. data.
Vector Decomposition II - database excludes U.S. data.

* P < .05
** P < .01
*** P < .001

Table 2-3. Impact of Size (GDP, Pop, and Area) with and without the United States, 1975-91.[59]

However, when the United States is excluded from the data base, only population size seems to be positively correlated with military expenditures (as a percentage of GDP).[60] This outcome suggests that, on average, members in the highest population category are likely to have higher military expenditures (as a percentage of GDP) than members with the smallest populations. While economy size does not matter when the United States is in the data set, the size of the economy has a negative, statistically significant relationship with military expenditures when the United States is excluded. This finding suggests that as wealth increases, military expenditures decrease in non-U.S. NATO nations. This finding does not support the exploitation of the great hypothesis.[61] The differences between the two data sets can be attributed to the pursuit of private goods by the United States and its role as the largest, most powerful NATO member. During this period, the United States was involved in several operations not related to NATO, such as Grenada and Panama, which increased its relative level of military expenditures. Additionally, as the largest ally, the United States would be expected to have a higher level of military expenditures.

These findings support the hypothesis that larger states shared a greater relative proportion of burdens than smaller states. However, these results do not suggest that NATO members characterize this disparity as exploitation.[62] Rather, this difference is an accepted outcome of NATO's progressive norms for burden sharing. As size increases, states are expected to contribute at a greater level. This norm is best demonstrated in the NATO common funding budgets.

NATO has institutionalized this progressive "ability to pay" philosophy in its common funding procedures.[63] There are three common fund budgets: the civil budget, the military budget, and the NATO Security Investment Program (NSIP) budget. NATO members make contributions to the three commonly funded budgets on an established cost share. These cost shares have been re-negotiated throughout the history of the Alliance, but have always included some consideration of the ability of the members to contribute based on relative GDP or GDP per capita. The common funding for infrastructure has been the most contentious area resulting in more frequent negotiations and adjustments. While these negotiations often consider net benefits and other political criteria in assigning costs shares, they also reflect on the state's ability to pay. Any changes in the three common funding cost shares requires Alliance consensus. During this period, the cost shares were adjusted in 1982 when Spain joined the Alliance.[64]

FORESHADOWING NEW MEMBERS: SPAIN

While there was only one new NATO member during this period, there are many parallels between Spain and the most recent wave of new NATO members. First, Spain had been ruled by a military dictator from 1939 until the death of General Francisco Franco in 1975. Therefore, Spain had spent most of the Cold War in semi-isolation from the rest of Western Europe.[65] Membership in NATO was seen as a way to reintegrate politically with the democracies of Europe. Second, Spanish leaders saw membership in NATO as a prerequisite to reintegration economically with Western Europe and the European Community. Finally, they also saw NATO membership as a way to strengthen democratic institutions and cement the subservience of the military to the political authorities.[66]

Spain's circumstances were unique in several aspects prior to accession. Spain had established basing agreements with the United States in 1953, while Franco was still in power. Thus, Spain had a history of cooperation with NATO, especially the United States, for almost 30 years prior to accession to NATO. Spain was also a major recipient of U.S. aid during the Cold War due to its strategic location and its possession of the Canary Islands. A major difference between Spain and the post-Cold War entrants was that Spain did not necessarily view the Soviet Union as a security threat.[67] Spain joined NATO, in part, to obtain greater leverage in negotiations with the United States over the existing basing treaties.[68] Anti-Americanism was also a common sentiment when Spain joined NATO in 1982.[69] Spain viewed its neighbors in Morocco and its own Basque separatists as greater security risks than the Soviet Union which was many miles away.[70]

Spain joined NATO while the center-right, *Union del Centro Democratico* (UCD), party was in power.[71] That same year, the Spanish Workers Socialist Party (PSOE) won the election and formed a new government. This party had been highly critical of U.S. basing agreements and NATO membership. Therefore, they suspended integration into the NATO military structure.[72] They also called for a public referendum on NATO membership, which was one of the items in their election platform.[73] In 1986, Spanish voters overwhelmingly supported NATO membership in a national referendum. In doing so, Spain also placed three conditions on continued membership in NATO.[74] First, Spain would continue to exclude nuclear weapons from its territory, as it had since 1979 (joining Denmark, Greece, and Norway that also prohibit nuclear weapons). Second, Spain would join Greece and France in being NATO members outside of the integrated military structure. They remained outside the military command structure until 1999. Finally, the U.S. military presence in Spain would have to be reduced. Spain notified the United States in 1987 that it would not renew the bilateral basing agreement.

During this period, Spain wanted to move away from a military focused on internal security to one focused on external threats. While there was some fluctuation over the 5-year period, 1977-81, Spain's average military expenditures were consistently below 2 percent of GDP. During the 5-year period following accession to NATO, 1982-87, Spain's military expenditures remained increased over 2 percent of GDP and remained relatively steady. While Spain's expenditures were consistently below the NATO average, this can be partially explained by its relatively benign threat environment compared to some of the other NATO members. What is more remarkable is that this steady level of expenditure occurred while a Socialist government was in power.

There was a substantial decline in military expenditures as a percentage of GDP after 5 years of membership (see Figure 2-4). This was largely due to Spain's economic prosperity during this period. Spain's GDP growth during this period (1987-91) had doubled over the previous 5 years. This rapid growth accounts for the declining percentage of GDP being spent on the military. In reality, from 1985 to 1990, Spain's real defense expenditures increased approximately 37 percent.[75] However, these defense expenditures continued to decline even after the Cold War.

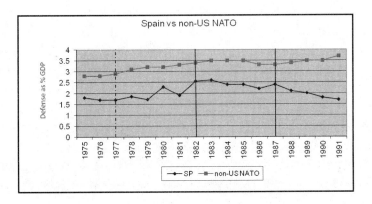

Figure 2-4. Spanish versus Non-U.S. NATO Expenditures as a Percentage of GDP.[76]

CONCLUSIONS FROM THE LATE-COLD WAR PERIOD

The results for the late-Cold War period are summarized in Table 2-4. The findings concerning the first hypothesis are mixed. All three measures of size (GDP, population, and area) are positive, and both population and area are statistically significant. These findings are consistent with the expectations of exploitation of the large by the small, as suggested by our first hypothesis.[77] However, when the United States is excluded from the data base, the first hypothesis is only supported for population size. Excluding the United States, as income increases, military expenditures decrease. This result suggests that wealthier non-U.S. NATO states tend to spend less, as a percentage of GDP, than poorer states. This data will be discussed further in the section on the post-Cold War. These findings also support the notion of NATO as a uniquely privileged group. A uniquely privileged group has one significantly larger member that is willing and able to bear most of the burdens of providing a public benefit regardless of the contributions of other members. As a uniquely privileged group, NATO members would therefore have strong incentives to free-ride on the United States.

		Results of Regression
H-1:	Large states will share greater relative proportion of burdens than small states	Supported for all three measures of size if the United States is included; If the United States is excluded: Supported for population, not GDP.
H-2:	Newer members will share greater relative proportion of burdens than older members	Supported if the United States is excluded. Not supported if the United States is included.
H-3:	New member burden sharing declines after NATO accession.	Only one new member
H-4:	The defense expenditures of NATO members, as percent of GDP, should increase as states are physically closer to Russia, or as Russian military expenditures increase.	Supported if the United States is excluded. Not supported if the United States is included.

Table 2-4. Summary of Findings from Regression.

The results of this chapter concerning age are also mixed. If the United States is excluded from the data set, the results support the second hypothesis that newer members of the Alliance will share a greater relative proportion of burdens than older members. As length of membership increased, military expenditures as a percentage of GDP decreased. This result was statistically significant and robust across all three methods. The findings suggest that the longer a member stayed in NATO, all things being equal, the more prone it was to free-riding behavior (see H2, Table 2-4). However, when the United States is included in the data set, the findings suggest that old members share a greater relative proportion of the burdens than new members. This result was statistically significant in two of the three methods.

Another interesting finding is the impact of threat perception on burden sharing decisions. Though U.S. and Soviet military expenditures were correlated, it appears that Soviet expenditures followed changes in U.S. military expenditures as a percentage of GDP. Not surprisingly, non-U.S. military expenditures were strongly correlated to changes in Soviet military expenditures during the portion of the late-Cold War period examined. When NATO is examined without the United States, military expenditures increase when Soviet military expenditures increase. However, the impact is conditioned by the distance from the Soviet Union; the closer the state is to the Soviet Union, the greater the impact.[78] This result is consistent with the theoretical expectations discussed earlier. This relationship will be examined in the next section to see if the improving strategic environment for NATO lessens the impact of Russian military expenditures.

The burden-sharing model presented in this chapter is both theoretically and empirically sound. The findings for most of the independent variables were robust. It was also possible to test the first two hypotheses during the late-Cold War period. However, with NATO adding only one new member during this period, Spain, it is difficult to make a conclusive argument about the impact of enlargement. For that, it is necessary to look at the post-Cold War period in the next section. The next section will also relook at the previous findings in the context of the new geostrategic environment.

POST-COLD WAR PERIOD: ENLARGEMENT (1992-2009)

Selected as the start point for this section is the year 1992.[79] The last section ended in 1991, the year the Soviet Union collapsed. This era marked a major shift in the strategic environment; 1992, the year that NATO drew up its work plan for Dialogue, Partnership, and Cooperation with the newly independent countries of Eastern Europe. This new policy represented an initial effort to explore increased cooperation with former Soviet satellite countries.[80] The data set ends in 2009, the year that Albania and Croatia became the newest members of NATO and the year before NATO's new Strategic Concept was approved.[81] The model used in the last section is applied to the post-Cold war data set.[82] The results confirm the validity of the demand function. The model explained approximately 79 percent of the annual variance in defense burdens in this period.

The relationship between economic growth (as measured by a change in GDP) and military expenditures as a percentage of GDP is negative and statistically significant at the .05 level.[83] For every percentage that GDP grows, military expenditures, as a percentage of GDP, decreases by .02 percent. This result was robust across multiple methods of analysis. This finding is different from our Cold War model in the last section, when economic growth of non-U.S. NATO states was not statistically significant. In the absence of the Soviet threat, it appears that military expenditures are more sensitive to economic growth. This phenomenon will be examined further later in this chapter.

There is also a statistically significant relationship between military expenditures as a percentage of

GDP and the 1-year lag of the dependent variable. For every 1 percent increase in military expenditures as a percentage of GDP, military expenditures increase .486 percent with the United States and .445 percent without. This finding is significant across multiple statistical methods at the .001 level. This result confirms the continued path dependency of military budgets as identified during the Cold War period.

Finally, states are less sensitive to the spending of their fellow allies during this period. This data is a change from the findings in the previous section.[84] The variable for spillover is positive, but the impact is smaller and not statistically significant. On average, military expenditures increase by only .127 percent for every 1 percent increase in military expenditures in the other NATO states. This result is not surprising. As threat decreases, states should be less concerned with the spending of their allies. In fact, average NATO military spending, as a percentage of GDP, has been in decline since the fall of the Soviet Union.

Analyzing the Threat.

The next step was to test the impact of threat on military expenditures as a percentage of GDP. Like the Cold War period, the value of the **threat** coefficient is very small. However, during this period, it is not statistically significant either with or without the United States included in the data set. This result is a change from the Cold War period, when **threat** had a significant impact on non-U.S. NATO spending. This finding supports the assertion that most NATO nations no longer perceive Russia as an imminent threat. However, interpreting these results requires greater analysis.

During this period, Russian military expenditures are positively and strongly correlated with U.S. military expenditures as a percentage of GDP.[85] U.S. military expenditures explain 68 percent of the variance in Russian military expenditures. This relationship is graphically explained for the United States in Figure 2-5. This correlation is stronger than in the Cold War period when U.S. military expenditures explained only 31 percent of the variance in Russian military expenditures. In both cases, increases in U.S. military expenditures, as a percentage of GDP, preceded increases in Russian military expenditures. For example, the increase in U.S. military expenditures in 2001 preceded increases in Russian military expenditures beginning in 2006. With the uncertainty and political upheaval in Russia and increasing disparity in relative power between the United States and Russia during this period, it is not surprising that Russian military expenditures were even more responsive to increased U.S. expenditures.

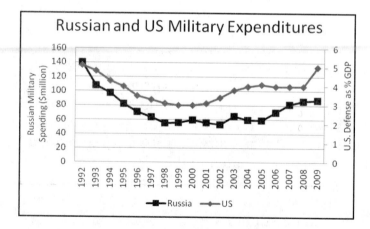

Figure 2-5. Impact of Threat on the United States in the Post-Cold War Period.[86]

As expected, threat from Russia no longer has a major impact on non-U.S. NATO spending. While non-U.S. military expenditures are positively correlated with Russian expenditures, there is a significant decrease from the Cold War period.[87] Russian military expenditures explain only 11 percent of the variance in non-U.S. NATO defense expenditures since 1992. Not only has NATO defense spending decreased steadily since 1992, non-U.S. defense expenditures continued to decline, even as U.S. and Russian levels began to increase. You can see this relationship graphically for the non-U.S. members of NATO in Figure 2-6. Clearly, Europe has a different perception of threat than either Russia or the United States. This assessment, validated in interviews conducted with NATO officials and representatives from NATO countries, will be discussed in greater detail in later chapters.

Figure 2-6. Impact of Threat on Non-U.S. NATO in the Post-Cold War Period.[88]

It is interesting to note that non-U.S. NATO expenditures have been in steady decline even though tensions have been building with Russia since the Iraq War in 2003. The year 2007 indicated a more dramatic shift in NATO-Russian relations. Three significant events suggested a more aggressive Russian policy toward NATO: the massive Russian cyber attack on Estonia, President Vladimir Putin withdrawing from the Conventional Forces in Europe (CFE) treaty and the resumption of Russian bomber flights.[89] This tension was heightened in 2008 with the Russian invasion of Georgia.

Russia was certainly upset by the two waves of NATO enlargements after the fall of the Soviet Union: one in 1999 and one in 2004. Additionally, U.S. efforts to place an anti-ballistic missile system in Poland and the Czech Republic coupled with the support of many NATO countries for Kosovo's independence all increased Russian apprehension regarding NATO's true intentions.[90] Yet, none of these events were significant enough to stem the decline of national defense budgets in Europe.

Controlling for Institutional Incentives: NATO and the EU.

As discussed during the late-Cold War period, membership in institutions such as NATO and the EU could also impact burden sharing decisions. In the post-Cold War period, the results for both the NATO and EU variables were negative. This is consistent with the logic of collective action which suggests that, on average, members in the EU or NATO are more prone to free-ride than nonmembers. However, the results were not statistically significant.[91]

The results also suggest that new member countries, on average, have higher military expenditures as a percentage of GDP than older NATO members. As in the Cold War, the value for the *age* coefficient was negative (-.025), suggesting that the longer a state remained in NATO, the more prone it was to free-ride. This data is consistent with the prediction in Hypothesis 2, new members would share a greater relative burden than older members. The results were statistically significant at the .05 level (see Table 2-5).[92]

Independent variables	PCSE I	PCSE II
Economic:	-0.16*	-.015*
Growth	(.009)	(.009)
DV LAG	.486***	.445***
	(.083)	(0.85)
SPILLOVER	.127	.183
(spillover)	(.202)	(.205)
THREAT	.001	.001
(threat)	(.002)	(.002)
NATO:	-.053	-.052
	(.131)	(.134)
EU	-.107	-.086
	(.149)	(.152)
AGE	-.025*	-.028*
	(.015)	(.015)

I- database includes U.S. data
II- database excludes
   P<.10
* P<.05
** P<.01
***P <.001

Table 2-5. Testing the Burden Sharing Model, 1992-2009.[93]

Next, variables were added to test the first hypothesis about size. This hypothesis, based on the logic of collective action, suggests that large states would share a greater relative proportion of burdens than small states. As in the previous section, three different independent variables were used to test this hypothesis: *gdpcat*, *popcat*, and *areacat*, (see Table 2-6).[94]

During the post-Cold War period, the coefficient for *gdpcat* was positive and statistically significant at the .001 level, with and without the United States included in the data set. On average, the richer a country was (as measured by GDP category), the less likely it was to free-ride. This result supports the assumption, based on the logic of collective action, that as the size of the country's GDP increases (richer countries), they would have higher levels of military expenditures. This relationship was not the case during the Cold War period. In addition, the coefficient for *popcat* was also positive and statistically significant at the .05 level, when the United States was excluded for the data set. This result, again, supports the "exploitation of the strong" hypothesis. The larger a country's population (as measured by population category), the greater its military expenditures as a percentage of GDP. The coefficient for *areacat* was not statistically significant in either case. Therefore, the geographic size of NATO states did not impact the relative level of military expenditures.

At this point, it would be useful to analyze the results in comparison with the late-Cold War. The main differences are noted among non-U.S. NATO members. Economic growth is the first difference between the post-Cold War period and the Cold War period. In the post-Cold War period, the economic growth had an inverse impact on military spending and was statistically significant for non-U.S. NATO allies. The results were not statistically significant for non-U.S. NATO allies during the late-Cold War period. These results support the earlier conjecture that military expenditures of our NATO allies are more sensitive to economic growth after the Cold War. The next difference between the post-Cold War period and the Cold War period is the results for spillover were not statistically significant. This weakens the earlier suggestion that defense goods were complementary during this period.[95] In fact, NATO allies do not appear to be sensitive to changes in allied military expenditures. The threat variable was not statistically significant in the post-Cold War period. In the late-Cold War period, the threat coefficients were positive and statistically significant for our NATO allies. This statistic reinforces the earlier assumption that the threat environment has changed in the post-Cold War period. This finding will be examined in greater detail later on in this chapter. Finally, the richer and more populous NATO allies tend to have higher military expenditures as a percentage of GDP. This notion, again, supports the "exploitation of the strong" hypothesis.

The main finding from Table 2-5 concerns the length of membership. As in the late-Cold War period, the *age* coefficient is negative (ranging from -.025 to -.028), suggesting that newer members, on average, have higher levels of military expenditures as a percentage of GDP.[96] These results are statistically significant at the .001 level. These findings support the hypothesis that new member states will burden share at a higher level than old member states.

The key findings are summarized in Table 2-7. The model explains approximately 80 percent of the annual variance in defense burdens and the results were robust across methods. The results support the first hypothesis that large states will share a greater relative proportion of burdens than small states. In addition, these findings support the second hypothesis that new member states should, on average, show higher levels of military expenditures as a percentage of GDP than older members of the Alliance. These results were statistically significant at the .05 level.

Independent variables	Vector Decomp I	Vector Decomp II
Economy:	.215***	.213***
(gdpcat)	(.036)	(.041)
Population:	.030	.066*
(popcat)	(.034)	(.036)
Area:	.017	-.022
(areacat)	(.018)	(.019)
Regression OLS I - database includes U.S. data		
Regression OLS II - database excludes U.S. data		

Table 2-6. Impact of Size (GDP, Pop, and Area) with and without the United States, 1992-2009.

		Results of Regression
H1:	Large states will share greater relative proportion of burdens than small states	Supported, for economic size.
H2:	New members will share greater relative proportion of burdens than old members	Supported and statistically significant.

Table 2-7. Summary Findings from Regression.

Alternative Test: Comparing Similar Cases.

Another method of comparison is to look at new members in comparison with old NATO members controlling for population size and ability to pay (GDP size). As discussed earlier, there is a statistically significant relationship between size and military expenditures as a percentage of GDP. Therefore, this section will examine the three new NATO members from the 1999 wave with comparable older NATO members using a most similar system (MSS) methodology.[97] Old and new NATO members are analyzed in dyads to control for population size: Belgium (10.3 million) and Hungary (10 million) are roughly the same population size as are Portugal (10 million) and the Czech Republic (10.3 million). In addition, Spain (39.5 million) compares closely with Poland (38.7 million). These same country pairs were used in an earlier study by Jeffrey Simon to evaluate the contributions of new NATO members.[98] While the physical size of these countries varies among each other, any impact of area should be constant over time, as their size does not change, with the exception of Czechoslovakia after 1992. This section will look at each of these dyads sequentially, beginning with Hungary and Belgium, the two allies with one of the lowest levels of military expenditures, as a percentage of GDP.

Hungary and Belgium are not identical in GDP size. Belgium has a much more advanced and richer economy than Hungary. Belgium's average GDP during this period was four times larger than Hungary's. As discussed earlier, there is a statistically significant relationship between GDP size and military expenditures as a percentage of GDP. There is also an ability to pay norm in NATO, discussed earlier, that accepts that richer nations should pay more than poorer members. Yet, using military expenditures, as a percentage of GDP, already controls for the ability to pay, unlike absolute military expenditures. Additionally, the magnitude of the wealth difference is relatively constant throughout this period. Therefore, we can look at the relationship between these two countries before and after Hungary's accession to NATO and compare the effect of membership on military expenditures as a percentage of GDP. Prior to joining NATO, Hungary's average GDP was $42.8 billion, while Belgium's average GDP was $247.9 billion. Hungary's economy was approximately 17 percent the size of Belgium's GDP. After joining NATO, Hungary's average GDP was $78.2 billion, while Belgium's average GDP was $301.9 billion. This data illustrates that Hungary's relative economic size increased to 26 percent the size of Belgium's GDP after accession to NATO. Based on the relationship between economic size and military expenditures, Hungary should have a lower relative demand for military expenditures than Belgium after 1998.

However, this relationship was not validated. Hungary's average military expenditures, as a percentage of GDP, before becoming a NATO member was 1.66 percent; roughly similar to Belgium's average military expenditures, as a percentage of GDP rate before 1999, 1.67 percent. After accession to NATO, Hungary's average military expenditures, as a percentage of GDP, decreased to 1.50 percent, while Belgium's average military expenditures, as a percentage of GDP decreased to 1.20 percent after 1998. While not meeting the NATO standard of 2 percent of GDP, Hungary did relatively better than Belgium after becoming a member of NATO (see Figure 2-7). This data provides further support that new members will share greater relative proportion of burdens than old members, controlling for both population and economy size.

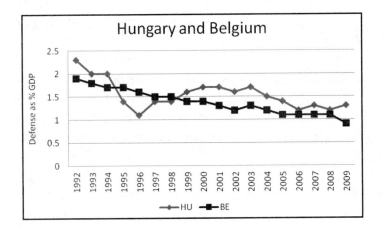

Figure 2-7. Hungarian versus Belgian Military Expenditures as a Percentage of GDP.[99]

The comparison of the Czech Republic and Portugal reveals similar findings. Portugal has a wealthier economy than the Czech Republic. The Czech Republic's average GDP was $71.3 billion during this period, while Portugal's average GDP was $129.8 billion. Prior to joining NATO, the Czech Republic's average GDP was $49.6 billion, while Portugal's average GDP was $107.3 billion. This information means that the Czech Republic's economy was approximately 46 percent the size of Portugal's GDP prior to accession. After joining NATO, the Czech Republic's average GDP was $90.3 billion, while Portugal's average GDP was $149.3 billion. Clearly, the Czech Republic's relative economic size increased to 60 percent the size of Portugal after accession to NATO. Therefore, the Czech Republic should have a lower relative demand for military expenditures than Portugal after 1998.

As with the first dyad, this result is not the case. The Czech Republic's average military expenditures, as a percentage of GDP, before becoming a NATO member was 2.7 percent, about 0.2 percent higher than Portugal's average military expenditures, as a percentage of GDP, before 1999 of 2.5 percent. After accession to NATO, the Czech Republic's average military expenditures, as a percentage of GDP rate, decreased to 1.8 percent. However, it remained higher than Portugal's average military expenditures, as a percentage of GDP, of 1.7 percent, after 1998. While the Czech Republic only met the NATO standard 2 percent of GDP during its first 4 years of membership, it did relatively better than Portugal after becoming a member of NATO (see Figure 2-8). This finding, again, supports the hypothesis that new members will share greater relative proportion of burdens than older members.

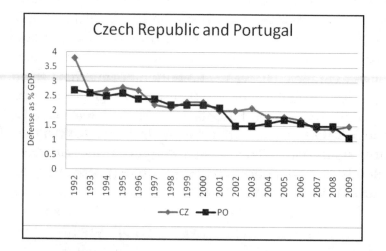

Figure 2-8. Czech versus Portuguese Military Expenditures as a Percentage of GDP.[100]

The final comparison looks at Poland and Spain. As with the earlier dyads, Spain has a wealthier economy than Poland. Poland's average GDP was $183.3 billion during this period, while Spain's average GDP was $722.2 billion. Prior to joining NATO, Poland's average GDP was $129.6 billion, while Spain's average GDP was $577.0 billion. In other words, Poland's economy was approximately 22 percent the size of Spain's GDP prior to accession. After joining NATO, Poland's average GDP was $230.4 billion, while Spain's average GDP was $849.2 billion. Thus Poland's relative economic size increased to 27 percent the size of Spain after accession to NATO. Since Poland's relative economic size grew over this period, Poland should have a lower relative demand for military expenditures than Spain after 1998.

In reality, Poland's average military expenditures, as a percentage of GDP, before becoming a NATO member was 2.4 percent versus Spain's average military expenditures, as a percentage of GDP, of 1.5 percent. After accession to NATO, Poland's average military expenditures, as a percentage of GDP rate, decreased to 1.9 percent. However, it was higher than Spain's average military expenditures as a percentage of GDP, 1.2 percent (see Figure 2-9), and was close to the NATO standard 2 percent of GDP. These findings are, again, consistent with the hypothesis that new members will share greater relative proportion of burdens than older members.

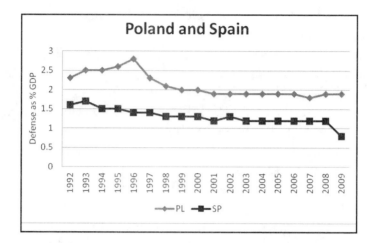

Figure 2-9. Polish versus Spanish Military Expenditures as a Percentage of GDP.[101]

Another factor to consider in these comparisons is that all three new members continued to use conscript forces during much of this period. Because conscripts are paid at below market rates, expenditure measures underestimate the true costs to states of their force structure. In earlier studies, Oneal adjusted defense spending by 10 percent to reflect the monetary value of conscription.[102] Therefore, new member contributions to NATO are underestimated using this measure. While Belgium ended conscription in 1994, Hungary continued to use conscripts until 2004.[103] Similarly, while Portugal ended conscription in 2003, the Czech Republic continued to use conscripts through 2005.[104] Finally, while Spain ended conscription in 2001, Poland continues to use conscripts.[105] If adjusted for conscription, Poland's levels of military expenditures as a percentage of GDP would meet the NATO goal. In sum, the Czech Republic, Hungary and Poland, while all not at the NATO goal of 2 percent, exceeded the expenditures of Belgium, Portugal, and Spain in the period following their membership into NATO (1999). While their levels of military expenditures dropped after attaining membership, they did so at a slower rate than older members.

DOES NEW MEMBER BURDEN SHARING DECLINE AFTER ACCESSION INTO NATO?

Related to the hypotheses about new versus old burden sharing, Hypothesis 3 states that new member burden sharing should decline after accession into NATO. In all three cases examined earlier, military expenditures dropped between accession to NATO in 1999 and 2004 when the second wave of NATO expansion took place. They continued to drop through 2009. However, their average levels of military expenditures exceed those of non-U.S. NATO members during this same period.[106] New member states are compared in cohorts, based on their year of admission to NATO. In Figure 2-10, we can see that the military expenditures, as a percentage of GDP, of the new NATO members from 1999 (the Czech Republic, Hungary, and Poland) decreased slightly in the years following NATO membership. However, this decline in military expenditures, as a percentage of GDP, is in line with the average expenditures of other NATO states which were declining at a similar rate.

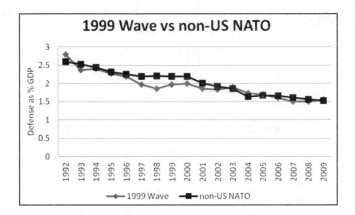

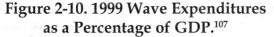

**Figure 2-10. 1999 Wave Expenditures
as a Percentage of GDP.[107]**

This result differs from Spain's experience during the Cold War (see the previous section) when
its level of military expenditures, as a percentage of
GDP, diverged from the non-U.S. NATO average after the 5-year mark. In fact, there is a convergence of
new member military expenditures as a percentage
of GDP on the NATO average after accession for the
1999 wave. This information suggests the decline in
military expenditures, as a percentage of GDP, is not
attributable to new member free-riding, rather to some
outside factor affecting all members of the Alliance.

Figure 2-11 tracks the military expenditures of the
2004 wave from 1992 to 2009. Again, military expenditures, as a percentage of GDP, do decline in absolute terms after accession into NATO. However, the
military expenditures of the new NATO members
from 2004 (Bulgaria, Estonia, Latvia, Lithuania, Romania, Slovakia, and Slovenia) are in line with the
average expenditures of other NATO states (excluding the United States). Unlike the earlier wave, they
begin to converge on the NATO average beginning

about 3 years before joining NATO. As with the first wave, they have remained in line with other NATO states since accession. This finding contradicts Hypothesis 3; new member burden sharing would decline after accession into NATO, due to the removal of conditionality.

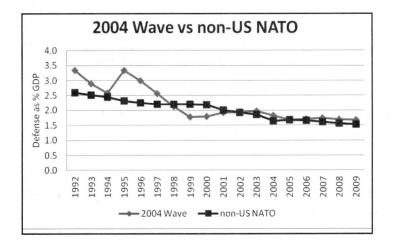

Figure 2-11. 2004 Wave versus Non-U.S. NATO Military Expenditures as a Percentage of GDP.[108]

Again, this finding is in contrast with NATO's previous experience with expansion in 1982. In Figure 2-12, we can see that the military expenditures of Spain diverged from the average expenditures of other NATO states after becoming a member. Also of interest is that Spain's military expenditures only begin to meet the NATO average in 1992 after the end of the Cold War. Even then, this convergence resulted more from falling NATO expenditures than any change in Spain's military expenditures.

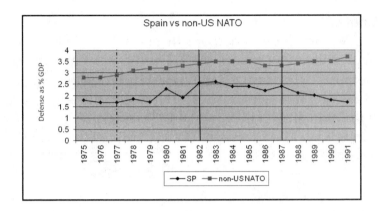

**Figure 2-12. Spain versus Non-U.S. NATO
Military Expenditures
as a Percentage of GDP.**[109]

Perhaps it was easier for new members to free-ride during the Cold War when both super powers were vying for potential allies and proxies. However, in the post-Cold War period, that does not appear to be the case. In sum, all of the tests conducted up to this point support the hypothesis that new members will share a greater relative proportion of burdens than old members. A summary status of the findings is presented in Table 2-8.

		Results of Regression
H1:	Large states will share greater relative proportion of burdens than small states	Supported for economic size.
H2:	New members will share greater relative proportion of burdens than old members	Strongly Supported
H3:	New member burden sharing declines after accession into NATO.	Supported, but no more than other members.

**Table 2-8. Initial Findings from
Alternative Methods.**

Controlling for the Threat.

The analysis discussed earlier suggests that new members will share greater relative proportion of burdens than old members because they want to establish credibility within the Alliance, especially with the Alliance leader, the United States. This is not to say that new members no longer fear Russia. In fact, they are very wary of Russian intentions and increasingly aggressive foreign policy. Rather, the argument is that new members' contributions are more directly linked to establishing their reputations than reacting to their historic adversary, Russia. At this point, it would be helpful to revisit an alternative explanation that could be made to illustrate these results.

Realists would contend that the new members' relatively greater military spending could be based on a desire to balance against their historic adversary, Russia. Since the Czech Republic, Hungary, and Poland are all closer to Russia than Belgium, Portugal, and Spain, and since they all were occupied by Soviet troops in the post-World War II period, a compelling argument can be made that a stronger threat perception is responsible for their greater military expenditures. If this were the case, we would expect that military expenditures, as a percentage of GDP levels, would rise as Russian military expenditures increased and would decrease as Russian military expenditures decreased. In order to control this alternative explanation, the average military expenditures, as a percentage of GDP, for the Czech Republic, Hungary, and Poland are compared to Russia's military expenditures before and after accession to NATO in 1999 (see Figure 2-13).

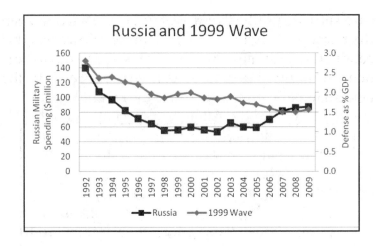

**Figure 2-13. Russian Military Expenditures
versus 1999 Wave Expenditures
as a Percentage of GDP.**[110]

As in the previous model, the military expenditures of the new member states are not responsive to increases in Russian military expenditures. While Russian military expenditures began to rise in 2006, the average defensive burden of these new members continued their gradual fall. Only after the Russian invasion of Georgia in 2008 did the average military expenditures of the Czech Republic, Hungary, and Poland increase, and then only 0.1 percent of GDP.

The same is true for the 2004 wave of new members, except that their average has remained constant at 1.7 percent of GDP from 2005-09 (see Figure 2-14). This result is not consistent with realist expectations (H4) that increased threat would lead to higher levels of military expenditures. Additionally, if Russia were the main factor driving burden sharing behavior, we would expect these new member states would not participate in NATO missions out of fear for their own security. Rather, they would be expected to keep their troops at home for self-defense. However, this conduct is also not the case. This element of burden sharing will be explored in greater detail in the next chapter.

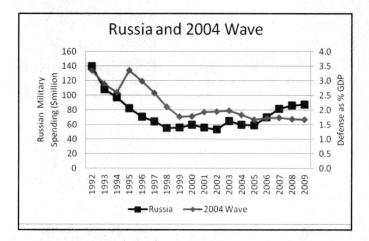

Figure 2-14. Russian Military Expenditures versus 2004 Wave Expenditures as a Percentage of GDP.[111]

Effect of Enlargement on Free-Riding.

The theory of collective action also suggests that as NATO enlarged, the incentives to free-ride would also increase. Larger groups have a more difficult time enforcing collective action. Therefore, as NATO almost doubled in size since 1999, there should be a relative decline in non-U.S. NATO defense spending. This conjecture adds another hypothesis for examination.

H5: Free-Riding Behavior Should Increase with NATO Enlargement.

This section will use two measures to test the hypothesis that enlargement increased free-riding behavior: average military expenditures versus the pre-enlargement trend, and NATO average military expenditures versus U.S. military expenditures.[112] One test to examine free-riding after NATO enlargement would be to look at the average rate of change of military expenditures, as a percentage of GDP, before and after NATO enlargement.

If enlargement of NATO did lead to greater free-riding, then we would expect the rate of change (in this case decline) in military expenditures as a percentage of GDP for non-U.S. members would increase after enlargement. In Figure 2-15, average NATO military expenditures are charted against the pre-enlargement averages and a linear trend line based on the pre-enlargement averages. If Hypothesis 4 is correct, the line representing the actual average NATO military expenditures should plot below the pre-enlargement trend line after NATO enlargements in 1999 and 2004. However, the results indicate that the rate of decline in military expenditures did not increase after enlargement. This data does not mean that NATO nations are not free-riding, rather that enlargement is not the culprit.

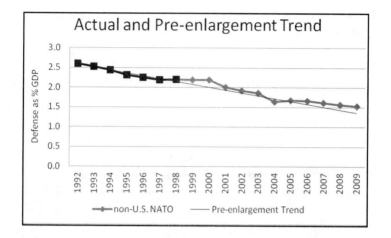

Figure 2-15. Average NATO Military Expenditures as a Percentage of GDP versus Trend Line.[113]

Another method of comparison would be to analyze the average annual non-U.S. NATO military expenditures versus the level of U.S. military expenditures from 1992 to 2009. As seen in previous figures, the average level of military expenditures declined in absolute terms throughout this period. Prior to the first wave of expansion, the average military expenditure levels dropped from 2.6 percent to 2.2 percent. This represents a 15 percent reduction. However, U.S. levels of military expenditures also dropped during this period, declining from 5.1 percent in 1992 to 3.1 percent in 1998, a 39 percent reduction. After NATO expansion in 1999, the average military expenditures for non-U.S. NATO members dropped from 2.2 percent to 1.7 percent. This result represents a 23 percent reduction. However, U.S. levels of military expenditures actually increased after 1999, from 3 percent in 1999 to 4 percent in 2004 (see Figure 2-16). Over the entire post-enlargement period, the annual rate of change for the U.S. was positive. This result bears further analysis.

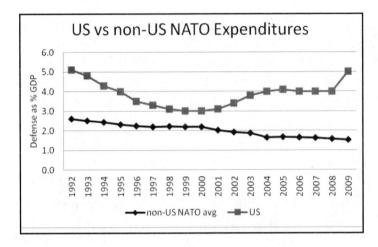

Figure 2-16. Non-U.S. NATO versus U.S. Military Expenditures as a Percentage of GDP.[114]

The relative decline in average rates of military expenditures for non-U.S. NATO members after enlargement could be cited as evidence of increased free-riding. However, it is first necessary to rule out alternative explanations. Increases in U.S. levels of spending could be the result of a relative increase in the power of the U.S. versus its NATO allies, leading to a greater provision of public goods by the United States. However, this is not likely. Non-U.S. NATO members had a slightly higher GDP growth rate (2.31 percent compared to 2.27 percent) than the United States during this period. Alternately, it could be the result of the United States pursuing private goods versus Alliance-wide public goods after 1999. The following section will examine these two ideas sequentially, looking for observable implications that might suggest whether or not there are more plausible explanations.

Alternative Explanations: Uniquely Privileged Groups.

As discussed in the previous section, NATO is often characterized as a uniquely privileged group.[115] As a uniquely privileged group, NATO members would therefore have strong incentives to free-ride on the United States, especially when U.S. power was increasing relative to Europe. Conversely, as the relative U.S. power declined, so too should free-riding behavior. Contrary to hypothesis five, evidence of this relationship would challenge the linkage between NATO enlargement and increased free-riding behavior during the post-Cold War period.

The data through 2000, shown in Figure 2-1, supports the alternative explanation attributing free-riding behavior to NATO being a uniquely privileged group. Between 1980 and 2000, the U.S. proportion of NATO military spending roughly paralleled changes in relative economic strength. As the proportion of the U.S. GDP to NATO's combined GDP increased, so did the proportion of U.S. military spending compared to NATO military spending (in U.S. dollars). However, after 2000, this practice is no longer the case. U.S. military expenditures, as a percentage of total NATO military expenditures, continued to increase even though the relative size of the U.S. economy (GDP) decreased. This finding suggests that either non-U.S. allies increased free-riding after NATO enlargement in 1999, or that the United States pursued more impure public or private goods after 2000, such as the Iraqi War or the War on Terrorism, which accounted for the divergence.

The Pursuit of Private or Impure Public Goods.

In 1991, Murdoch and Sandler critiqued the hegemonic power relationship with military expenditures as discussed earlier and suggested that the joint product model better explained military expenditures behavior within NATO.[116] Analyzing different types of weapon systems, they suggested that military expenditures did not uniformly yield public goods, but rather could also produce private and "impure" public goods. For example, long range strategic weapons (such as nuclear weapons) yield pure public benefit. First, the benefits produced (deterrence) are characterized by nonrival consumption. If more states fall under the protective umbrella of the U.S. nuclear arsenal, it does not diminish the deterrent benefits for the original members. Second, it is difficult to exclude members from the benefit of nuclear deterrence, even if they are free-riders. Other weapon systems, such as protective weapons, yielded either impure public or private benefits. For example, allies can be excluded from the benefit of a conventional weapon such as coastal artillery.

If we extend Murdoch and Sandler's joint product model to military operations, as well as weapon systems, we can then test our preliminary conclusions regarding burden sharing after enlargement. However, the characteristics of some military operations are more like public goods than others. In order for NATO to undertake any mission, it requires consensus. Every member would have to agree that the mission is in the best interest of the Alliance, or at least that it would not have a net detrimental impact on its national interest. NATO operations in the Balkans are one example. The benefits produced from the Balkan operations, deterrence of further inter-ethnic conflict and demonstration of NATO resolve and capability, were characterized by nonrival consumption. All European countries benefitted from the post-operation stability without reducing the benefit for the other members of the Alliance. Second, every member of NATO benefits from a more stable Balkan region and a stronger Alliance, whether or not it contributed its fair share to the mission. This phenomenon is an example of nonexclusion. In fact, all European countries, with the possible exception of Serbia, benefitted from these operations. Therefore, contributions to NATO approved missions could be characterized as public goods. In addition, expenditures in support of these NATO operations would rightly be included in burden sharing discussions.

The case of Operation IRAQI FREEDOM (OIF) is a different story. The war in Iraq was not a NATO mission. In fact, many NATO allies disagreed with the war and thought that it would lead to greater insecurity. Using Murdoch and Sandler's description, OIF was in pursuit of "country specific goals" and thus yielded private benefits. Troops and equipment committed to the defense of Iraq were unavailable for use elsewhere (therefore, rival). This manner of conduct became increasingly true for NATO operations in Afghanistan, where the Alliance has had a continued shortfall of required capability and the United States was unable to fully meet the demands for troops. As the Supreme Commander Allied Powers Europe stated during an interview in 2008:

> From a purely military perspective, I think the U.S. would be very stretched if it were required to undertake operations in Afghanistan without NATO support, given the level of commitment in Iraq.[117]

Clearly, U.S. expenditures in Iraq fell under the category of rival consumption and yielded questionable benefits to the Alliance; they were not an Alliance public good. In addition, the benefits of OIF were excludable. For example, the United States initially banned three critics of the war (France, Germany, and Russia) from competing for post-conflict reconstruction contracts.[118] Therefore, any military expenditure by the United States, in support of OIF, should not be counted in burden sharing comparisons with non-U.S. allies. The following analysis compares U.S. military expenditures as a percentage of GDP to the NATO average during this period.

If OIF was a private good, the U.S. military expenditures should be adjusted to get the true U.S. contribution to NATO public goods. According to data published by the General Accounting Office (GAO), U.S. military obligations in support of OIF amounted to approximately $267 billion dollars between 2003 and 2006.[119] This figure represented about 0.6 percent of GDP. Other estimates put the cost of the war in Iraq even higher. For example, the Congressional Research Service (CRS) estimates would increase this figure to 0.7 percent of GDP and the Congressional Budget Office (CBO) estimates for Iraq and Afghanistan, at $1.4 trillion between 2001 and 2012, would increase this figure to 0.85 percent of GDP.[120] All of this analysis understates the amount of private benefits contained in U.S. defense expenditures, since much of this spending supports America's global interests outside of NATO.

Using the more conservative number, if we adjust U.S. military expenditures as a percentage of GDP by 0.6 percent, then the average level of U.S. military expenditures between 2003 and 2008 would actually be around 3.4 percent. With this adjustment for private goods, U.S. levels of burden start at 3 percent in 1999 and finish at 3.4 percent in 2008, while non-U.S. NATO averages start at 2.2 percent in 1999 and finish around 1.6 percent in 2008. Not only did non-U.S. military expenditures decline after enlargement, the gap between the United States and non-U.S. NATO average expenditures increased even after accounting for the U.S. pursuit of private goods during OIF. This finding supports Hypothesis 4 that free-riding behavior increased with NATO enlargement, though this increase cannot be directly attributed to enlargement.

Conclusions from the Post-Cold War Period.

The findings for the post-Cold War period directly address most of the hypotheses in this project. A summary of the results is listed in Table 2-9. The "exploitation of the great" hypothesis (H1) appears to be a valid phenomenon during this period as measured by GDP (economic size).[121] The results also appear to support the second hypothesis (H2) that new member states share burdens at a higher level than existing members. While new member burden sharing did decline after accession into NATO (H3), it declined relatively less than for other NATO members.

		Results of Regression
H1:	Large states will share greater relative proportion of burdens than small states.	Supported, for economic size.
H2:	New members will share greater relative proportion of burdens than old members.	Supported.
H3:	New member burden sharing declines after accession into NATO.	Supported, but no more than old members.
H4:	The defense expenditures of NATO members, as percent of GDP, should increase as states are physically closer to Russia, or as Russian military expenditures increase.	Not supported.
H5:	Free-riding behavior should increase with NATO enlargement.	Supported, but causality questionable.

Table 2-9. Summary Findings from 1992-2009.

Another interesting finding is that defense expenditures of NATO members did not increase as Russian military expenditures increased (H4), as realists might predict. Finally, the results are mixed as to whether enlargement of NATO increased free-riding behavior (H5). The fact that few NATO states are now meeting the 2 percent benchmark is irrefutable. This data is consistent with the expectations of the logic of collective action in that the expansion of NATO from 16 to 26 members should have resulted in greater free-riding.

However, there were other contributing factors to the declining levels of military expenditures by non-U.S. NATO members. First, the rate of change in military expenditures as a percentage of GDP for non-U.S. members did not increase after enlargement. If enlargement caused a declining level of burden sharing, military expenditures should have decreased at a higher rate after enlargement.[122]

Second, rising levels of U.S. military expenditures after 2001 are largely explained by the pursuit of private benefits by the United States. The U.S. war in Iraq was responsible for a large portion of the increase in U.S. military expenditures during this period. Finally, declining military expenditures can be best explained by a declining conventional threat perception on the part of the NATO allies, especially the older, more prosperous members of the Alliance. Those countries without global interests find it increasingly difficult to justify defense expenditures in the absence of a recognized threat and in the face of increasing economic pressures.

The analysis to this point has focused on the traditional measures of burden sharing in NATO: defense expenditures as a percentage of GDP. While this is certainly an important aspect of the burden sharing debate, this measure alone gives an incomplete picture of burden sharing. The next chapter focuses on outputs in the form of troop contributions to NATO.

ENDNOTES - CHAPTER 2

1. Robert Gates, Secretary of Defense, *NATO Strategic Concept Seminar*, Washington, DC, National Defense University, February 23, 2010, available from *www.defense.gov/speeches/speech. aspx?speechid=1423*.

2. See Simon Duke, *The Burdensharing Debate*, New York: Saint Martin's Press, 1993, pp. 124-150; Simon Lunn, *Burden Sharing in NATO*, London, UK: Royal Institute of International Affairs, 1983, pp. 17-18; Keith Hartley and Todd Sandler, *The Political Economy of NATO*, New York: Cambridge, 1999, p. 28; and Wallace Theis, *Friendly Rivals: Bargaining and Burden-Shifting in NATO*, Armonk, NY: M. E. Sharpe, 2003, p. 182.

3. Stephen M. Walt, "Alliance Formation and the Balance of World Power," *International Security*, Vol. 9, No. 4, Spring 1985, p. 9; Peter K. Forster, and Stephen J. Cimbala, *Multinational Military Intervention: NATO Policy, Strategy and Burden-Sharing*, Burlington, UK: Ashgate, 2010, p. 206.

4. Mancur Olson, Jr., *The Logic of Collective Action: Public Goods and the Theory of Groups*, Rev. Ed., New York: Schocken Books, 1971, p. 176.

5. See, for example, Lincoln Gordon, "Economic Aspects of Coalition Diplomacy — The NATO Experience," *International Organization*, Vol. 10, Issue 4, 1956, pp. 529-543; Mancur Olson, Jr., and Richard Zeckhauser, "An Economic Theory of Alliances," *The Review of Economics and Statistics*, Vol. 48, No. 3, 1966; John R. Oneal and Mark A. Elrod, "NATO Burden Sharing and the Forces of Change," *International Studies Quarterly*, Vol. 33, 1989; John R. Oneal, "The Theory of Collective Action and Burden Sharing in NATO," *International Organization*, Vol. 44, No. 3, 1990; Todd Sandler, "Impurity of Defense: An Application to the Economics of Alliances," *Kyklos*, Vol. 30, 1977, pp. 443–460; Todd Sandler, "NATO Burden Sharing: Rules or Reality?" Christian Schmidt and Frank Blackaby, eds., Peace, Defence and Economic Analysis, London, UK: Macmillian, 1987; Todd Sandler, "The Economic Theory of Alliances: A Survey," *Journal of Conflict Resolution*, September 1993; Todd Sandler and John F. Forbes, "Burden Sharing, Strategy, and the Design of NATO," *Economic Inquiry*, Vol. 18, 1980; Keith Hartley and Todd Sandler, *The Political Economy of NATO: Past, Present, and Into the 21st Century*, London, UK: Cambridge University Press, 1999; and James C. Murdoch and Todd Sandler, "Nash-Cournot or Lindahl Behavior? An Empirical Test for the NATO Allies," *The Quarterly Journal of Economics*, Vol. 105, No. 4, 1990.

6. Olson, *The Logic of Collective Action*.

7. *Ibid.*, pp. 28–29.

8. Joseph Lepgold, "NATO's Post-Cold War Collective Action Problem," *International Security*, Vol. 23, No. 1, 1998, p. 104.

9. Olson, *The Logic of Collective Action*, p. 35.

10. Olson and Zeckhauser, p. 275.

11. Oneal and Elrod, pp. 435–456.

12. *Ibid.*, p. 447.

13. See also Bruce M. Russett, *What Price Vigilance? The Burdens of National Defense*, New Haven, CT: Yale University Press, 1970.

14. Oneal, "The Theory of Collective Action and Burden Sharing in NATO," p. 389.

15. James C. Murdoch and Todd Sandler, "Controversy: Alternative Approaches to the Study of Alliance Burden Sharing," *International Studies Quarterly*, Vol. 35, 1991, p. 113.

16. Oneal and Elrod, p. 111.

17. NATO Information for Press, "NATO-Russia Compendium of Financial and Economic Data Relating to Defence," Brussels, Belgium: NATO Headquarters, December 20, 2007, and June 10, 2010, available from *www.nato.int/issues/defence_expenditures/index.html*. For GDP data, see World Economic Outlook Database, International Monetary Fund, available from *www.imf.org/external/pubs/ft/weo/2010/02/weodata/index.aspx*.

18. Celeste Wallander and Robert Keohane, "Risks, Threats, and Security Institutions," Robert Keohane, ed., *Power and Governance in a Partially Globalized World,"* New York: Routledge Press, 2002, p. 95.

19. Alexandria Gheicu, "Security Institutions as Agents of Socialization: NATO and the New Europe," *International Organization*, Vol. 59, No. 4, 2005.

20. Jeffrey Checkel, "International Institutions and Socialization in Europe: Introduction and Framework." *International Organization*, Vol. 59, No. 4, 2005.

21. Judith Kelley, "International Actors on the Domestic Scene: Membership Conditionality and Socialization by International Institutions," *International Organization*, Vol. 58, 2004.

22. Gülnur Aybet, "NATO Conditionality in Bosnia and Herzegovina: Defense Reform and State-Building," *Problems of Post-Communism*, Vol. 57, September-October 2010.

23. See D. Fritz-Assmus and K. Zimmerman, "West German Demand for Defence Spending," London, UK: Routledge, 1990; Robert Looney and Stephen Mehay, *United States Defence Expenditures: Trends and Analysis*, London, UK: Routledge, 1990; and Murdoch and Sandler, "Nash-Cournot or Lindahl Behavior?"

24. Stephen M. Walt, "Alliance Formation and the Balance of World Power," *International Security*, Vol. 9, No. 4, Spring 1985.

25. *Ibid.*, p. 9.

26. In this monograph, the distance was measured in kilometers (capitol to Moscow).

27. Hartley and Sandler, *The Political Economy of NATO*, p. 31.

28. I also added a variable to account for a possible impact of the composition of the government (on a left-right scale) on military expenditures as a percentage of GDP. This model used a dichotomous variable, *lrparty*, to represent whether or not the head of state (Prime Minister) is from a left or right party. As might be expected from the literature, a government with a prime minister from a left party (*lrparty=1*), on average, had a lower level of military expenditure as a percentage of GDP. However, the impact was not large, and the results were not statistically significant. Thus, the party variable was removed from the model.

29. The main source for this information comes from NATO Information for Press, "NATO-Russia Compendium of Financial and Economic Data Relating to Defence."

30. At the Prague Summit in 2002, NATO established a new benchmark for allied military expenditures as 2 percent of GDP.

31. This data comes from the International Institute for Strategic Studies, *The Military Balance*, London, UK: Routledge, 1977-91.

32. A lagged dependent variable (DVLagit-1) is added to the model to account for the path dependency of defense spending instead of using the relative price of defense goods (PRICE). The demand for military expenditures is largely inelastic. The bureaucratic nature of the military budget process and the domestic political considerations that influence military expenditures cause an inelastic demand function. The decision to remove PRICE is in line with Sandler and Hartley's earlier work on the demand for military expenditures and other quantitative studies that suggest this is appropriate when using military expenditures as a percentage of GDP as the dependent variable. This project also excludes the variable, STRATEGIC, from the demand function since the military doctrine of the Alliance was relatively constant during this period as was the threat. In 1967, NATO adopted a strategic concept of flexible response. This doctrine espoused an integration of conventional and nuclear capabilities to provide an appropriate response to potential threats. NATO upgraded its strategic concept to forward defense in the 1980s at the same time the U.S. Army developed its Airland Battle concept. According to Sandler and Hartley, both flexible response and forward defense reduced the incentives to free ride due to the "complementarity of strategic and conventional weapons." The demand equation for NATO defense expenditures also changed during this period due to NATO's transition first to the flexible response strategy and then to the forward defense strategy. The "threat" environment during this period was one of moderately stable confrontation between the West and the Warsaw Pact. However, this does not imply a benign strategic environment. The Soviet invasion of Afghanistan in 1979 certainly heightened tensions between east and west, as did the declaration of martial law in Poland in 1981. The Reagan military buildup also occurred during this period.

33. This book uses a different measure of threat than Sandler and Hartley. In their model, THREAT represented the defense outlays of Alliance enemies (e.g. the USSR). If Stephan Walt is correct, the closer a NATO state is to the Soviet Union, the greater its perception of threat. Therefore, this model uses a new threat variable, *threat*, which is derived by dividing Soviet military expenditures (in $1 billion) by the distance (in 1,000 kilometers) be-

tween the NATO capital and Moscow. This project also excludes the variable, STRATEGIC, from the demand function. Rather, two separate data sets are used to account for changed strategic environments and corresponding changes to the Alliance military doctrine. The first data set covers the period from 1975 to 1991. Chapter 3 covers the period after 1992.

34. This is important because regression estimates of coefficients are often subject to omitted variable bias.

35. The ordinary least squares regression (OLS) model analyzes pooled cross sectional time series data on NATO members from 1975 to 1991. Iceland is not included in the data since it does not maintain a military force.

36. OSCE, "Conference on Security and Co-operation in Europe Final Act," 1975, available from *www.osce.org/documents/mcs/1975/08/4044_en.pdf.*

37. OSCE, "History of the OSCE," *OSCE Handbook,* October 11, 2007, available from *www.osce.org/publications/sg/2007/10/22286_955_en.pdf.*

38. These findings are not robust when checked with other statistical methods. In order to test the robustness of the findings in the model, three different methods of estimation were used: Panel Corrected Standard Errors (PCSE), Generalized Least Squares (GLS), and Fixed Effects Vector Decomposition (FEVD). Because I am using panel data, only panel corrected standard errors (PCSE) are presented in the table. First order autocorrelation is accounted for using the correlation (ar1) command with the STATA command, XTPCSE. In order to get rid of the serial correlation, the model was also tested using Generalized Least Squares (GLS) method. While autocorrelation does not cause biased estimates, it can cause the model to underestimate the variance of coefficients which makes tests of significance suspect. Using Vector Decomposition is also appropriate since it allows estimation of time invariant variables in a panel using fixed effects. These methods are also applied to two different data sets (with and without the United States).

39. The R-squared for the base model (model 7) was .962 and the coefficient for dvlag was .497. This means that, on average, current military expenditures as a percentage of GDP increase by .497 for every one percent increase in previous year's military expenditures as a percentage of GDP. In order to examine just how much explanatory power was driven by the lagged dependent variable, the lagged dependent variable was removed from the model in Model 11. However, the R-squared remains high at .94. These findings suggest that the model is sound even without the lagged dependent variable, dvlag.

40. Benjamin E. Goldsmith, "Bearing the Defense of Burden, 1886-1989," *Journal of Conflict Resolution*, Vol. 47, No. 5, 2003, p. 569.

41. While the results are not statistically significant when the United States is excluded from the database, they are also positive.

42. See, Oneal and Elrod, p. 451; Hartley and Sandler, *The Political Economy of NATO*, p. 37.

43. Hartley and Sandler, *The Political Economy of NATO*, p. 39.

44. However, it was statistically significant using GLS (at the .05 level) and using FEVD (at the .001 level).

45. The coefficient was the same and was statistically significant at the .001 level using both GLS and using FEVD.

46. NATO Information for Press, "NATO-Russia Compendium of Financial and Economic Data Relating to Defence."

47. *Ibid.*

48. *Ibid.*

49. However, NATO membership was statistically significant using GLS and FEVD (at the .05 level) with the United States included. Without the United States, the relationship of NATO membership to expenditures was not statistically significant using either GLS or FEVD.

50. However, it was not statistically significant using GLS and was only statistically significant (at the .05 level) using FEVD.

51. Statistically significant, using all three methods at the .001 level.

52. Endnote 50. Standard errors in parentheses. This model uses panel corrected standard errors to account for autocorrelation. Autocorrelation violates one of the assumptions in regression models: that the error terms are independent of one another. Autocorrelation is a frequent problem in working with panel data. While autocorrelation does not cause biased estimates, it can cause the model to underestimate the variance of coefficients which makes tests of significance suspect. Both GDP and military expenditures tend to change cyclically and therefore successive observations may be interdependent in this model. This data was checked in STATA using the *xtserial* command. The results of this test were significant, indicating that serial correlation was present.

53. Olson, *The Logic of Collective Action*, p. 29.

54. For example, Murdoch and Sandler used population as an independent variable in their study of defense expenditures in Sweden. See James C. Murdoch and Todd Sandler. "Swedish Military Expenditures and Armed Neutrality," Hartley and Sandler, eds., *The Economics of Defence Spending*, p. 148.

55. A collinearity test between the variables *gdpcat, popcat, areacat* and the country variables was run. Since the tolerance values were all lower than 0.1, these variables could be considered as a linear combination of the country variables. This is largely due to the fact that these measures of size are relatively time invariant within cases. Therefore, the country variables are deleted from the model while testing this hypothesis. For data, see International Institute for Strategic Studies, *The Military Balance*; Central Intelligence Agency, "World Factbook," Undated, available from *https://www.cia.gov/library/publications/the-world-factbook/geos/pl.html*.

56. These values were generated by taking the log of the actual GDP in $billions, as reported by the International Monetary

Fund for 1980 to 1991 and by International Institute for Strategic Studies for 1975 to 1979.

57. Central Intelligence Agency, "World Factbook."

58. A process developed by T. Plumper and V. Troeger, called Vector Decomposition, allows estimation of time invariant variables in a panel using fixed effects. One of the problems with ordinary fixed effects models is that they cannot estimate the effects of time-invariant variables. Fixed effects models can also lead to inefficient estimation. Vector decomposition isolates those fixed effects attributable to time invariant variables through a three stage process. The first stage estimates unit effects. The second stage reduces the fixed effects to those explained by the time invariant variables and those effects that are unexplained. The third stage re-estimates the model including the time invariant variables and the unexplained fixed effects. Not only does this method permit the use of a fixed effects model, it can also result in a more efficient estimate. The vector decomposition method is used on both data bases (with and without the United States) in order to test the robustness of our findings.

59. Endnote 57: Standard errors in parentheses.

60. This result is statistically significant at the .001 level.

61. Without the United States, the results for area were not statistically significant.

62. See, for example, Gordon; and Ronald Ritchie, *NATO: The Economics of an Alliance*, Toronto, Ontario, Canada: Ryerson Press, 1956. These references note the ability to pay norms of the Alliance since the very beginning of NATO.

63. NATO Public Diplomacy Division, *NATO Handbook*, Brussels, Belgium: NATO, 2001, p. 206.

64. "NATO: History of Common Funded Cost Shares," Report GAO/NSIAD-98-172, Washington, DC: General Accounting Office, May 1998, available from *www.gao.gov/assets/230/225915.pdf.*

65. Federico G. Gil and Joseph S. Tulchin, eds., *Spain's Entry into NATO: Conflicting Political and Strategic Perspectives*, Boulder, CO: Lynne Rienner Publishers, 1988, p. 1; and Inocencio Felix Arias, "Spanish Media and the Two NATO Campaigns," *Spain's Entry into NATO*, p. 31.

66. In fact, there had been an unsuccessful military coup attempt as late as 1981.

67. The Soviet Union was a major support of the Republic during the Spanish Civil War, while the United States and Western Europe supported Franco. See Joaquin Abril Martorell, "Spain, A Singular Ally," Gil and Tulchin, eds., p. 42.

68. Arias, p. 30.

69. Many Spaniards resented U.S. support of the Franco regime and its attitude toward Latin America. See Gil and Tulchin, eds., p. 2.

70. *Ibid.*, p. 3.

71. Colonel F. R. Stevens. Jr., USA, "Spain and NATO: Problems and Prospects." *Air University Review*, March-April 1980, available from *www.airpower.maxwell.af.mil/airchronicles/ aureview/1980/mar-apr/stevens.html.*

72. David García Cantalapiedra, "Spain, Burden-Sharing, and NATO Deterrence Policy," *Strategic Insights*, Vol. VIII, No. 4, September 2009, available from *edocs.nps.edu/npspubs/institutional/ newsletters/strategic%20insight/2009/garciaSep09.pdf.*

73. Emilio A. Rodriguez, "Atlanticism and Europeanism," Gil and Tulchin, eds., *Spain's Entry into NATO*, p. 64.

74. Glenn H. Snyder, "Spain in NATO: The Reluctant Partner," Gil and Tulchin, eds., *Spain's Entry into NATO*, p. 140.

75. Germany showed a similar drop in military expenditures after 1987 Germany's real defense expenditures increased 17 percent during this same period. Again, their expanding economy contributed to the decline as a percentage of GDP.

76. NATO Information for Press, "NATO-Russia Compendium of Financial and Economic Data Relating to Defence."

77. This result is also supported when looking at another traditional indicator of burden sharing, what Simon Duke called one of the output measures: force structure. This measure has been used from the very beginning of the Alliance starting with the Lisbon defense planning goals of 1952. As expected, the U.S. total armed forces, as a percentage of its labor force, (3.3, 2.9, 2.8, and 2.6, respectively) exceeded the NATO average (3.1, 2.8, 2.7, and 2.5, respectively) in 1975, 1980, 1985, and 1990. This result also supports the hypothesis concerning exploitation of the large by the small. See NATO Press Release M-DPC-2 (75)18, dated December 9, 1975, "Financial and Economic Data Relating to NATO Defence," and NATO Press Release PR/CP (2009)009, dated February 19, 2009, "Financial and Economic Data Relating to NATO Defence."

78. These findings were statistically significant at the .01 level and robust across all three methods.

79. The reasons for delineating this as a separate period of study are backed up by statistical rationale. A Chow Test was conducted to test whether or not the two time periods (pre- and post-Cold War) could be pooled together. Using 44 parameters in the data set, $f(44,598) = 2.14$. This was greater than the critical value (1.39) at .05 level of significance. Therefore, we can reject the hypothesis that the function is the same in the two time periods.

80. It is also the year that Czechoslovakia separated into two separate states: the Czech Republic and the Slovak Republic. This would normally be a slightly unbalanced panel due to this separation. In order to balance the panel, data for Czechoslovakia is used for both the Czech Republic and the Slovak Republic in 1992 only. Due to the large number of observations in the panel, this should not significantly skew the final results.

81. Albania and Croatia are excluded from this dataset for two reasons. First, they lack a sufficient track record as new NATO members. Second, both Albanian and Croatian military expenditures were inflated during the Croatian war of independence (1991-95) and the conflicts in Bosnia-Herzegovina during

the same period. The year 2009 was also selected as the end point because it was the last year for which there was complete data available.

82. The data set is a pooled cross sectional time series.

83. As mathematically expected, military expenditures as a percentage of GDP decrease when the denominator (GDP) increases.

84. See, for example, Oneal and Elrod, p. 451; Hartley and Sandler, *The Political Economy of NATO*, p. 37.

85. The have a correlation coefficient of .87.

86. NATO Information for Press, "NATO-Russia Compendium of Financial and Economic Data Relating to Defence."

87. During this period, they had a correlation coefficient of .34.

88. *Ibid.*

89. See "NATO Sees Recent Cyber Attacks on Estonia as Security Issue," *Deutsche Welle*, May 26, 2007, available from *www.dw-world.de/dw/article/0,2144,2558579,00.html*; Pavel Felgenhauer. "Putin Cancels CFE until NATO countries Properly 'Adhere' to Its Provisions," *Eurasia Daily Monitor*, May 2, 2007, available from *www.jamestown.org/edm/article.php?article_id=2372138*; Anton Troianovski, "Russia Resumes Its Long-Range Air Patrols," *The Washington Post*, August 18, 2007, p. A07, available from *www.washingtonpost.com/wp-dyn/content/article/2007/08/17/AR2007081702265.html*.

90. Fred Weir, "Post-Soviet 'Frozen Conflicts' Heat up as Big-Power Interests Collide," *The Christian Science Monitor*, June 25, 2008, available from *www.csmonitor.com/2008/0626/p06s01-woeu.html#*.

91. Normally the model would include independent variables for both NATO and EU membership and an interactive term. This interactive variable could be the product of the two dichotomous variables: NATO and EU. However, there are no EU countries in

the dataset that are not in NATO. Therefore, there is not enough leverage to test the interaction between NATO and EU. Only the two dichotomous variables, *nato* and *eu*, are included.

92. The model was tested using three statistical methods: Generalized Least Squares (GLS), Panel Corrected Standard Errors (PCSE), and Fixed Effects Vector Decomposition (FEVD). A common method of analysis uses Ordinary Least Squares (OLS), or Generalized Least Squares (GLS). However, because we are using panel data, panel corrected standard errors (PCSE) is more appropriate. This method permits the use of a fixed effects model. In order to account for first order autocorrelation, the (ar1) command is used with the STATA command, XTPCSE. Using Vector Decomposition is also appropriate since it allows estimation of time invariant variables in a panel using fixed effects. The results were consistent using all three methods of estimation and different data sets (with and without the United States). The results using FEVD were even more convincing.

93. Using the Vector Decomposition method developed by Plumper and Troeger allows estimation of time invariant variables in a panel using fixed effects. Not only does this method permit the use of a fixed effects model, it can also result in a more efficient estimate. This method is used on both data bases (with and without the United States) in order to test the robustness of our findings using OLS. Using the Vector Decomposition method increases the explanatory power of the model to 83 percent, with the United States, and 81 percent without the U.S. data. Vector decomposition also increases the statistical significance of the spillover variables.

94. See International Institute for Strategic Studies, *The Military Balance*; Central Intelligence Agency. "World Factbook."

95. Hartley and Sandler, *The Political Economy of NATO*, p. 32.

96. This result was consistent using GLS and the Vector Decomposition method.

97. Other than Iceland, which does not have a military, there are no cases where older NATO members have smaller economies than the new NATO members.

98. Jeffrey Simon, "The New NATO Members: Will they contribute?" *Strategic Forum*, No. 160, April 1999, Institute for National Strategic Studies, available from *www.ndu.edu/inss/strforum/SF160/forum160.html*.

99. NATO Information for Press, "NATO-Russia Compendium of Financial and Economic Data Relating to Defence."

100. *Ibid.*

101. *Ibid.*

102. Oneal.

103. Cindy Williams, "From Conscripts to Volunteers: NATO's Transitions to All-Volunteer Forces," *Naval War College Review*, 2005, p. 37.

104. *Ibid.*

105. *Ibid.*

106. In order to control for the unique U.S. role in NATO as the leader of the Alliance and its sole superpower, the new members are compared only to their non-U.S. allies.

107. NATO Information for Press, "NATO-Russia Compendium of Financial and Economic Data Relating to Defence."

108. *Ibid.*

109. *Ibid.*

110. *Ibid.*

111. *Ibid.*

112. A simple method used in previous studies to examine free-riding was to look at the standard deviation between defense burdens. See Russett; Oneal, "The Theory of Collective Action and Burden Sharing in NATO." The standard deviation represents the average deviation from the mean of NATO military expenditures

as a percentage of GDP. In this earlier study, as the value of the standard deviation got smaller, it was interpreted that burdens were shared more equally among member states. The use of the standard deviation has been absent in the more recent literature on burden sharing. One reason is that using standard deviation as measure of free-riding can be misleading. It is equally possible that declining standard deviations actually represent more uniform free-riding behavior. Given that few NATO countries are currently meeting the NATO benchmark of 2 percent of GDP for military expenditures, this might be a more plausible explanation. As the Supreme Allied Commander Europe General Bantz J. Craddock told the author in February 2008, "Since then [2002], we have actually regressed in levels of spending. Only six of 26 NATO members are meeting the 2% figure."

113. NATO Information for Press, "NATO-Russia Compendium of Financial and Economic Data Relating to Defence."

114. *Ibid.*

115. Oneal and Elrod, p. 448.

116. *Ibid.*

117. General John McColl, Deputy Supreme Allied Commander Europe, interview by author, SHAPE Headquarters, Mons, Belgium, February 1, 2008.

118. Douglas Jehl, "A Region Inflamed: The Reconstruction; Pentagon Bars Three Nations from Iraq Bids," *The New York Times*, December 10, 2003, available from *query.nytimes.com/gst/fullpage. html?res=9D00E5D91F3DF933A25751C1A9659C8B63.*

119. "Global War on Terrorism: Reported Obligations for the Department of Defense," Report GAO-08-423R, Washington, DC: General Accounting Office, January 30, 2008, p. 5, available from *www.gao.gov/new.items/d08423r.pdf.*

120. "The Cost of Iraq, Afghanistan, and Other Global War on Terror Operations Since 9/11," Report RL33110, Washington, DC: Congressional Research Service, July 14, 2008, p. 20, available from *www.fas.org/sgp/crs/natsec/RL33110.pdf;* "Iraq and Afghani-

stan," Washington, DC: Congressional Budget Office, 2007, *www. cbo.gov/topics*; Joseph Stilitz and Linda Bilmes, *The Three Trillion Dollar War*, New York: W. W. Norton, 2008, estimated the actual costs of the war in Iraq at $539 billion dollars between 2001 and 2007.

121. This result is also supported when looking at force structure since 2004 as in Endnote 71. The U.S. total armed forces (as a percentage of its labor force) exceeded the NATO average in every year after 2004. See NATO Press Release PR/CP (2009)009, dated February 19, 2009, "Financial and Economic Data Relating to NATO Defence."

122. Another contributing factor was that non-U.S. NATO members had an average growth rate of 2.31 percent compared to 2.27 percent for the United States during this period. Thus relative expenditures as a percentage of GDP should be lower for NATO allies.

CHAPTER 3

SHARING RISK:
CONTRIBUTIONS TO NATO MISSIONS

ANALYSIS OF CONTRIBUTIONS TO
NATO MISSIONS

> The NATO Treaty, written in 1949, speaks about "shared risk and shared responsibility" as a founding principle of the Alliance—we need that commitment as much today as we did in 1949.

> Victoria Nuland
> Former United States
> Ambassador to NATO 2007[1]

Shared risk and responsibility are key components of burden sharing. Ambassador Claudio Bisogneiro, the North Atlantic Treaty Organization's (NATO) Deputy Secretary General, defined burden sharing in political terms. "[Burden sharing] is first and foremost a political issue and has to do with political will."[2] Political will is most important when discussing Alliance outputs, such as contributions to NATO missions. Without political will, it is difficult for an Alliance member to initiate or sustain military operations. Military contributions to NATO missions represent a key indicator of burden sharing that is especially applicable to the on-going policy debates within NATO today.

The findings in this chapter reinforce the results from the last chapter on burden sharing. As expected from the collective action literature, size has an impact on contributions to NATO missions. For example, larger states usually provide greater air contributions than smaller NATO states. When it comes to troop contributions, the results are better explained by the joint product model. Where larger states were clearly pursuing private benefits (the United States in Afghanistan and Big 4 European nations in Bosnia/ Kosovo), they tended to provide a greater proportion of ground forces. Conversely, when smaller states are pursuing private benefits such as credibility (especially with the United States), they tended to provide an equal or greater proportion of ground forces.[3]

The results for the second hypothesis are mixed. During Bosnia and Kosovo, older member states, on average, provided greater troop contributions than new NATO members. This finding generally reflects a lack of military capability by new members immediately after accession into NATO. However, new member contributions generally increased over the duration of these missions as their capabilities increased. During the NATO mission to Afghanistan, newer member states provided greater troop contributions than older NATO members. This finding suggests that the pursuit of private benefits (credibility) by new members often mitigated the incentives to "free ride."

The results also suggest that free-riding behavior did not increase with NATO enlargement. In both Bosnia and Kosovo, the average troop contributions of small states equaled or exceeded their percentage of population after enlargement. While this phenomenon was not the case in Afghanistan, it was largely due to the delayed and initially limited role of NATO during the earlier years of operations in Afghanistan. In fact, the United States initially wanted to be free from Alliance constraints during Operation ENDURING FREEDOM (OEF). The fact that NATO assumed control of International Security Assistance Force (ISAF) in 2003 in the midst of an ongoing and contentious debate over Iraq suggests that NATO nations wanted to demonstrate their commitment to the Alliance and its leader, the United States. Thus, allied contributions increased steadily in the subsequent years in the face of significant domestic, political and economic constraints.

The results of this chapter also suggest a distinction between willingness and capability to burden share. This distinction is observable in two areas. First, there is a division of labor in NATO. This arrangement is agreed upon during NATO force planning and generation processes. Large NATO states are expected to have a relatively larger air force structure than smaller states, reflecting a deliberate choice by the Alliance to reduce redundant, high tech capabilities. Where smaller NATO states have a comparative advantage, as in conventional or niche troops, they are more willing and able to contribute. The analysis in these case studies shows a disproportionate contribution of air forces by large NATO states, reflecting the division of labor and their comparative advantage in high technology and financial resources. These contributions compensate for the times when larger states appear to free-ride in the provision of troops.

The second indication of this distinction concerns the limited ability of new members to contribute to missions outside their borders. Oftentimes, what appears to be free-riding behavior actually reflects a lack of capability versus a lack of willingness to contribute. As military capabilities increased, so too did new member contributions to NATO missions.

Not surprisingly, the willingness to participate is often constrained by individual national military capabilities and political realities. This fact is true for all NATO members. As Jamie Shea, former NATO spokesman and current Director of Policy Planning stated, "In the final analysis, how to count contributions to the Alliance is in the eye of the beholder. All national contributions are driven by political constraints."[4] While this reality may lead to a sub-optimal provision of public goods, it does not imply a rational calculation to free-ride. This idea is explored in greater detail in Chapter 5.

In this chapter, relative and proportional contributions of member states are analyzed during four NATO missions: one humanitarian and three peacekeeping/peace enforcement. The deployment of the NATO Response Force to Pakistan is analyzed as an example of a humanitarian mission. This mission was the first and only operational employment of ground elements from the NATO Response Force. The three peacekeeping missions represent the three largest NATO missions involving ground forces to date. The NATO mission in Bosnia (SFOR) and the NATO mission in Kosovo (KFOR) are examples of peace enforcement and peacekeeping missions. The NATO mission in Afghanistan (ISAF) has progressed from peacekeeping to stability and reconstruction to a counterinsurgency mission. These particular missions began during three distinct periods of interest for this book: before NATO enlargement, immediately following the first wave of NATO enlargement in 1999, and immediately preceding the last wave of NATO enlargement in 2004. These different start dates allow maximum variation in membership and enlargement status.

Two measures are used as proxies for burden sharing in support of NATO missions: air and troop contributions.[5] While both contributions are important, there is a definite distinction between the two.

Air contributions are largely constrained by existing military capability and technology. For example, few NATO countries had precision strike capability during these missions. Therefore, larger, wealthier countries that have these systems in their inventories should be able to bear a larger proportion of these burdens. Troop contributions, on the other hand, depend less upon technology and are largely constrained by political will and population (size and demographics). The decision to send soldiers into harm's way is a difficult political decision and the subsequent loss of life in these operations can hurt public support for a government. Therefore, while both air and ground contributions are analyzed, the emphasis is on troop contributions.[6]

WHY TROOP CONTRIBUTIONS?

In many ways, participation in NATO missions is a more valid measure of burden sharing than military expenditures. First, support for NATO missions carries greater political risk than do military expenditures. The human costs of these deployments are concentrated (usually within a professional military), while the benefits are distributed across society. Second, troop contributions are more clearly linked to a common goal of the Alliance.[7] Thus, contributions to NATO missions are more clearly attributable to a collective good than military expenditures, which are more difficult to identify as either public or private goods.

Each NATO mission requires approval through NATO's consensus procedures. Any NATO member, even the smallest and least powerful, can break silence and stop NATO from acting. Consensus decisionmaking ensures that these missions contribute to the pursuit of a common goal. This rule is a major factor in NATO's survival. During interviews conducted at NATO headquarters in Brussels, Belgium, in 2008, NATO officials placed a great deal of stock in consensus and its salience in the burden sharing debate.

> Consensus is important when countries commit to dangerous missions and accept great political risk. Consensus is the strength of Alliance and it provides legitimacy and demonstrates unity.[8]

Once NATO is committed to a mission, every NATO member benefits from the resulting increased security or stability, regardless of whether or not they directly contribute to the mission. Thus, the benefits are nonexcludable. Nonrival consumption means that the number of actors benefiting from the good or service does not diminish the amount available to others. The direct benefits of these NATO missions, whether increased security, stability, or good will, apply to all members without reducing the benefits to other members. All NATO states also gain from the indirect benefits of these missions, such as greater interoperability within the Alliance and increased deterrence to threats outside of the Alliance. These missions also satisfy the requirement of nonrival consumption.

Contributions to NATO missions are qualitatively and substantively different measures of burden sharing from military expenditures. Placing troops in a dangerous situation entails greater political risk than increasing defense spending or contributing to NATO common funding. Therefore, it should be more difficult to overcome the rational incentives to free-ride when sending troops to NATO missions, especially when those missions are difficult to directly link to a national interest. This is especially true when looking at humanitarian missions.

THE NATO RESPONSE FORCE IN PAKISTAN

Humanitarian operations represent a new type of NATO mission, though they build on earlier NATO civil emergency planning activities.[9] Humanitarian missions are designed to alleviate human suffering in the wake of natural disasters or as a result of on-going conflicts. Among NATO's new missions, Joseph Lepgold characterized humanitarian operations as public goods (both nonexcludable and nonrival) so long as they were of short duration and limited scope.[10] They are also more difficult to link to national interests of the contributing nations, making them more susceptible to free-riding behavior.

The NATO Response Force (NRF) mission to Pakistan was intended to provide assistance after the earthquakes in 2005. This mission was certainly limited in both scope and duration. The NATO mission in Pakistan was to transport humanitarian relief supplies and provide engineering and medical support to the government and the people of Pakistan. This mission lasted a little over 5 months, from October 2005 until February 2006.[11] NATO chose the NRF to support this humanitarian mission in order to showcase the NRF capabilities. A quick review of the background and composition of the NRF will provide a context for interpreting contributions by NATO nations.

The NRF is made up of air, land, and sea forces that are on a 6-month standby rotation to support NATO missions.[12] All forces participating in the NRF go through a training and certification process before going into the standby window. Like most NATO missions and exercises, contributions to the NRF are based on national offers to fill NRF requirements. These requirements and contributions are hashed out during annual Force Generation conferences.[13]

Once the North Atlantic Council (NAC) makes the decision to employ the NRF, member states are supposed to transfer authority of the forces to the Supreme Allied Commander Europe (SACEUR). However, the cost of operating those forces largely remains a national responsibility. For example, during the NRF 5 mission to Pakistan, operations were handled under NATO's customary policy of costs lying where they fell. This means that states were responsible for costs incurred by their forces even though they were under NATO control.

The development of the NRF was an evolutionary process. NRFs 1 and 2 were used as test cases to develop concepts and procedures for the NATO force.[14] NRF 3 demonstrated the capabilities of the response force concept during exercise Destined Glory, 2004, and was part of the certification process for the initial operating capability. During the first 6-month rotation after the initial operating capability, the land component command was filled by the NATO Rapid Deployable Corps-Italy, with the United Kingdom (UK) in charge of the maritime forces and the United States having the Air Component Command out of Izmir, Turkey. Italy (IT) provided approximately 70 percent of the personnel for the land forces, with the remainder coming from other NATO countries.

The first real mission of the NRF took place in support of the Summer Olympics in Greece during 2004, although only select units were deployed. An Italian battalion from NRF 3 was also deployed to Afghanistan in support of the presidential elections in 2004, though the NRF was not formally activated.[15] NRF 4 built on the lessons learned from NRF 3 and was in the rotation from January to June 2005. The land component command for NRF 4 was the German Netherlands Corps, with the UK in charge of the maritime forces and the United States having the Air Component Command out of Izmir.

NRF 5 took over responsibilities in July 2005. In September 2005, the NAC activated NRF 5 to provide airlift support for aid during Hurricane Katrina. Some 15 NRF cargo aircraft from France (FR), Germany (GE), Greece, IT, and the UK consolidated contributions in GE prior to shipment to the United States.[16] Twelve aircraft coming from Canada, Turkey, and NATO's Airborne Early Warning Fleet were used to ship these supplies to the United States from GE. Ukraine, a member of the Partnership for Peace, also donated a large portion of these cargo planes. In total, all NATO members offered assistance in addition to 14 members of the Euro-Atlantic Partnership Cell.[17]

On October 8, 2005, Pakistan was struck by a devastating earthquake that killed over 73,000 people and injured even more.[18] On October 10, 2005, Pakistan requested assistance in dealing with the aftermath of the earthquake. The next day, the NAC approved the deployment of air assets to bring in relief supplies and on October 21, 2005, approved the deployment of land elements of the NRF. This action represented the first operational deployment of both land and air forces from the NRF. NRF 5, on call during this period, consisted of the NATO Rapid Deployable Corps—Spain, the Italian Maritime Forces, and the Joint Forces Air Component Command (JFACC) under French command.[19]

The NRF mission to Pakistan should have led to free-riding behavior and an exploitation of the great by the small, if Lepgold's characterization of humanitarian missions as public goods was correct. This tendency should have been even greater if the major NATO states were pursuing private benefits in supporting this humanitarian operation. Larger NATO countries certainly had more economic and strategic interests in this region.

This situation is especially true for the United States since Pakistan was vital, not only to the "Global War on Terror," but to operations being conducted in Afghanistan under U.S. OEF. While NATO relied on Pakistani cooperation for its operations in Afghanistan (ISAF), it was not as reliant as America. Therefore, those nations that benefited the most from the humanitarian operation and had the most ambitious objectives, such as the United States, should have contributed more than other allies. The rational incentives to free-ride should have been magnified by the fact that the NRF was not common funded and that each NATO member paid for the costs incurred by their individual forces.

Large Versus Small.

Under NRF 5, NATO deployed some 170 flights in support of the humanitarian operation in Pakistan from October 2005 to January 2006.[20] A majority of these came from large NATO member states, although smaller states provided funding contributions in some cases. For example, the UK alone contributed 25 percent of all NRF flights.[21] Additionally, the United States provided over 140 airlifts, using its own assets, in addition to six U.S. military ships delivering aid.[22]

The same level of contribution was true for the deployment of helicopters. NRF 5 had a total of five helicopters deployed in support of earthquake relief operations in Pakistan; 80 percent of those coming from one country, GE, and the other 20 percent from Luxemburg.[23] On its own, the United States provided at least 24 helicopters to relief efforts, outside of NRF 5, compared to 40 helicopters provided by the Alliance as a whole.[24]

These results suggest that the United States and the other major powers in NATO provided a disproportionate share of air assets during NATO's Pakistan earthquake relief operation, supporting the hypothesis of an exploitation of the great by the small. However, this discrepancy reflects differing military capabilities rather than the willingness to assume burdens. Contributions to land forces provide a better measure for analyzing any free-riding behavior.

The troops required to support earthquake relief efforts were primarily engineers and medical personnel. At the time, the United States was not on standby to provide either of those assets to NRF 5. However, the United States made a significant bilateral troop contribution to the relief effort which can be compared to those of NATO (see Figure 3-1). According to the logic of collective action, the troop contributions of the Americans to the humanitarian mission should be larger than the other NATO members because they are the largest member of NATO and because they have more to gain and lose from such missions.

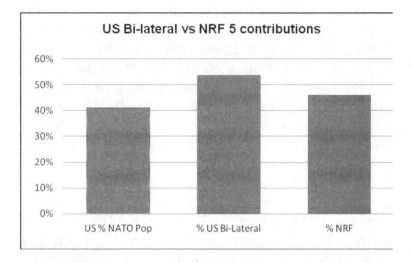

Figure 3-1. U.S. Troop Contributions as a Percentage of Combined U.S./NRF 5 Force.[25]

During the mission to Pakistan, the United States provided over 1,000 troops and two large medical teams consisting of over 200 personnel each.[26] This assistance exceeded the total NATO contributions under NRF 5 of 1,000 troops and 200 medical personnel. If this support was compared to the combined U.S. and NATO aid, the U.S. proportion of troops exceeded its percentage of NATO population at the time. This finding reinforces the results from the air contributions that large states will share greater relative proportion of burdens than small states.

Looking at the contributions from the Big 4 European states reveals a different picture. Within NRF 5, large European states (IT and the UK) provided about 26 percent of the engineers, and FR and the UK provided about 20 percent of the medical personnel.[27] At 25 percent of the NRF, this contribution was less than the Big 4 proportion of NATO population at the time (see Figure 3-2). Even though these states were not committed to provide any more forces during this NRF rotation, this result is not consistent with the hypothesis that larger states would share a greater proportion of the burden. This finding suggests that while large states honored their commitments to the NRF, they did not share a greater relative proportion of the burdens (with the exception of the United States). The more important question is whether or not the smaller NATO states met their commitments to the NRF during this operation.

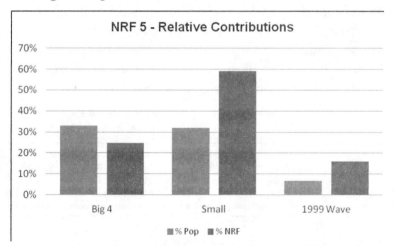

Figure 3-2. Relative NATO Troop Contributions to NRF 5.[28]

The contributions of small NATO states represented about 59 percent of the NRF, including 74 percent of the engineers and 80 percent of the medical personnel. In particular, Spain contributed 37 percent of the NRF engineering force, with only 5 percent of the NATO population, and the Netherlands contributed 65 percent of the medical personnel for NRF 5, with less than 2 percent of the total NATO population.

This behavior is consistent with Lepgold's argument that side payments or incentives could mitigate the logic of free-riding.[29] For example, since Spain had the command of the Land Forces during NRF 5, there was prestige rewards involved with leading the land forces. Therefore, it is not surprising that Spain fulfilled its commitments to the NRF. The leader of the Spanish contingent summed this sentiment up nicely: "This (was) the first real operation of the NATO Response Force and Spain (was) proud to lead it."[30] Similarly, the Dutch contingent was responsible for leading the NATO field hospital and thus earned the benefits of command with its large contribution to the mission. These findings do not support the hypothesis that large states will share greater relative proportion of burdens than small states (see Table 3-1).

		Humanitarian Operations
H1:	Large states will share greater relative proportion of burdens than small states	Supported for air operations and bilateral U.S. troop contributions. Not supported for troop contributions to the NRF mission.

Table 3-1. Initial Findings from NRF Troop Contributions.

If the results from the previous chapter are consistent, new member states should have contributed a larger portion of the NRF force than their proportion of the NATO population.[31] In comparing the contribution of the 1999 cohort (the Czech Republic, Hungary, and Poland) to its relative population size, the 1999 cohort exceeded its fair share of the NRF force. The total contribution of the 1999 wave represented 16 percent of the NRF, compared to its percentage of the NATO population, 6.8 percent (see Figure 3-2). Together, they represented 17 percent of the NRF engineering force, with Poland providing 14 percent and the Czech Republic 3 percent.[32] The 1999 wave of new members also comprised 12 percent of the NRF medical force, with the Czech Republic alone providing 24-30 medical personnel serving at the Netherlands Field Hospital.[33] Other new members contributed to the mission as well. For example, the Lithuanians provided one of the four water purification teams sent with the NRF, and Slovenia sent one of the two NRF Civil Military Coordination teams. These results suggest that these new NATO members did not free-ride during the NRF 5 mission and contributed more than their fair share to the NATO hurricane relief mission.

New Versus Old.

Figure 3-3 shows relative troop contributions of new versus old members to NRF 5.[34] Participation in these missions can also be used to look at the difference between new and old members. If Hypothesis 2 is correct, the contributions of new members should be relatively larger than the contributions of existing NATO members, controlling for population size.[35] As in the previous chapter, contributions of the 1999 wave are compared with those of existing NATO members (controlling for size). Total contributions by the Czech Republic (CZ) and Hungary (HU) to the NATO missions exceeded their percentage of NATO population. They also exceeded the contributions of comparable NATO states: Belgium (BE) and Portugal (PO). If new members were free-riding, neither of these findings would be true. The total contributions by the largest new member, Poland (PL), also exceeded its percentage of NATO population though it did not exceed the contributions made by Spain (SP) to the NRF mission. As discussed earlier, Spain's contribution was commensurate with its level of command, which was at a higher level than that of the Poles.

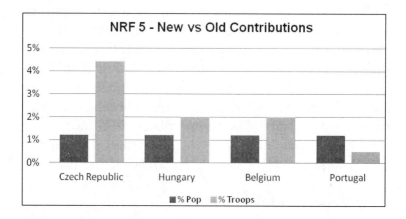

Figure 3-3. Relative Troop Contributions of New versus Old Members to NRF 5.

This case study yields mixed results. The first hypothesis was supported under two conditions. If bilateral American troop contributions are compared to the troop contributions from NRF 5, then the United States did share a greater relative proportion of burden than other NATO states. This information is not surprising given the private benefits of this aid to U.S. interests in the region. The first hypothesis is also supported when looking at air contributions to the earthquake relief efforts. Since these large states had an advantage in air capability, it is again not unexpected that they contributed these assets at a higher level than smaller NATO states. However, the first hypothesis is not sustained for small state troop contributions to the

NRF mission. The contributions of small NATO states to NRF 5 exceeded their proportion of the combined NATO population. (See Figure 3-4.)

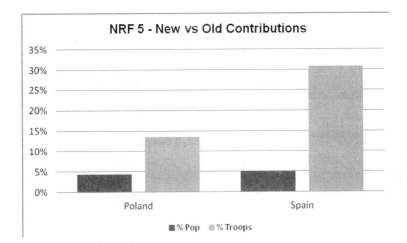

Figure 3-4. Relative Troop Contributions of Poland versus Spain to NRF 5.[36]

Hypothesis 2 is supported for the Czech Republic in comparison with Belgium and Portugal. However, it is not supported for Spain, as leader of NRF 5, in comparison with Poland. In general, the findings suggest that both small states and new member states attempted to fulfill their obligations to NATO, even during a humanitarian mission in a distant country. There is an important caveat to these findings. Since member nations commit forces to the NRF in advance, too much cannot be read into these results. Since commitments to the NRF are established on a rotational basis, it is not possible to generalize the findings from NRF 5 to other NRFs. However, as the only NRF to actively deploy ground forces to date, NRF 5 does shed some light on the burden sharing issue. Not only did small states and new members commit significant troops to NRF 5, they also followed through with this commitment when the NRF was deployed at great costs to their individual countries. Table 3-2 summarizes the results of this case study.

		Humanitarian Operations
H1:	Large states will share greater relative proportion of burdens than small states.	Supported for air operations and bilateral U.S. troop contributions. Not supported for troop contributions to the NRF mission.
H2:	New members will share greater relative proportion of burdens than old members.	Supported for Czech Republic

Table 3-2. Findings from NRF Case Study.

PEACEKEEPING MISSIONS: BOSNIA

Peacekeeping became an official NATO mission after the Oslo Summit in June 1992.[37] Unlike humanitarian and deterrence missions, peacekeeping and peace enforcement operations are potentially even more detrimental to Alliance burden sharing since they are both nonexcludable and rival. Lepgold makes one key distinction between these types of missions; peacekeeping missions are "designed to influence the political incentives of the actors in a conflict."[38] Because the benefits are nonexcludable both inside and outside the Alliance, the logic of collective action would suggest that these missions would lead to greater levels of free-riding. If members do not contribute fully or bear proportional risk, they still receive the benefit of the ensuing peace. Peacekeeping missions are also rival

112

in that the forces committed to one mission are not necessarily available for other Alliance missions.[39]

When peace operations are both nonexcludable and rival, this is the worst of both worlds. In this case, states have incentives to under supply the forces while the demand for these types of missions increases. Lepgold notes that since peace operations are "politically and legally discretionary,"[40] they are also more prone to free-riding behavior. For example, it is difficult to mobilize political will and resources to defend people in a faraway land. This challenge is especially relevant during an economic crisis when there is a greater competition for resources. As mentioned in Chapter 2, even if Alliance members reach consensus on conducting a peacekeeping mission, individual domestic incentives can often encourage free-riding in the execution of that mission.

The first peacekeeping mission examined is NATO's intervention into Bosnia. This task was NATO's first major peacekeeping operation and took the Alliance outside of the territory of member states. It is also significant because it occurred prior to NATO enlargement. Therefore, this mission can serve as a baseline for comparing new members' burden sharing before and after enlargement. European states attempted to deal with the situation in Bosnia mainly through the auspices of the United Nations (UN) from 1991 through 1993.[41] During this early phase, the United States was against American involvement in the Balkans and characterized it as a European problem, suggesting a private good.[42] The location of the crisis in the Balkans was especially threatening to European states and neighboring countries particularly IT and Greece. Because of its recent experience in Somalia, the United States was extremely hesitant to commit forces, especially ground forces, to the efforts in Bosnia. However, given the failure of European efforts, the United States eventually decided to intervene. This decision was partly made over concerns about maintaining the credibility of the UN and the European forces committed to that effort.

In a juxtaposition of the burden sharing argument in Afghanistan after 2003, it was the European nations that complained about the Americans unwillingness to equally share the risks involved in the peacekeeping efforts during Bosnia. Playing to its strategic, comparative advantage in airpower and considering its unwillingness to accept potential U.S. casualties, the Bill Clinton administration recommended a two pronged approach: lifting the arms embargo on the Bosnian Muslims and using precision bombing to punish Serbian forces. The United States did not immediately commit to providing land forces to augment the Alliance efforts.

> European allies complained that the plan would endanger their troops while the United States watched from a safe distance. As a result, many allied officials said NATO should do everything to avoid a situation where European and United States officials do not face comparable risks on the ground.[43]

Thus, while NATO encourages a division of labor, it also encourages all members to bear the political risks, especially those associated with troop deployments.

Large Versus Small.

NATO's first major air operation in the Bosnian crisis was Operation DENY FLIGHT. Operation DENY FLIGHT began in April 1993 and lasted until December 1995. It was approved by the NAC on April 8, 1993, and its purpose was to enforce the no fly zone established by the UN under UN Security Council Resolution (UNSCR) 816, provide close air support to UN troops, and to conduct limited air strikes. It was during this NATO mission that the Alliance fired its first shots in conflict. The forces of 14 NATO countries were deployed in support of Operation DENY FLIGHT, with only Iceland and Luxemburg not participating.[44] However, the United States provided the majority of planes, 43 percent, and most of the precision strike capability.[45] If the other four major powers in NATO are included, the UK, FR, GE, and IT, these larger states provided over 84 percent of the aircraft.[46]

The same is true of the subsequent air campaign, Operation DELIBERATE FORCE, conducted in response to the shelling of Sarajevo by Bosnian Serbs on August 28, 1995. Operation DELIBERATE FORCE lasted from August 29, 1995, to September 14, 1995, and was intended to compel the Serbian forces to comply with UN resolutions. In total, the forces of 12 NATO countries were deployed in support of Operation DELIBERATE FORCE. The exceptions were Iceland (with no military force), Greece, Luxemburg, and Portugal. This time, however, the United States provided almost 66 percent of the sorties flown in support of Operation DELIBERATE FORCE.[47] This effort included the use of sophisticated Tomahawk missiles that other allies did not possess.[48] During this operation, the other major powers in NATO (UK, FR, GE, and IT) provided over 86 percent of the aircraft.[49] These results suggest that the Americans and the other major powers in NATO did bear a disproportionate share of the military burdens during Operations DENY FLIGHT and DELIBERATE FORCE, suggesting the exploitation of the great by the small. However, this situation may result more from differing military capabilities than a lack of willingness to assume burdens. These five nations combined account for over 81 percent of NATO's total gross domestic product (GDP).[50] Therefore, they would be expected to provide a greater proportion of the expensive and technologically advanced air support required for these operations (see Table 3-3). This topic is explored in greater detail in Chapter 5, Capability versus Willingness to Burden Share.

		Operation Deny Flight and Deliberate Force
H1:	Large states will share greater relative proportion of burdens than small states.	Supported for contributions to air operations.

Table 3-3. Initial Findings from SFOR Air Contributions.

There is a significant difference between the commitment of air power and the commitment of ground troops. Up to this point, most of the land forces in the Bosnia area of operation were European. As mentioned in Chapter 2, the political risk of land contributions is significantly higher than that of air and naval forces. The political risk is exacerbated when the mission does not pose a direct threat to the security of the intervening states. This argument was prevalent in the discussions concerning U.S. troop contributions to Bosnia. Many states were upset that the United States, as the leader of the Alliance, was initially unwilling to put its own troops on the ground.

It is not burden sharing to say, 'You guys go out and take the risk of getting killed, and if there are problems, we will provide air support'. Putting American forces at risk is fundamental to assuring that there is a political commitment from Washington. American feet on the ground [are] vital.[51]

Therefore, the next section focuses on the land contributions to the two NATO missions in Bosnia: Implementation Force (IFOR) and Stabilization Force (SFOR).

IFOR and SFOR were the two NATO missions that were approved by the NAC to enforce the Dayton Peace Accords and entailed placing NATO forces in Bosnia-Herzegovina. The UNSCR 1031 gave NATO a 1-year mandate to enforce the Dayton Peace Accords through IFOR. IFOR's mission began on December 20, 1995. After the first set of Bosnian elections, NATO approved a follow-on force to take the place of IFOR. SFOR was activated on December 20, 1996, and was authorized by the UN under UNSCR 1088.[52] While containing only half of the forces that were in IFOR, SFOR represented a sustained commitment to the peacekeeping mission in Bosnia. In both IFOR and SFOR, every NATO nation with a national military contributed to the mission. This largely successfully mission was passed on to the European Union (EU) in 2004.

According to the first hypothesis, the troop contributions of the United States and the Big 4 European states to SFOR should have been larger than the other NATO members because they had more to gain and lose from these missions. In looking at the participation between 1995 and 2004, the contributions of the largest members of NATO only met or exceeded their proportion of NATO population 50 percent of the time. According to the fourth hypothesis, the level of free-riding should also increase after NATO enlargement. If this were the case, the relative U.S. contribution and the Big 4 European NATO members should have increased after NATO enlargement in 1999. However, these states actually appear to shoulder less than their fair share of the burdens after enlargement in 1999 than before NATO expanded (Figure 3-5). These results do not support either the first or fourth hypotheses. The data could suggest either that smaller states were not free-riding, or that the results were skewed due to free-riding behavior by either the United States or the other four major powers within NATO.

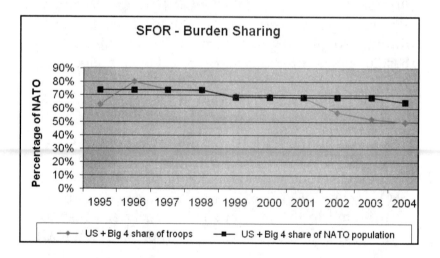

Figure 3-5. Relative U.S. and Big 4 SFOR Troop Contributions.[53]

In Figure 3-6, only the contributions of the Big 4 European NATO states are analyzed. In looking at their contributions between 1995 and 2004, the allocations of the largest members of NATO (excluding the Americans) exceeded their proportion of NATO population throughout the operation. This data is in stark contrast to the results including the United States. While the support from the Big 4 peaked in 1999 (coinciding with the first wave of NATO expansion), it never dropped below the proportion of the NATO population. These states appear to shoulder their fair share of the burdens, both before and after enlargement in 1999. These results do not support either the first or fourth hypotheses. The outcome could indicate that either the United States was free-riding, or that the level of support fell due to increasing operational tempo. For example, declining contributions after 2001 could reflect the competing demands from the pursuit of the "Global War on Terror."

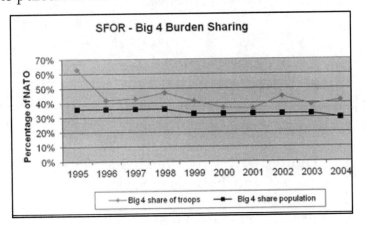

**Figure 3-6. Relative Big 4 European States'
Troop Contributions to SFOR.**[54]

Analysis of the smaller NATO states also supports these findings. The contributions of smaller NATO states between 1995 and 2004 met or exceeded their proportion of NATO population 70 percent of the time. Even more compelling, after the first phase of NATO enlargement in 1999, smaller NATO states consistently met their fair share of the burdens of the SFOR mission (see Figure 3-7). The contributions of these smaller NATO states also continually increased as a percentage of the total NATO force after NATO enlargement. Therefore, the first and fifth hypotheses are not supported (see Table 3-4). These findings are surprising; according to the logic of collective action, enlargement should have led to greater free-riding, especially by the smaller states.

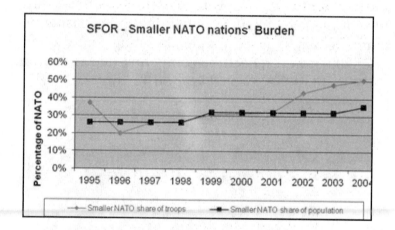

Figure 3-7. Relative Small State Troop Contributions to SFOR.[55]

Impact of NATO Enlargement.

Troop contributions of NATO members before and after enlargement in 1999 can also be examined. If NATO expansion did increase free-riding behavior (H5), the contributions small countries should decrease relative to their percentage of population after NATO enlargement. Rather, the contribution of small

NATO countries increases in almost every year following NATO expansion in 1999 (see Figure 3-7). It would
also follow that the combined, relative contributions
of the United States and Big 4 European NATO countries would increase after enlargement. However, the
combined, relative contribution of the Americans and
Big 4 NATO countries decreases in almost every year
following NATO expansion in 1999 (see Figure 3-5).
These findings suggest that NATO expansion did not
lead to greater free-riding behavior in the Alliance
(see Table 3-4).

		Troop Contributions
H1:	Large states will share greater relative proportion of burdens than small states.	Not Supported for the U.S.; supported for the Big 4 European NATO states till 2001.
H5:	Free-riding behavior should increase with NATO enlargement.	Not Supported

Table 3-4. Initial Findings from SFOR Case Study.

Did Free-Riding Increase after Membership?

NATO's intervention into Bosnia (SFOR) started
prior to the first wave of enlargement in 1999. Prior
to this date, states from the 1999 wave were members
of the Partnership for Peace Program. As these states
vied for membership in NATO, it was natural for
them to demonstrate their credibility and their potential contributions to the Alliance. One would expect
strong support prior to membership. However, once
these states became members in 1999, they should
have been tempted to free-ride. Therefore, only new
member participation from 1999 onward is analyzed.[56]

In their first year of NATO membership, participation in SFOR was at approximately the same level, 4 percent of the NATO force, as in 1998 when these countries were not yet members of NATO. Therefore, there was no precipitous drop after membership. However, during the 6 years following accession to NATO, the 1999 wave's troop contributions to SFOR never exceeded its percentage of NATO population. The contributions of the 1999 wave to SFOR averaged 3.9 percent of the total NATO force throughout the post-membership period. This average level of support is well below the percentage of the total NATO population (7 percent), but is approximately at the same level as when these countries entered NATO. This result indicates that, while new members did not necessarily provide their fair share of the burdens (as defined earlier in the chapter), the new members did not free-ride at a greater rate after membership (H3). In order to test the competing second and third hypotheses, it is necessary to compare the contributions of new members with those of existing NATO members of comparable size (see Figure 3-8).

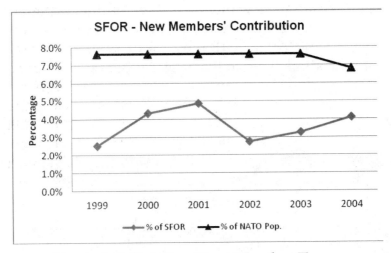

Figure 3-8. Relative New Member Troop
Contributions to SFOR.[57]

New Versus Old.

Figure 3-9 compares the troop contributions of the 1999 wave with comparable, existing NATO members (controlling for size). From 1999 to 2001, the Czech Republic and Hungary provided troops at a comparable level to Belgium and Portugal. However, the commitment level of both new members dropped in 2002, 3 years after membership. On average, over the period, the Czech Republic and Hungary provided 1.0 percent of the NATO force while each comprised approximately 1.3 percent of the NATO population. This commitment was relatively less than the two existing NATO members of similar size. On average, Belgium and Portugal provided 1.6 percent of the NATO force while each comprised approximately 1.3 percent of the NATO population. This information suggests that old members might share greater relative proportion of burdens than new members. This finding is primarily due to the drop in new member commitments after 2001. From 1999 to 2001, these new members contributed their fair share to the NATO mission.

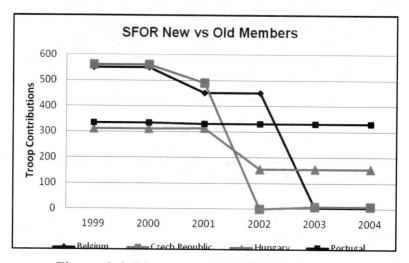

Figure 3-9. New versus Old Member Troop Contributions to SFOR.[58]

The picture is different when comparing the largest state in the 1999 wave with an existing NATO member (controlling for size). Poland consistently contributed less to the SFOR mission than Spain, despite the fact that these two nations had a comparable population size. On average, Poland provided 1.9 percent of the NATO force, while comprising 4.4 to 5 percent of the combined NATO population. This commitment was significantly less than its fair share (as defined earlier) and less than the contributions of aid from Spain. On average, Spain provided 6.5 percent of the NATO force while comprising 4.8 to 5 percent of the combined NATO population. This finding is consistent with the above and supports the third hypothesis that old members will share greater relative proportion of burdens than new members (see Figure 3-10). However, it could be that troop support to SFOR was constrained by concurrent commitments to the other NATO missions, such as Kosovo. If commitments to Kosovo were to blame for this drop in support to SFOR, there should be increased commitments from the 1999 wave to the KFOR mission in 2002. After summarizing the findings to this point, this chapter examines the relative contributions of the 1999 wave to the NATO mission in Kosovo.

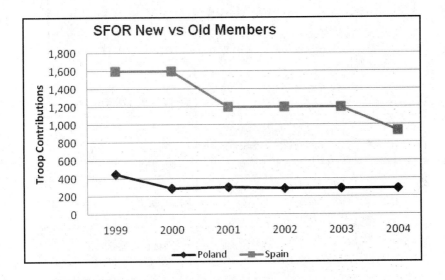

Figure 3-10. Poland versus Spain Troop Contributions to SFOR.[59]

The examination of NATO member contributions to the SFOR missions in Bosnia yielded the following findings (see Table 3-5). The results for the first hypothesis are mixed. If only considering air contributions and the Big 4 European NATO states until 2001, it appears that large states shared a greater relative proportion of burdens than small states. However, this finding is not supported when looking at troop contributions, especially after 2001. In fact, the United States (the largest and most powerful member of the Alliance) could be considered a free-rider if only looking at troops on the ground. In this mission, it appears that the United States bore the greatest burden in those areas where it had the advantage in military capabilities and where it had the political willingness to use those capabilities. Air capabilities depend upon both technical knowledge and economic strength. Therefore, it is not surprising that the United States has an advantage. The use of air power is also less hindered by domestic political constraints than the use of ground forces.

		Contributions to SFOR
H1:	Large states will share greater relative proportion of burdens than small states.	Supported for Air and for Big 4 European NATO states till 2001; Not supported for U.S. troop contributions.
H2:	New members will share greater relative proportion of burdens than old members.	Not Supported.
H3:	New member burden sharing declines after accession into NATO	Supported for Poland and only after 2001 for CZ & HUN.
H5:	Free-riding behavior should increase with NATO enlargement.	Not Supported.

Table 3-5. Findings from SFOR Case Study.

The findings also support the third hypothesis that old members will share greater relative proportion of burdens than new members. On average, the annual contributions by older NATO members exceeded those of new members of equal size. They also partially support the corollary hypothesis that new member burden sharing would decline after accession into NATO. However, there was also a decline in contributions of older members during this period. One plausible explanation for the lower troop contributions from the new member states is the lack of interoperability and low military readiness of these former Warsaw Pact forces. Most new members entered the Alliance with outdated Soviet equipment, Warsaw Pact operating procedures, and limited English skills. If capability is, in fact, the reason new members lag in troop contributions, versus the desire to free-ride, this gap should close over time as new member capabilities increase. Another possible explanation is that these forces were shifted to support another NATO mission. Finally, the findings do not support the hypothesis that free-riding behavior should increase with NATO enlargement. If anything, the relative contribution of smaller states increased after enlargement.

PEACEKEEPING MISSIONS: KOSOVO

The next case study examines NATO's involvement in Kosovo. NATO intervened into Kosovo partly to prevent a humanitarian disaster and partly to preserve the reputation and relevance of the Alliance. As the U.S. Secretary of Defense stated before Operation ALLIED FORCE, "NATO's credibility remains on the line."[60] The Kosovo Force (KFOR) mission presented more problems for the Alliance than SFOR. There was more domestic political opposition to the NATO mission in Kosovo. The mission was conducted without a UN resolution. Many European countries felt that a UN resolution was necessary to legitimize the use of force. KFOR took place during the same year three new members were added to NATO. Given these greater problems, this should have led to added free-riding behavior. This makes KFOR a good test case for the hypothesis that new member burden sharing would decline after accession into NATO, *ceteris paribus*.

As with Operations DENY FLIGHT and DELIBERATE FORCE, the United States heavily supported NATO's air operations during the Kosovo crisis, Operation ALLIED FORCE. Similar to the air operations in Bosnia, Americans provided the bulk of sophisticated military capabilities such as "stealth capabilities, precision-guided munitions, and sophisticated communications equipment."[61] The United States also provided the majority of the aircraft flown in support of Operation ALLIED FORCE, 63 percent. With only 48 percent of NATO's GDP, this U.S. level of contribution supports the hypothesis that large states will share a greater relative proportion of burdens than small states. (See Table 3-6.)

		Operation Allied Force
H1:	Large states will share greater relative proportion of burdens than small states.	Supported for contributions to air operations.

**Table 3-6. Initial Findings from KFOR
Air Contributions.**

Like the NATO mission in Bosnia, the United States and the Big 4 European states did not provide a relatively larger portion of the ground forces in KFOR.

On average, these large states met, but did not exceed their fair share of NATO forces (see Figure 3-11). Between 2003 and 2004, the largest members of NATO did not even contribute their fair share.

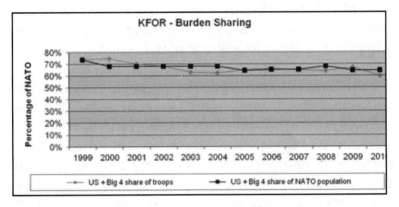

Figure 3-11. Relative U.S. and Big 4 European States' Troop Contributions to KFOR.[62]

This finding contradicts the expectations of the first hypothesis that the troop contributions of the United States and the Big 4 European states to KFOR should be larger than the other NATO members because they have more to gain and lose from such missions. These results do not support the hypothesis that the level of free-riding should increase after NATO enlargement in 1999. However, as mentioned, there appeared to be an equalization of burdens after the second wave of NATO enlargement. As with the Bosnian case, these results could suggest that the Americans were actually free-riding within NATO.

In order to check whether these results were due to U.S. or European free-riding, the contributions of the Big 4 European NATO states are analyzed separately (see Figure 3-12). In looking at their contributions between 1999 and 2008, the support from the four largest members of NATO (minus the United States) significantly exceeded their proportion of NATO population throughout the operation. These large states appeared to have shouldered their fair share of the burdens after both waves of enlargement in 1999 and 2004. These results suggest that the United States might have been free-riding. It could also be that European members were pursuing private benefits.[63] Certainly, the crisis in the Balkans had potentially greater externalities for European countries (such as migration, refugees, cross-border spillover of the conflict, and internal ethnic unrest) than it did for the United States. The German Secretary of Defense expressed a popular sentiment perfectly with his statement: "We want to do everything in our power to keep corpses from piling up in the Balkans and to ensure that there isn't a new stream of refugees into Europe."[64]

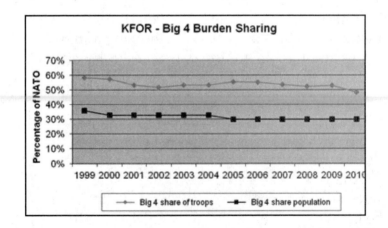

Figure 3-12. Relative Big 4 Troop Contributions to KFOR.[65]

Comparable to the Bosnian operation, the White House was reluctant to send ground forces to the Balkans. Even as late as April 1999, U.S. Secretary of Defense William Cohen prohibited Supreme Allied Commander Europe (SACEUR) General Wesley Clark, from discussing a ground option at a NATO summit. Cohen's instructions to Clark were, ". . . nothing about ground forces. We have to make this air campaign work."[66] During this same time frame, the author was working with the ad hoc planning team developing potential ground options in Kosovo at Supreme Headquarters Allied Powers Europe (SHAPE) Headquarters in Mons, Belgium. The sentiment in the team was not that the United States did not want to win or to do its fair share; rather, it was believed that the domestic political opinion did not support a heavy American ground commitment. Therefore, SACEUR was explicitly constrained from formally planning for a ground intervention. Even after the successful NATO intervention into Kosovo, *The New York Times* highlighted the reluctance to commit U.S. ground forces into the Balkans in 2000.

> . . . The American contingent has shrunk, and the Europeans are bearing most of the burden. The United States' peacekeeping force in Bosnia and Kosovo totals 11,400 troops . . . less than one-fifth of the 65,000-member NATO peacekeeping force in the region.[67]

Analysis of the contributions of smaller NATO states suggests that there was not an exploitation of the great by the small. On average, the smaller NATO states provided their fair share of the troops during the KFOR mission of 32 percent, which exactly corresponds to their proportion of the NATO combined population of 32 percent. While the contributions of smaller NATO states decreased after the first wave of enlargement in 1999, they increased significantly in

2003 when the White House began to pull its troops to support Operation IRAQI FREEDOM (OIF). These results reflect the dynamic nature of burden sharing within the Alliance where other states often have to compensate for the domestic constraints of their allies and where allies tend to contribute according to their capabilities. For example, during operations in Kosovo, Greece was under intense domestic pressure and its contributions were constrained by negative public opinion during the campaign. While the country did not participate in NATO air strikes, Greece did provide significant logistical support and facilitated the onward movement of NATO forces into Kosovo.

Impact of NATO Enlargement.

If NATO expansion did increase free-riding behavior (H5), there should be decreased contributions of small countries relative to their percentage of population after NATO enlargement. In KFOR, the support of small NATO countries increased in almost every year following NATO expansion in 1999 (see Figure 3-13). In addition, while these contributions decline after 2004, they remain approximately at the same level as their percentage of NATO population. If the fourth hypothesis is correct, that free-riding behavior would increase after NATO enlargement, then the combined, relative contributions of the United States and Big 4 NATO countries should also increase after enlargement. As in SFOR, the combined, relative contribution of the Americans and Big 4 NATO countries decreases in almost every year following NATO expansion in 1999 (see Figure 3-12). While the proportional contribution of the United States and Big 4 NATO countries increased after 2004, it is largely due to the reduction of the total force from approximately 20,000 to 18,000.

In fact, none of these countries increased the actual number of troops committed after 2004. These findings suggest that NATO expansion did not lead to greater free-riding behavior in the Alliance. During both NATO operations in Bosnia and Kosovo, the Big 4 European countries and the smaller NATO states, on average, provided their share of troops to both of these missions. These results suggest that the first and fifth hypotheses were not supported. (See Table 3-7.)

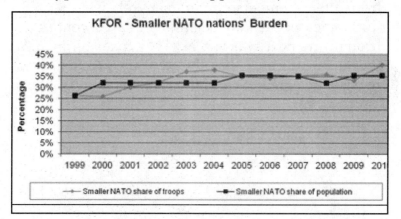

Figure 3-13. Relative Small State Troop Contributions to KFOR.[68]

		Troop Contributions
H1:	Large states will share greater relative proportion of burdens than small states.	Not Supported for the U.S.; supported for the Big 4 NATO.
H5:	Free-riding behavior should increase with NATO enlargement.	Not Supported.

Table 3-7. Initial Findings from KFOR Case Study.

Decline of Burden Sharing after Accession.

NATO's intervention into Kosovo began 10 days after NATO enlargement in 1999. In their first year of NATO membership, new member participation in KFOR comprised approximately 3.6 percent of the NATO force, similar to the 4 percent level of contribution to SFOR in that year. There was no precipitous drop after membership; in fact, relative contributions increased steadily beginning in 2002, continuing through the next wave of NATO expansion in 2004. This data indicates that the new members did not free-ride at a greater rate after membership (H3). (See Figure 3-14.)

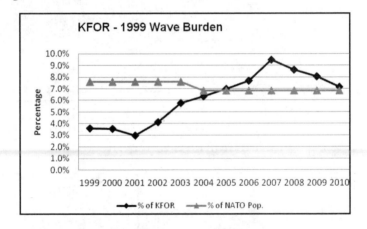

Figure 3-14. Relative New Member Troop Contributions to KFOR.[69]

It was only following the second wave of NATO enlargement in 2004 that the 1999 wave's relative contributions to KFOR exceeded its percentage of NATO population. In 2005 and 2006, contributions to KFOR averaged 7.3 percent of the total NATO force, while the percentage of NATO population had declined to

6.8 percent. This trend continued through 2010. This level of contribution represented an increase over the troops committed to SFOR and supports the argument that as capabilities of these new members increased, so did new member contributions to NATO missions. Not only did capabilities improve after enlargement, but also the desire to demonstrate credibility to the Alliance continued even after the new members entered NATO. A statement made in 2001 by Hungarian Ambassador Andras Simonyi supports this conjecture that the new member states wanted to demonstrate their credibility to the Alliance during the KFOR operations.

Hungary was also a brand new member that had to prove itself. But we also had to prove that enlargement was not a mistake, and that Hungary together with Poland and Czech Republic will not weaken the solidarity and cohesion of the Alliance.[70]

New Versus Old.

The new member contributions also stacked up well in comparison to similarly sized older members. While the troop contributions of the Czech Republic and Hungary were consistently below the level of Belgium, their involvement actually increased after NATO membership in 1999 and surpassed the contributions of both Belgium and Portugal in 2006 (Figure 3-15). On average, the Czech Republic and Hungary provided 1.43 percent of the NATO force while each comprising 1.3 percent of the NATO population. This commitment was relatively less than the two existing NATO members, Belgium and Portugal, but represented a fair share of the NATO force. On average, Belgium and Portugal provided 1.92 percent of the

NATO force while each comprising 1.2 to 1.3 percent of the NATO population. This finding suggests that old members shared a greater relative proportion of burden during KFOR than new members, even though the new members' percentage of the NATO force increased in every year after 2001 and surpassed that of Belgium and Portugal from 2006 to 2008. These findings suggest that new member contributions increased as military capability increased and domestic constraints waned.

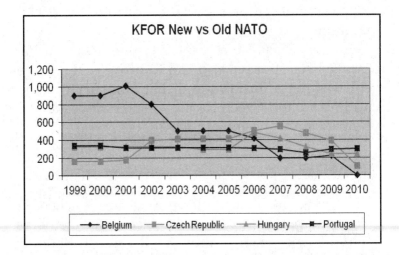

Figure 3-15. New versus Old Member Troop Contributions to KFOR.[71]

Initially, Hungary and the Czech Republic faced significant domestic political opposition to military action in Kosovo. Karel Kovanda, former head of the Czech delegation to NATO, explained some of the challenges faced by new NATO members:

The Kosovo campaign started 12 days after we became members of the Alliance, and I think the manner in which NATO makes its decisions took our politicians in Prague somewhat by surprise. And so, in the first days of the Kosovo campaign, our leadership found itself in two difficulties. One was the unfamiliarity with the decisionmaking process and the other difficulty was public opinion, which was reflected in the view of some of our politicians: public opinion, which for a variety of reasons, was staunchly against the bombing and in favor of Belgrade, even if it was the Belgrade of a Milosevic.[72]

The comparison between the two countries in the larger dyad is also of interest. On average, Poland provided 2.3 percent of the NATO force, while comprising more than 4.4 percent of the NATO population. This commitment was relatively less than the existing NATO member, Spain, for most of this period. On average, Spain provided 3.9 percent of the NATO force while comprising 4.8 to 5 percent of the NATO population. (It is interesting to note that Spain's contribution to KFOR spiked in 2001 after President Aznar was reelected in 2000 with a majority government and began a gradual decline under the Zapatero regime starting in 2004.) Yet, in 2009 and 2010, Poland's contributions to KFOR exceeded those of Spain. (See Figure 3-16.)

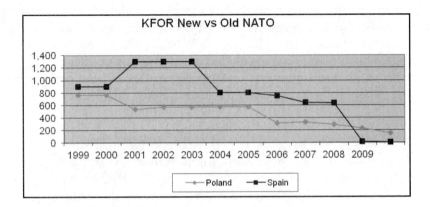

Figure 3-16. Poland versus Spain Troop Contributions to KFOR.[73]

The findings refute the alternative explanation from the Bosnia case study which suggested that declining contributions to SFOR were attributable to a shift in forces from SFOR to KFOR. Only the Czech Republic increased its ground forces in KFOR in 2002, by 225 soldiers. Even in this case, the increased commitment to KFOR did not compensate for the reduction of their commitment to SFOR (from 490 to 0) in 2002. Troop levels for both Hungary and Poland remained relatively stable from 2001 to 2005. Thereafter, Hungary increased its commitment to KFOR while Poland decreased its commitment.

The results from the examination of NATO contributions to the KFOR mission in Kosovo are listed in Table 3-8. Considering only air contributions, large states shared a greater relative proportion of the burden than small states. Again, this suggests that the difference in air power contributions is more a matter of capabilities rather than willingness to bear burdens. The troop contributions of the Big 4 NATO states are also consistent with this finding, though this was not the case when looking at U.S. troop contributions. If looking only at troop support, the largest and most powerful member of the Alliance would be considered a free-rider. However, given the extensive level of U.S. contributions to the air campaign, this actually reflects the division of labor in NATO.

		Contributions to KFOR
H1:	Large states will share greater relative proportion of burdens than small states.	Supported for Air and for Big 4 European NATO states troops; Not supported for the U.S. troop contributions.
H2:	New members will share greater relative proportion of burdens than old members.	Not Supported.
H3:	New member burden sharing declines after accession into NATO.	Not Supported, except for Poland.
H5:	Free-riding behavior should increase with NATO enlargement	Not Supported

Table 3-8. Findings from KFOR Case Study.

The findings do not support the hypothesis that new member burden sharing would decline after accession into NATO. On the contrary, contributions from both the Czech Republic and Hungary increased after attaining NATO membership. Finally, the findings do not support the hypothesis that free-riding behavior should increase with enlargement. On average, the relative contribution of smaller states increased after enlargement.

PEACE ENFORCEMENT MISSION: AFGHANISTAN

The NATO mission in Afghanistan represents an ideal case for free-riding behavior to occur. First, the ISAF is NATO's first peacekeeping mission outside of Europe. Second, while the core mission consists of stability and reconstruction, NATO forces are also more or less involved in combat operations, depending upon the location of the forces and the caveats imposed by their governments. Jamie Shea, NATO Director of Policy Planning, characterized ISAF as several distinct missions. "Peacekeeping is required in the north of the country, but combat and counterinsurgency operations are needed in the south."[74] These two factors place significant strains on NATO's cohesion and ability to field sufficient forces to accomplish the mission. In this regard, it should be difficult for NATO to overcome the rational incentives to free-ride during ISAF. If free-riding were ever to occur, it should occur when the domestic political costs are high (due to potential casualties and lack of public support), and the potential benefits are hard to articulate (due to the distance from both Europe and North America and a lack of clear connection to national interests).

The American-led mission that deposed the Taliban government in Afghanistan was OEF, launched in the aftermath of the attack by al-Qaeda on the United States on September 11, 2001 (9/11). Beginning in October 2001, this operation was a largely American one with limited participation of coalition partners. OEF, in addition to its stabilization and reconstruction mission, has always had a combat component to conduct counterinsurgency operations against the Taliban and remnants of al-Qaeda. While NATO nations participated in these missions, OEF was not a NATO operation. The commitment of forces to the NATO mission in Afghanistan in 2003 certainly supported U.S. objectives under OEF. Therefore, the subsequent NATO mission in Afghanistan could be considered a joint product, having both public benefits for NATO and private benefits for the United States. If this were true, then the United States would be expected to bear a larger proportion of the burdens in ISAF.

The ISAF mission in Afghanistan was created under UNSCRs 1386, 1413, and 1444. It was established in the aftermath of the invasion as a parallel mission to the on-going U.S. OEF mission. While ISAF was initially led by successive NATO nations—the UK, Turkey, and GE/Netherlands—the NATO Alliance did not take responsibility for the mission until August 2003.[75] Once NATO took command of ISAF, it began to expand its role in Afghanistan gradually. During Stage One of ISAF, NATO took control in the northern part of Afghanistan with predominantly French and German forces. The purpose of this mission was largely to provide security to the government in the capital of Kabul.[76] The mission later expanded with the deployment of provisional reconstruction teams (PRTs). These civil military teams were designed to help extend governance and reconstruction efforts. In Stage Two, NATO expanded into western Afghanistan under UNSCR 1623, with Italy and Spain providing the bulk of the forces. Both of these sectors were largely peaceful when NATO assumed control. This stage lasted from May 2005 until July 2006.[77] During this stage, the Alliance members were largely in agree-

141

ment as to the nature of the mission and the strategy to be employed by ISAF.

Starting in July 2006, Stage Three brought the deployment of NATO troops to southern Afghanistan, an area with significant Taliban activity and the focal point for OEF operations. The American, British, Canadian, and Dutch forces represented the largest contingent of the NATO force in southern Afghanistan. The beginning of Stage Three heralded a divergence of views within the Alliance. While the allies agreed on the mission, they disagreed on the strategy to accomplish that mission. Many NATO nations imposed caveats on where and when their forces could be used. These restrictions not only hampered military effectiveness, but also caused considerable strain within the Alliance. In September 2006, the NATO mission in Afghanistan was extended for 1 year by UNSCR 1707. Finally in Stage Four, NATO assumed control over the entire country in October 2006. In September 2007, the NATO mission in Afghanistan was again extended for 1 year by UNSCR 1776.[78] This mandate was extended again in September 2008 with UNSCR 1833.[79] While the level of violence increased considerably in Afghanistan after 2008, the UN continued the ISAF mandates in UNSCRs 1833, 1890, and 1917. It is in this context that the ISAF mission is examined.

Large Versus Small.

In ISAF, the United States and the largest NATO nations consistently provided a relatively greater portion of the ground forces, especially after the mission was transferred to NATO in 2003 (Figure 3-17). Unlike either SFOR or KFOR, the Big 4 European NATO states consistently provided a smaller proportion of the NATO force relative to their proportion of the NATO population. This account was especially true after 2008, following large increases in U.S. forces by President George W. Bush and President Barack Obama.

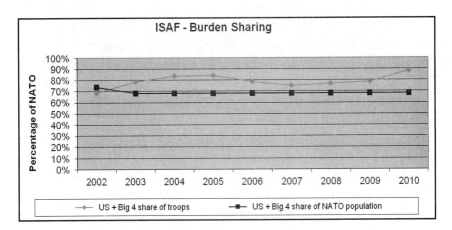

Figure 3-17. Relative U.S. and Big 4 Troop Contributions to ISAF.[80]

There are several possible rationales for this outcome. The first is that these states were attempting to free-ride on the United States. This explanation is certainly in line with the logic of collective action. Without a doubt, the rhetoric found in many U.S. publications would suggest that states were free-riding.

This relatively lower level of participation could also be seen as a backlash against American unilateralism. Many European nations were disenchanted with U.S. leadership in the aftermath of the Iraq war in 2003. For example, a 2003 survey indicated that the Iraq war had "undermined America's standing with Europeans."[81] In addition, many allies felt slighted by U.S. earlier refusal to assign a larger role to NATO nations during the opening phase of the conflict with Afghanistan. However, this explanation is inconsistent with the continued expansion of ISAF's area of responsibility from 2003 through 2006.

A more persuasive argument is that the United States was pursuing private benefits during ISAF and that this accounts for the relatively smaller contributions of non-U.S. NATO allies. However, separating public from private benefits is a difficult proposition. One indication that a country is pursuing a private benefit is when the expected benefits have "a direct link to self-interests."[82] In the wake of the 9/11 attacks on the United States, operations in Afghanistan were more closely linked to American interests than to those of other NATO nations. Additionally, the impact of a resurgent al-Qaeda and the Taliban within Afghanistan would have a great impact on U.S. security and international prestige in addition to the credibility of the new administration. (See Figure 3-18.)

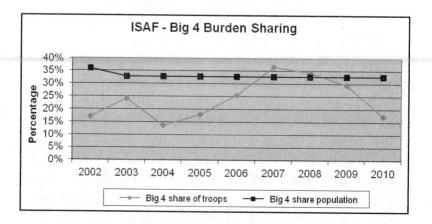

**Figure 3-18. Relative Big 4 European States'
Troop Contributions to ISAF.[83]**

Another indication that the United States was pursuing distinct private benefits is that NATO and the United States differed in the strategies employed during the mission. Initially, the Americans viewed ISAF as a supporting operation to its more combat oriented mission in Afghanistan, OEF, which was initially designed to topple the Taliban regime and to attack al-Qaeda bases in Afghanistan. The OEF mission has since focused on counter terrorism and bringing a general level of security to Afghanistan. The ISAF mission, while also committed to helping establish security and stability in Afghanistan, focuses more on reconstruction, economic development, and the establishment of good governance. According to former OEF Commander Lieutenant General David Barno, NATO countries were pursuing different objectives in Afghanistan than the United States.

> NATO was psychologically on a Peace Keeping Operation. It was very apparent that politically this was what they signed up for [peacekeeping operation]. NATO came in when Taliban was flat on its back and that was how the U.S. characterized the mission to NATO.[84]

NATO nations only reluctantly accepted a more active military role as the Taliban began to regain strength.

Similarly, the smaller European states, on average, shouldered a smaller share of the burden than the United States and their proportional share based on population (Figure 3-19). On average, the smaller NATO states provided only 21 percent of the troops during the ISAF mission, which is significantly below their proportion of the NATO combined population, 32 percent. Again, this disparity grew after significant American increases in forces after 2008. These results can, again, be explained using a private benefits framework to analyze the ISAF mission. As mentioned earlier, it was difficult for smaller NATO countries to explain the security risk posed to their citizens from the Taliban and al-Qaeda in Afghanistan. There was also a great deal of debate within European nations as to the desirability and suitability of conducting combat operations in Afghanistan as the level of Taliban violence surged. A 2008 poll provides support for this divergence of interests. While most NATO allies demonstrated strong support for the mission, only 43 percent of Europeans supported the conduct of combat operations, compared to 76 percent of Americans.[85] The argument that the United States is pursuing private benefits is also supported by the fact that free-riding behavior did not occur during either SFOR or KFOR.

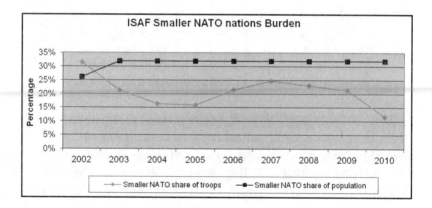

Figure 3-19. Relative Small State Troop Contributions to ISAF.[86]

The previous findings support the hypothesis that large states will share greater relative proportion of burdens than small states. Not only has the United

States contributed most of the forces to Afghanistan, it has also borne most of the casualties. Through 2010, the United States suffered over 1,342 fatalities in ISAF, representing 63 percent of the total killed. Of the Big 4 European NATO states, only Britain comes close, with approximately 16 percent of the ISAF killed in actions (KIA). More so than any other indicator, this data suggests that the Americans have done the heavy lifting in ISAF. See Table 3-9.

		Troop Contributions
H1:	Large states will share greater relative proportion of burdens than small states.	Supported for the U.S.

Table 3-9. Initial Findings from ISAF Case Study.

Impact of NATO Enlargement.

Participation in ISAF before and after enlargement in 2004 can also be analyzed. If NATO expansion did increase free-riding behavior (H5), contributions of small countries should have decreased, relative to their percentage of population after NATO enlargement. As in the previous NATO missions, the average contribution of small NATO countries actually increased following NATO expansion in 2004 (see Figure 3-19). This increase continued until 2007, when their relative contributions began to fall. This relative decline mirrors that of the Big 4 European NATO countries whose contributions also fell after 2007 (see Figure 3-17). Yet, the relative contributions of both the Big 4 European NATO states and the smaller European states, on average, increased between NATO enlargement in 2004 and 2007, and increased in absolute terms through 2010. This result does not support the hypothesis that free-riding behavior would increase with NATO enlargement. These initial findings are summarized in Table 3-10.

		Troop Contributions
H5:	Free-riding behavior should increase with NATO enlargement.	Not Supported.

Table 3-10. Enlargement Findings from ISAF Case Study.

Decline of Burden Sharing after Accession.

The contributions of new members to ISAF are also of note. In the first year of ISAF under NATO command (2003), the troop support of the 1999 wave comprised approximately 3.7 percent of the NATO force, similar to the level of contributions to KFOR in its first year. There was a temporary drop in the percentage of the total NATO force by the 1999 wave, down to 2.4 percent in 2004. However, this decline was attributable to a dramatic increase in American contributions (which increased by over 113 percent), rather than increased free-riding on the part of new members. In fact, the combined contribution of the 1999 wave actually increased between 2003 and 2004. While the contributions of the 1999 wave were consistently below their proportion of the NATO population, they did steadily increase after 2005. From 2008 until 2010, they were nearly equal to their percentage of population. This stability occurred at the same time the relative contributions of other NATO members were declining (see Figures 3-18 and 3-19). This statistic indicates that the new members did not free-ride at a greater rate after gaining membership (H3).

The contributions of the 2004 wave of new NATO members supports this claim (see Figure 3-20). As was the case earlier, the relative contribution of new members increased after they became NATO members. This information indicates that the new members did not free-ride at a greater rate after membership (H3). Rather, troop contributions increased as capability increased. In a 2007 interview by the author, the Supreme Allied Commander Europe, General John Craddock, supported this assessment. "By and large, new members are carrying their weight, although they have limited capabilities. Some good examples are Czech Republic, Estonia, Lithuania, Poland, and Romania."[87]Certainly, new NATO members responded to calls for additional troops from 2006 through 2010, even in the face of growing resistance from the Taliban.

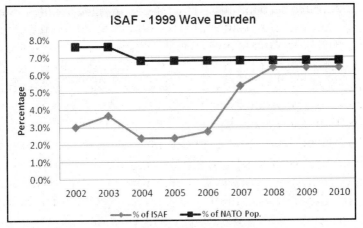

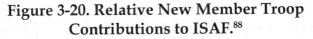

Figure 3-20. Relative New Member Troop Contributions to ISAF.[88]

New Versus Old.

The results are confirmed when comparing new versus old members using dyads based on size. Troop contributions by the Czech Republic and Hungary were consistently at or above the level of troops contributed by Belgium and Portugal (Figure 3-21). Between 2002 and 2008, the Czech Republic contributed about 1.5 percent of the NATO force, while comprising between 1.2 and 1.3 percent of NATO's population. During this same period, its support also exceeded those of both Belgium and Portugal. Hungary contributed a much smaller proportion of the NATO force, on average 0.5 percent during this period, but its contributions consistently exceeded those of Portugal and surpassed those of the Czech Republic in 2010. This calculation suggests that new members were burden sharing at a greater rate than existing NATO members (see Figure 3-22). As a previous U.S. Ambassador to NATO stated:

> We have been impressed by the commitment of all our new Allies to bring as much as they can to the table. Some countries are really punching above their weight class, like Lithuania, which runs its own Provincial Reconstruction team in Ghor Province in Afghanistan.[89]

150

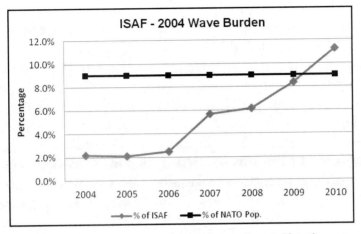

Figure 3-21. Relative 2004 Wave Contributions to ISAF.[90]

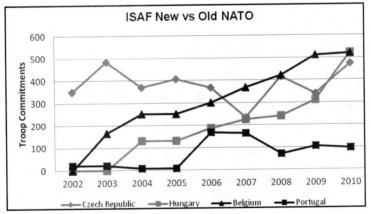

Figure 3-22. New versus Old Member Troop Contributions to ISAF.[91]

When comparing the larger states (Poland and Spain), Poland initially appears to free-ride more than Spain in contributions to ISAF (see Figure 3-23). On average, Poland contributed less than 1 percent to the NATO force between 2003 and 2006. However, Poland increased its support substantially between 2006 and 2010, in response to repeated SACEUR requests for additional NATO troops. Poland increased its contributions to 1,200 troops in 2008 and this number increased again to 2,488 in 2010.[92] In addition, Poland committed to providing eight badly needed helicopters in support of ISAF, with the first two arriving in August 2008.[93] More importantly, Poland's initial level of contributions to ISAF was constrained by commitments to the American-led OIF operation in Iraq. Poland's contributions to ISAF increased as troops came home from Iraq. Poland's contribution to OIF is examined in the next section.

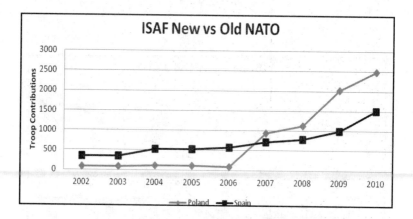

Figure 3-23. Poland versus Spain Troop Contributions to ISAF.[94]

New NATO members have also assumed a relatively larger portion of the risks in ISAF than other NATO countries. Many new NATO members have fewer restrictions on their forces in Afghanistan than older members. This practice not only improves the effectiveness of the forces committed, it also demonstrates a greater commitment to the success of the mission. This willingness to accept the political risks of ISAF is also reflected in their casualties. Through 2010, the new NATO member states (both 1999 and 2004 waves) have suffered 55 fatalities in representing ISAF. While relatively small in comparison to the United States, this signifies 2.6 percent of the total killed in ISAF. This number exceeds the KIA rates of three Big 4 European NATO states (FR, GE, and IT), with casualty rates of 2.3 percent, 1.5 percent, and 1.5 percent, respectively.[95] Again, this data suggests a sincere willingness to share in the burdens of the ISAF mission.

The analysis of NATO member contributions to the ISAF mission in Afghanistan yielded the following findings (see Table 3-11). If referring to the largest NATO member, the results support the hypothesis that large states will share a greater relative proportion of burdens than small states. As discussed earlier, this data may be attributable to the United States pursuing private benefits. This finding is not supported when looking at the Big 4 non-U.S. countries. Unlike SFOR and KFOR, the largest and most powerful members of the Alliance fell short in the relative contribution of the ground forces in ISAF.

The findings support the second hypothesis that new members will share a greater relative proportion of burdens than old members. The troop contributions for the Czech Republic and Hungary exceeded those of older members (controlling for size) for most of this period. The same is true for Poland during the last 4 years of ISAF. The average annual contributions of the 1999 wave are roughly equal to those of comparable older members. Finally, the findings do not support the hypothesis that free-riding behavior should increase with NATO enlargement.

		Contributions to ISAF
H-1:	Large states will share greater relative proportion of burdens than small states.	Supported for the U.S.
H-2:	New members will share greater relative proportion of burdens than old members.	Supported, especially after 2006.
H-3:	New member burden sharing declines after accession into NATO.	Not Supported.
H-5:	Free-riding behavior should increase with NATO enlargement.	Not Supported.

Table 3-11. Findings from ISAF Case Study.

The relative contribution of both the Big 4 European and smaller states increased after enlargement in 2004 until 2007, but declined after 2008. These findings for ISAF are summarized in the Table 3-11. The next step is to look at the impact of OIF on contributions to ISAF.

THE PURSUIT OF PRIVATE GOODS: OPERATION IRAQI FREEDOM

The relatively strong support of ISAF by the 1999 new members is even more remarkable when considering the competing demands for their forces during this period. While their level of contributions to ISAF never met their percentage of NATO population, this may have been due to their strong support of the U.S.-led OIF. Certainly, OIF was a controversial operation within the Alliance. New members were under conflicting pressures and unlike the previous NATO missions, there was no clear-cut definition of appropriate behavior. In fact, President Jacques Chirac suggested in 2003 that East European support of American policies in Iraq were counter to what Europe expected from its new members and could jeopardize their membership in the EU.[96] An analysis of the contributions by new member states suggests that they were pursuing private benefits, the demonstration of credibility to the United States, during OIF. According to Todd Sandler and Keith Hartley, "private or ally-specific benefits occur when a jointly produced defense output assists the provider, but the output's benefits are not received by other allies."[97] This would certainly be a good characterization of support to OIF.

OIF began in 2003 with the invasion of Iraq in order to topple the regime of Saddam Hussein. While many NATO members participated in the Multinational Forces in Iraq, OIF was not a NATO mission. In fact, there was considerable disagreement and dissention among the Allies brought about by the invasion. As an indication of the level of disagreement, U.S. Secretary of Defense Donald Rumsfeld derided two staunch NATO allies, GE and FR, as members of "old Europe" for their lack of support for OIF. However, new NATO members took advantage of this situation to establish their reliability to the leader of NATO, the United States. "Germany has been a problem, and FR has been a problem," said Rumsfeld, a former NATO ambassador. "But you look at vast numbers of other countries in Europe. They're not with FR and Germany on this; they're with the United States."[98]

In evaluating new member participation in OIF, the relative support from new members was compared to the contributions of non-U.S. NATO members. U.S. contributions were excluded since it appeared to be pursuing significant private benefits in this mission. This ratio was then compared to the 1999 wave's percentage of the total NATO population. In this American-led mission, OIF, the combined contributions of the three new NATO members (the Czech Republic, Hungary, and Poland) exceeded their percentage of non-U.S. NATO population in every year examined. From 2003 to 2007, their combined contributions to OIF averaged 14 percent of the total non-U.S. force coming from NATO nations, while their percentage of the NATO population decreased from 7.8 percent to 6.8 percent. This level of support represented an increase over the contributions made to both SFOR and KFOR, which were NATO missions. This finding suggests that new members were trying to build credibility with the United States by providing a greater level of support to OIF (see Figure 3-24).

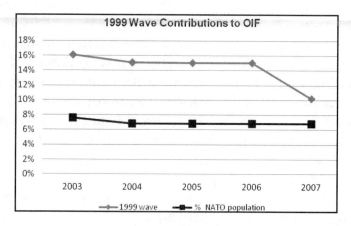

Figure 3-24. Relative 1999 Wave Contributions to OIF.[99]

This level of contribution to OIF might also explain the shortfalls in contributions to the NATO mission in ISAF. Had the OIF contributions over and above the percentage of NATO population been added to the NATO force in ISAF, the troop support from the three new members would have exceeded their population levels from 2003 onward. From 2002 until 2006, the average contribution to ISAF would have been 10.8 percent versus their 6.8 percent of NATO population. This finding supports the alternative explanation that new members were not necessarily free-riding during ISAF, but perhaps seeking credibility with the Americans by providing a greater level of support to OIF.

New versus Old.

The results are similar when comparing dyads based on size. On average, Portugal's contribution to OIF was consistently less than both the Czech Republic and Hungary, and ended in 2005. Belgium did not even contribute troops to OIF. This finding does not necessarily indicate free-riding by the older members of NATO. After all, many NATO countries, including Belgium, were opposed to the Iraq war. Rather, this finding suggests that new members were pursuing a private benefit in their level of support for OIF, and this may have affected their level of support to KFOR and ISAF post-2002. (See Figure 3-25.)

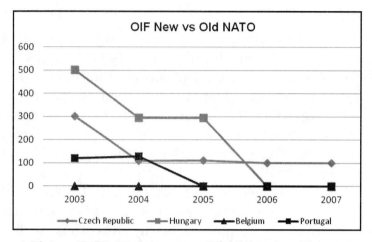

Figure 3-25. New versus Old Member Troop Contributions to OIF.[100]

The results are similar when comparing the two medium-sized countries. Throughout this period, Spain's contribution to OIF was consistently less than Poland's. In addition, Spain discontinued their contributions to OIF in the wake of the Madrid bombings and the change of government in 2004. Again, this finding does not indicate free-riding by Spain, but rather the pursuit of private benefits by Poland, namely credibility with the United States. Poland's significant contribution to OIF certainly constrained its ability to provide additional forces for the NATO mission in KFOR and ISAF. During the first 3 years of OIF, Poland was one of the largest troop contributors (over 2,000 troops) to the Multinational Forces in Iraq. While Poland decreased its force size to 900, these forces remained in OIF until October 2008. While this mission represented a significant cost to Poland, OIF provided political capital and enhanced the practical experience of Poland's military forces.[101] (See Figure 3-26.)

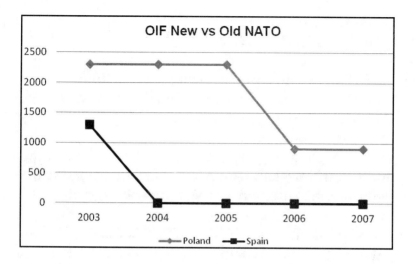

Figure 3-26. Poland versus Spain Troop Contributions to OIF.[102]

These results help to better understand the findings from ISAF concerning the contributions of the 1999 new NATO members. These findings also weaken the evidence for the third hypothesis that old members will share greater relative proportion of burdens than new members. Results from ISAF represent a marked difference from the findings in SFOR and KFOR. These findings support the conjecture that the indications of free-riding by new members were actually a lack of capability to contribute versus a lack of will to contribute to NATO missions. In each subsequent mission, the contribution of new NATO members increased relative to older NATO members. The next chapter covers this increased commitment in greater detail.

NATO IN LIBYA: OPERATION UNIFIED PROTECTOR

Following an uprising in February 2011, Muammar Qadhafi mounted increasingly violent attacks on his own citizens in Libya. In response, the UNSC adopted Resolutions 1970 imposing an arms embargo on Libya. On March 8, NATO sent Airborne Warning and Control System (AWACs) aircraft to monitor the deteriorating situation. On March 17, 2011, under UNSCR 1973, NATO embarked upon a mission with the stated position to protect civilians in Libya, enforce an arms embargo, and maintain a no fly zone.[103] FR was a key proponent and leader for NATO's involvement in this operation. NATO's participation in this operation consisted mainly of air and naval assets with over 250 aircraft and 20 ships.[104]

The commitment of forces to the NATO mission in Libya supports the findings that the largest states of the Alliance will share greater relative burdens in NATO missions. In Libya, the United States, France, and Great Britain alone provided about 70 percent of all strike sorties.[105] Belgium, Canada, Denmark, and Norway provided aircraft for combat operations; Italy provided reconnaissance aircraft and basing support (as did Greece).[106] Spain and Turkey also helped enforce the no fly zone. While the United States provided 26 percent of all sorties (and 97 percent of Tomahawk cruise missiles and 75 percent of all aerial refueling and reconnaissance flights), Britain and FR, together, provided about 50 percent of the aircraft.[107] This operation yielded public benefits for all NATO members and private benefits for larger Mediterranean countries and trading partners with Libya. Using the joint product model, it is not surprising, therefore, that FR provided about a third of the overall sorties, about 10 percent more than the United States. Given the lack of ground involvement and a reliance on air and naval forces, it is also not surprising that the participation of both new and small members of NATO was limited. These results confirm the findings in the earlier missions already examined that large states would share a greater relative proportion of burdens than small states when considering air forces. While the participation of aircraft is noticeably absent, Bulgaria and Romania provided naval forces in support of the arms embargo, and Poland sold precision munitions to participating allies.[108]

FINDINGS FROM THE ANALYSIS
OF NATO MISSIONS

A summary of the findings concerning the contributions to the three main NATO peacekeeping missions is listed in Table 3-12. The results for the first hypothesis are mixed. There is support for the hypothesis that the largest states of the Alliance will share greater relative burdens in peacekeeping missions under two conditions. First, this is true when talking about providing air support, where the American and large NATO allies have a comparative advantage in capabilities. Second, this appears to be true when the large states are pursuing private benefits (the United States in Afghanistan; Big 4 European nations in Bosnia/Kosovo). However, when smaller states are pursuing private benefits, such as credibility (especially with the United States) or fulfilling their commitments to the NATO Response Force, they tended to provide an equal or greater proportion of ground forces than their larger NATO allies.

		Results
H-1:	Large states will share greater relative proportion of burdens than small states.	Supported for Air and for European troop contributions; Not supported for SFOR after 2001.
H-2:	New members will share greater relative proportion of burdens than old members.	Not Supported (Except for ISAF).
H-3:	New member burden sharing declines after accession into NATO.	Supported for SFOR and KFOR (Poland).
H-5:	Free-riding behavior should increase with NATO enlargement.	Not Supported.

Table 3-12. Summary of Findings from Peacekeeping Missions.

The results for the second and third hypotheses are mixed. During Bosnia and Kosovo, older member states, on average, provided greater troop contributions than new NATO members. This finding generally reflects a lack of military capability by new members immediately after accession into NATO. However, in ISAF, as in OIF, the new member contributions from the 1999 wave equaled or exceeded those of similar sized older NATO members. The increasing level of relative contributions by new members over time suggests that the earlier disparity was more likely caused by capability shortfalls rather than deliberate free-riding behavior. This conjecture will be examined further in the next chapter. The findings did not support the corollary hypothesis that new member burden sharing would decline after accession into NATO, except during SFOR. Rather, the contributions of the new members, on average, increased over time after gaining membership.

Finally, the results did not support the fourth hypothesis that free-riding behavior would increase with NATO enlargement. In both Bosnia and Kosovo, the average troop contributions of small states equaled or exceeded their percentage of population. While this was not the case in Afghanistan, this was largely due to the delayed and initially limited role of NATO during the earlier years of operations in Afghanistan. The United States wanted to be free from Alliance constraints during OEF.

These results also reflect a division of labor agreed upon during NATO force planning and generation processes. These agreements are made to the mutual benefit of all allies. Similar to the economic concept of comparative advantage, all allies benefit from this division of labor by reducing their opportunity costs for redundant military capability. Smaller NATO states have a comparative advantage in conventional or niche troops, whereas large NATO states have a comparative advantage in high technology weapons.

CONCLUSIONS

In reviewing the results from the last three chapters, there are several interesting general findings (see Table 3-13). First, the logic of collective action does not apply in every case. The nature of the Alliance "products" pursued (public, impure public, or private) are important, albeit difficult to categorize precisely. The results also vary between measures used and by the strategic context under which burden sharing was examined. Where there were private benefits or disagreements over the strategy and the nature of the mission, it seems that free-riding behavior increased.

		Military Expenditures	Contributions to Operations
H-1:	Large states will share greater relative proportion of burdens than small states.	Supported, if size is measured by GDP and also by population if the U.S. is excluded.	Supported for Air operations and when states are pursuing private goods. Not supported for troop contributions to the NRF mission.
H-2:	New members will share greater relative proportion of burdens than old members.	Supported.	Supported for ISAF.
H-3:	New member burden sharing declines after accession into NATO.	Not Supported.	Mixed results; Supported for SFOR; Not supported KFOR/ISAF.
H-5:	Free-riding behavior should increase with NATO enlargement.	Mixed Results.	Not supported

Table 3-13. Summary of Findings.

There are several circumstances or conditions that mitigate the rational incentives for NATO members to free-ride. States are more willing to contribute to Alliance missions when they are given incentives or side-payments, such as command positions. Since NATO traditionally assigns higher-level commands based on the level of troop contributions, this can mitigate the incentives for free-riding. In addition, states attempting to establish credibility with the leader of the Alliance, the United States, are also more likely to prioritize their contributions to missions led by the Americans over their contributions to other NATO missions. Finally, when states are pursuing private benefits, it may be more difficult to distinguish free-riding behavior.

Second, there is a difference between the willingness and the capability to contribute to NATO public goods. The results consistently support the first hypothesis that large states will share greater relative proportion of burdens than small states when looking at air power and high tech capabilities. It is difficult for smaller states to maintain the full range of these capabilities. In fact, NATO encourages member states to develop niche capabilities, (nuclear, biological, chemical defense and detection; counter-mine; and medical) while discouraging the development of certain capabilities, such as air superiority and nuclear weapons. Since high tech capabilities tend to cost more than conventional forces, it is no surprise that large NATO states, on average, devote a greater percentage of their GDP to military expenditures.

The results generally support the first hypothesis, though with some caveats. Whether looking at inputs (defense expenditures as a percentage of GDP) or outputs (air and troop contributions to NATO missions) there is some support for the hypothesis that the largest states of the Alliance will share a greater relative burden. However, there were some surprising findings in this area. First, the largest NATO states (in terms of geographic area) did not necessarily have the highest defense expenditures as a percentage of GDP. Second, the United States, as the largest and wealthiest NATO state, did not always contribute a relatively larger share of troops to NATO missions. Much depended upon the perceived private benefits and risks associated with a particular mission. The results also reflect the division of labor in NATO where the United States and large NATO allies contributed a greater percentage of air capabilities, an area where they have a comparative advantage.

There are mixed results for the hypothesis that new members will share greater relative proportion of burdens than old members. Certainly, new members fared better in trying to meet NATO's spending targets than many other members, partly due to their desire to prove their credibility to the Alliance and the United States. But this phenomenon also reflects their need to modernize their armed forces and their willingness to develop compatible NATO capabilities. In regards to troop contributions to NATO missions, it appears that as their capabilities and levels of interoperability increased, new member states have been more willing to take on additional responsibility and burdens. This data is also supported by the fact that new member contributions to NATO missions generally increased after gaining membership and after the 2004 wave of NATO expansion. This result is studied in greater detail in the next chapter.

Finally, the findings linking enlargement and free-riding are mixed. When looking at NATO's 2 percent spending benchmark, the results support the hypothesis that free-riding behavior increased with NATO enlargement. However, these results could be epiphenomenal. There were other equally important economic or geopolitical reasons for these trends. As mentioned earlier, the findings from the three peacekeeping missions do not support the hypothesis that free-riding behavior increased with NATO enlargement. The results also bring out the necessary distinction between willingness and capability to contribute.

ENDNOTES - CHAPTER 3

1. Victoria Nuland (U.S. Ambassador to NATO), "Ambassador Discusses Security Issues on Eve of NATO Ministerial," web chat on December 5, 2007), available from *www.america.gov/st/ washfile-english/2007.*

2. Claudio Bisogneiro, Deputy Secretary General of NATO, interviewed by author, January 31, 2008, NATO Headquarters, Brussels, Belgium.

3. Peter K. Forster and Stephen J. Cimbala, *The US, NATO and Military Burden sharing*, New York: Frank Cass, 2005, pp. 121-127.

4. Jamie Shea, Director of Policy Planning, interviewed by author, January 31, 2008, NATO Headquarters, Brussels, Belgium.

5. As much as possible, demographic information and data on contributions to NATO missions were extracted from NATO documents. Where not found in NATO documents, data comes from another common source used in previous studies: *The Military Balance*, published annually by the International Institute for Strategic Studies. This method is consistent with previous studies such as John R. Oneal and Mark A. Elrod, "NATO Burden Sharing and the Forces of Change," *International Studies Quarterly*, Vol. 33, 1989. See also Keith Hartley and Todd Sandler, *The Political Economy of NATO*, New York: Cambridge University Press, 1999.

6. Data was systematically collected from other credible published sources, international organizations (such as the OECD) and relevant NATO documents. For each cased study, this project uses the same procedure to analyze the data to increase the reliability of the findings. The data is evaluated in groupings relevant to the hypotheses tested: large versus small and old versus new. New member troop contributions are aggregated by cohorts, controlling for population, and examined against similar sized old NATO members. This chapter concentrates its analysis on the 1999 wave since they were NATO members during all four NATO missions under study.

As discussed in the previous chapters, the appropriateness of using contributions to NATO peacekeeping operations as a measure of burden sharing is founded on the notion of a public good. Contributions of member states to NATO peacekeeping operations are appropriate measures of burden sharing because they are generally considered to be a public good. These missions must also have the qualities of nonexcludability and nonrival consumption. Nonexcludability means that those who do not contribute to the provision of a particular good or service cannot feasibly be kept from benefiting from it. Once NATO is committed to a mission, every NATO member benefits from the resulting increased security or stability regardless of whether or not they directly contribute to the mission. Thus the benefits are nonexcludable. Nonrival consumption means that consumption of the good or service by one actor does not diminish the amount available to others. The direct benefits of these NATO missions, whether increased security, stability, or good will, apply to all members without reducing the benefits to other members. All NATO states also gain from the indirect benefits of these missions such as increased interoperability within the Alliance and increased deterrence to threats outside of the Alliance. Thus these missions also satisfy the requirement of nonrival consumption.

However, there are cases where these contributions are also made in the pursuit of private benefits. Certainly quelling the ethnic violence in the Balkans offered private benefits to neighboring states and those with ethnic minorities in the region. The same could be said about the U.S. contributions to the "Global War on Terror" (i.e., Afghanistan and Iraq). In addition, troop contributions made to gain favor with the United States could yield private benefits such as enhanced credibility. Since credibility is excludable, contributions to these missions in the pursuit of credibility could also mitigate free-riding behavior. This project attempts to identify were potential private benefits have had a significant impact on the contributions to these NATO missions and adjust the findings to account for these instances.

7. Forster and Cimbala, p. 164.

8. Colonel (Ret.) Steven Mirr (former military aide to General Jones and Director of the Defense Operations Division, U.S. Delegation to NATO); based on interviews conducted on January 31, 2008, at NATO Headquarters, Brussels, Belgium.

9. NATO Public Diplomacy Division, *NATO Handbook*, Brussels, Belgium: NATO, 2006, p. 297.

10. Joseph Lepgold, "NATO's Post-Cold War Collective Action Problem," *International Security*, Vol. 23, No. 1, Summer 1998, p. 82.

11. NATO Euro-Atlantic Disaster Response Coordination Center (EADRCC), Daily Situation Reports, *Earthquake Pakistan, Final Situation Report No. 23*, Brussels, Belgium: NATO, February 15, 2006, available from *www.nato.int/eadrcc/2005/pakistan/060215-final.pdf*.

12. NATO Allied Command Operations, "The NATO Response Force," available from *www.nato.int/shape/issues/shape_nrf/nrf_intro.htm*.

13. NATO Allied Command Operations, "NATO Response Force Q & A's." available from *www.nato.int/shape/issues/shape_nrf/nrf_q_a.htm*.

14. NATO Allied Command Operations, "NATO Launches Response Force," October 15, 2003, available from *www.nato.int/shape/news/2003/10/i031015.htm*.

15. *Ibid*.

16. NATO Allied Command Operations, "NATO Response Force Continues Relief Effort," *SHAPE News*, September 6, 2005, available from *www.nato.int/SHAPE/news/2005/09/050914a.htm*.

17. NATO Allied Command Operations, "The Last NATO Cargo Shipment Arrived in the United States," *SHAPE News*, October 4, 2005, available from *www.nato.int/SHAPE/news/2005/10/051005b.htm*.

18. Islamic Republic News Agency (IRNA), "Pakistan: Italian Engineers to Jjoin NATO Forces in Kashmir," *Relief Web*, December 2, 2005, available from *www.reliefweb.int/rw/rwb.nsf/db900sid/VBOL-6JPE8W?OpenDocument*.

19. NATO Allied Command Operations, "The NATO Response Force."

20. NATO Allied Command Operations, "NATO Disaster Relief Operation in Pakistan," February 28, 2006, available from *www.nato.int/shape/news/2005/pakistan_trifold.htm.*

21. UK Ministry of Defence, "Pakistan Earthquake Relief Operations: MOD Assistance Provided to the Relief Effort," undated Fact Sheet, available from *www.mod.uk/DefenceInternet/Fact-Sheets/OperationsFactsheets/PakistanEarthquakeReliefOperationsMod AssistanceProvidedToTheReliefEffort.htm.*

22. U.S. Department of State, Office of the Spokesman, "U.S. Response to Pakistan's Earthquake Disaster," November 9, 2005, available from *www.state.gov/r/pa/prs/ps/2005/56703.htm.*

23. NATO Allied Command Operations, "All NATO Countries Contribute to Pakistan Relief," February 28, 2006, available from *www.nato.int/shape/news/2005/pakistan_contributions.htm.*

24. See Jaap de Hoop Scheffer, "Statement by the Secretary General on enhanced NATO assistance for Pakistan," NATO Press Release 2005(134), October 21, 2005, available from *www. nato.int/docu/pr/2005/p05-134e.htm;* and Vince Crawley, "NATO Faces Challenge in Pakistan Earthquake Response," The Washington File 16, Washington, DC: U.S. Department of State, Bureau of International Information Programs, November 2005, available from *www.globalsecurity.org/military/library/news/2005/11/ mil-051116-usia03.htm.* Also see Office of the Spokesman, "U.S. Response to Pakistan's Earthquake Disaster," Washington, DC: U.S. Department of State, November 19, 2005, available from *2001-2009.state.gov/r/pa/prs/ps/2005/57154.htm.*

25. See Crawley. Also see Office of the Spokesman, "U.S. Response to Pakistan's Earthquake Disaster."

26. Crawley.

27. See NATO Allied Command Operations, "NATO Disaster Relief Operation in Pakistan;" and "Pakistan: Italian Engineers to Join NATO Forces in Kashmir."

28. NATO Allied Command Operations, "NATO Disaster Relief Operation in Pakistan."

29. Lepgold, "NATO's Post-Cold War Collective Action Problem," p. 79.

30. "Misiones Internacionales" ("International Missions"), *Revista Espanola de Defensa*, ano 18, No. 214, December 2005, pp. 18-20.

31. Note: Percent of NATO force > percent of combined NATO population.

32. Czech Ministry of Defense, "MOD History of Czech Military Operations Abroad (1990-2007)," July 3, 2008, available from *www.army.cz/scripts/detail.php?id=5717*. Also see Sergeant Claude Flowers, "CENTCOM Public Affairs 2006-07-27," Warsaw, Republic of Poland: Ministry of National Defense, July 27, 2006, available from *www.mon.gov.pl/en/artykul/2100*.

33. NATO EADRCC, *Earthquake Pakistan*. Also see Ministry of Defence and Armed Forces of the Czech Republic, available from *www.army.cz/scripts/detail.php?id=5807*.

34. See "MOD History of Czech Military Operations Abroad (1990-2007)," Prague, Czech Republic: Ministry of Defence and Armed Forces of the Czech Republic; and Flowers.

35. Note: Number of troops new members > Number of troops old members.

36. NATO Allied Command Operations, "All NATO Countries Contribute to Pakistan Relief."

37. William R. Gates and Katsuaki L. Terasawa, "Reconsidering Publicness in Alliance Defence Expenditures: NATO Expansion and Burden Sharing," *Journal of Defence and Peace Economics*, October 2003, p. 373.

38. Lepgold, "NATO's Post-Cold War Collective Action Problem," p. 83.

39. Lepgold assumes that the actors have the same objectives or interests in the mission. When interests or benefits diverge, these missions tend to more closely resemble joint products, having both public and private benefits.

40. *Ibid.*, p. 85.

41. NATO also supported the UN arms embargo starting in 1991 with naval forces.

42. Forster and Cimbala, pp. 121-126.

43. Michael R. Gordon, "The 2000 Campaign: The Military; Bush would stop U.S. Peacekeeping in Balkan Fights," *The New York Times,* October 21, 2000, available from *query.nytimes.com/gst/fullpage.html?res=9C07E4DE1E3EF932A15753C1A9669C8B63&sec=&spon=&pagewanted=3.*

44. Iceland does not maintain a military force.

45. "SFOR Air Component," AFSOUTH Fact Sheets, NATO, August 18, 2003, available from *www.afsouth.nato.int/factsheets/SFORAirComponent.htm.*

46. *Ibid.*

47. "Operation Deliberate Force," AFSOUTH Fact Sheets, NATO, August 18, 2003, available from *www.afsouth.nato.int/factsheets/DeliberateForceFactSheet.htm.*

48. "Operation Deny Flight," AFSOUTH Fact Sheets, NATO, July 18, 2003, available from *www.afsouth.nato.int/operations/deny-flight/DenyFlightFactSheet.htm.*

49. AFSOUTH, "SFOR Air Component."

50. International Monetary Fund, "Reports for Selected Countries and Subjects," *World Economic Outlook Database,* April 2008, available from *www.imf.org/external/data.htm.*

51. Gordon.

52. SFOR, "History of the NATO-led Stabilisation Force (SFOR) in Bosnia and Herzegovina," NATO, undated, available from *www.nato.int/sfor/docu/d981116a.htm*.

53. *The Military Balance*, London, UK: International Institute for Strategic Studies, 1999-2005.

54. *Ibid.*

55. *Ibid.*

56. Only contributions made through 2004 are included as NATO turned over the mission to the EU in 2005.

57. *The Military Balance*, 1999-2005.

58. *Ibid.*

59. *Ibid.*

60. Dana Priest and Charles Trueheart, "Issue of NATO Airstrikes Rises Again; Cohen Warns Alliance Credibility at Stake When It Comes to Milosevic and Kosovo," *The Washington Post*, January 21, 1999.

61. "NATO Burden sharing after Enlargement," Congress of the United States, Washington, DC: Congressional Budget Office, August 2001, available from *www.cbo.gov/showdoc.cfm?index=2976 &sequence=2&from=0*.

62. *The Military Balance*, 1999-2005. For contributing nations and troop numbers, see Kosovo Force (KFOR) NATO graphic, available from *www.nato.int/kfor/structur/nations/placemap/kfor_ placemat.pdf*.

63. Forster and Cimbala.

64. Nina Werkhäuser, "Ten Years On, Germany Looks Back at Return to War in Kosovo," *Deutsche Welte*, March 24 2009, available from *www.dwworld.de/dw/article/0,,4123734,00.html?maca= en-rss-en-all-1573-rdf*.

65. *Ibid.*

66. General Wesley K. Clark, "Waging Modern War," *Public Affairs*, 2001, p. 269.

67. Gordon.

68. *The Military Balance*, 1999-2005. For contributing nations and troop numbers, see KFOR NATO graphic.

69. *Ibid.*

70. Ambassador Andras Simonyi, "Hungary in NATO—after Two Years of Membership," speech to NATO in 2001, available from *www.atlanticcommunity.org/Hungary%20in%20NATO.html.*

71. See *The Military Balance*, 1999-2005. For contributing nations and troop numbers, see KFOR NATO graphic.

72. Dita Asiedu, "NATO's Six Years of Dramatic Change—How Has the Czech Republic Fared?" *Český rozhlas 7*, Radio Praha, March 11, 2005, available from *www.radio.cz/en/article/64286.*

73. See *The Military Balance*, 1999-2005. For contributing nations and troop numbers, see KFOR NATO graphic.

74. Jamie Shea, "A NATO for the 21ST Century: Toward a New Strategic Concept," Fletcher Forum, *World Affairs*, Vol. 31, No. 2, Summer 2007, p. 44.

75. *NATO Handbook*, p. 155.

76. Ryan C. Hendrickson, "The Miscalculation of NATO's Death," *Parameters*, Spring 2007, p. 105.

77. Paul Gallis, "NATO in Afghanistan: A Test of the Transatlantic Alliance," CRS-3, Washington, DC: Congressional Research Service, July16, 2007.

78. *United Nations Security Council Resolution 1776 (2007)*, New York: United Nations, September 19, 2007, available from *www. nato.int/isaf/topics/mandate/unscr/resolution_1776.pdf.*

79. United Nations, *United Nations Security Council Resolution 1833 (2008)*, New York: United Nations, September 22, 2008, available from *www.nato.int/isaf/topics/mandate/unscr/resolution_1833.pdf*.

80. *The Military Balance*, 2004-08, London, UK: International Institute for Strategic Studies. For contributing nations and troop numbers, see NATO, ISAF "International Security Assistance Force and Afghan National Army Strength and Lay Down," 2006-08, available from *www.nato.int/isaf/docu/epub/pdf/isaf_placemat.pdf*.

81. German Marshall Fund of the United States and the Compagnia di San Paolo, "Transatlantic Trends 2003: Key Findings," 2003, available from *www.transatlantictrends.org/trends/doc/2003_english_key.pdf*.

82. Forster and Cimbala, p. 123.

83. *The Military Balance*, 2004-08. For contributing nations and troop numbers, see NATO, ISAF "International Security Assistance Force and Afghan National Army Strength and Lay Down."

84. Lieutenant General (Retired) David W. Barno, former Commander, OEF, and Director, NESA Center at National Defense University; interview by author at Carlisle Barracks, PA, on January 25, 2008.

85. "Transatlantic Public Opinion Survey Shows Support for NATO Rising," *NATO News*, September 11, 2008, available from *www.nato.int/docu/update/2008/09-september/e0911c.html*.

86. *The Military Balance*, 2004-08. For contributing nations and troop numbers, see NATO, ISAF "International Security Assistance Force and Afghan National Army Strength and Lay Down."

87. General John Craddock (Supreme Allied Commander Europe) interview by author, SHAPE Headquarters, Mons, Belgium, February 1, 2008.

88. *The Military Balance*, 2004-08. For contributing nations and troop numbers, see NATO, ISAF "International Security Assistance Force and Afghan National Army Strength and Lay Down."

89. Nuland, "Ambassador Discusses Security Issues on Eve of NATO Ministerial."

90. *The Military Balance*, 2008-08. For contributing nations and troop numbers, see NATO, ISAF "International Security Assistance Force and Afghan National Army Strength and Lay Down."

91. *Ibid.*

92. Polish Press Agency, "Polish Premier Starts Visit to Afghanistan," Reston, VA: U.S. Open Source Center, August 22, 2008, available from *https://www.opensource.gov.*

93. Polish Press Agency, "Poland Sends First Two Helicopters for Afghan Contingent," Reston, VA: U.S. Open Source Center, August 4, 2008, available from *https://www.opensource.gov.*

94. *The Military Balance*, 2004-08. For contributing nations and troop numbers, see NATO, ISAF "International Security Assistance Force and Afghan National Army Strength and Lay Down."

95. Associated Press, News Research Center Web Services, available from *nrcdata.ap.org/afghancasualties/default.aspx?username=casualty&password=2005battle.*

96. Craig S. Smith, "Threats and Responses: Brussels; Chirac Scolding Angers Nations that Back U.S.," *The New York Times*, February 19, 2003, available from *query.nytimes.com/gst/fullpage.html?res=9E01E2DC173DF93AA25751C0A9659C8B63&sec=&spon=&pagewanted=1.*

97. Sandler and Hartley, p. 35.

98. John Hooper and Ian Black, "Anger at Rumsfeld attack on 'old Europe'," *The Guardian*, January 24, 2003, available from *www.guardian.co.uk/world/2003/jan/24/germany.france.*

99. *The Military Balance*, 2002-08, London, UK: International Institute for Strategic Studies; "Iraq Coalition Troops, February 2007," *Global Security.org*, available from *www.globalsecurity.org/military/ops/iraq_orbat_coalition.htm.*

100. *Ibid.*

101. "Poland Withdraws Troops from Iraq," *The Warsaw Voice Online*, October 6, 2008, available from *www.warsawvoice.pl/newsX. php/6999/2549017099/printVer/*.

102. *The Military Balance*, 2002-08; *Global Security.org*, "Iraq Coalition Troops, February 2007."

103. NATO, "NATO and Libya—Operation Unified Protector," available from *www.nato.int/cps/en/SID-C7C31DC0-306B0BDC/natolive/topics_71652.htm?*

104. *Ibid.*

105. C. J. Chivers and Eric Schmitt, "Libya's Civilian Toll, Denied by NATO," *The New York Times*, December 18, 2011.

106. Ivo H. Daalder and James G. Stadvridis, "NATO's Victory in Libya: The Right Way to Run an Intervention," *Foreign Affairs*, Vol. 91, No. 2, March-April 2012, pp. 2-7.

107. Eric Westervelt, "NATO's Intervention In Libya: A New Model?" National Public Radio, September 12, 2011, available from *www.npr.org/2011/09/12/140292920/natos-intervention-in-libya-a-new-model*.

108. Daalder and Stadvridis, pp. 2-7.

CHAPTER 4

UNDERSTANDING NEW MEMBER BURDEN SHARING BEHAVIOR

Addressing Unanswered Questions.

> At the end of the day, political solidarity is more important than specific notions of equal numerical contributions. NATO leaders need to use alliance psychology recognizing that the pull of solidarity and mutual obligation works better than public criticism.
>
> Dr. Jamie Shea,
> Director of Policy Planning[1]

While the preceding analysis, based on a quantitative examination of empirical data, identified several patterns in burden sharing behavior, it was unable to answer a fundamental question: why burden sharing decisions are made. The logic of collective action, which dominates the burden sharing literature, assumes that states are rational, egoistic actors. This would suggest that burden sharing can be explained on a cost versus benefit basis. However, there are other plausible theoretical explanations for burden sharing behavior. This chapter examines these explanations to better understand the logic(s) behind burden sharing behavior. Not surprisingly, the discourse used by North Atlantic Treaty Organization (NATO) members and officials suggests that multiple, possibly contending logics influence burden sharing decisions. The findings suggest that while rational motivations (such as concerns over credibility and side payments) influence burden sharing decisions, those choices are shaped (and often supported publicly) using arguments based on identity. This data is consistent with results from Judith Kelley's 2004 study of European Institutions that found socialization efforts often guided rational decisions.[2]

The last chapter also suggested that burden sharing performance might result from a lack of capability versus a lack of will on the part of the nations' leaders. In this chapter, this distinction is examined further using interviews of NATO officials. The findings suggest that new members have the political will to bear their fair share of NATO burdens, however, they often lack the capability to fully contribute. This situation was especially true immediately after accession into NATO.

The chapter is divided into two main sections. The first section begins with a review of the noncollective action, theoretical basis for burden sharing: credibility and appropriateness. It also examines how NATO socialized new members, who gradually changed their preferences to more closely reflect NATO's burden sharing norms. These concepts provide the framework for the remaining analysis and guide the direction of the interviews covered in the next section. Standardized open-ended interviews of NATO and NATO member officials are analyzed to get a qualitative assessment of the burden sharing discourse. This section looks at the rhetoric used by NATO members and officials to explain burden sharing behavior. It examines how elites from NATO and NATO member states assess the burden sharing behavior of new members. This analysis suggests that new members are able to overcome the rational incentives to free-ride in order to prove their credibility; in fact, they see their contributions in terms of appropriateness. This finding fits nicely within the literature concerning the logic of consequences versus the logic of appropriateness, as discussed in detail by scholars in the rational choice and constructivist schools of international relations.[3] The results also lend credence to the assessments made in the previous chapters that new members were burden sharing within their capabilities.

METHODOLOGY

Up to this point, this project has used quantitative methods to explain burden sharing behavior in NATO. These numerical measures provided an insight into what has happened in NATO with regards to defense expenditures and contributions to NATO missions. This chapter focuses on qualitative methods to better understand these findings. The standardized, open-ended interviews specifically examine burden sharing discourse. This interview format increases the reliability of the results by asking the same basic questions in each interview. These inquiries were conducted with the primary stakeholders in the burden sharing decisions: political and military elites from NATO Headquarters and senior military officials from NATO member countries.

Two different social settings were selected for these interviews. The first dialogues took place at the National Defense University in Washington, DC, and the U.S. Army War College in Carlisle, PA. In this social setting, these NATO officers represent a minority. Most of the officers are U.S. Soldiers, and the curriculum is founded on U.S. military doctrine, norms, and procedures. Many of these officers have recently returned from deployments in either Iraq, Afghanistan or both. In this environment, officers from new NATO countries could feel compelled to justify the contributions of their states to NATO and the War on Terrorism. Therefore, it would be expected that credibility should be more prevalent in the discourse given in this social setting.

The second set of interviews was conducted at NATO Headquarters (Brussels, Belgium) and Supreme Headquarters Allied Powers Europe (SHAPE) in Mons, Belgium. In these military environs, the effects of institutional socialization are most likely to be present, and therefore discourse indicating the logic of appropriateness should be more prevalent. The political and military elites interviewed come from the International Staff (including the Deputy Secretary General) and the SHAPE, including the Supreme Allied Commander Europe (SACEUR) and the Deputy Supreme Allied Commander Europe (DSACEUR). These officials are filling NATO billets and therefore are supposed to pursue the Alliance's collective interests over national interests. The senior military officials come from the National Military Representatives of NATO members at SHAPE Headquarters. Those officers interviewed are filling national positions (pursuing national interests) but are operating in a NATO headquarters where NATO norms and procedures are prevalent. As much as possible, the interviews were conducted with members from the same NATO countries in both settings. The number of interviews was limited by resources (the amount of time and money available) and the composition of the student body at the National and Army War Colleges.

A RATIONAL CHOICE EXAMINATION
OF FINDINGS

The rational choice explanation for continued burden sharing by new members of NATO after accession emphasizes the benefits of maintaining a reputation as a credible partner. Certainly, members join and remain in NATO for both the tangible and the intangible benefits of being in a powerful alliance. With a combined population of almost 880 million and a combined gross domestic product (GDP) of $28.5 trillion,[4] NATO membership offers a degree of physical and psychological security to its member states.

The rational benefits of being in an alliance have also been studied in international relations theory. In his game-theoretic study of alliances, Alastair Smith found that defensive alliances deterred aggression. The more reliable the alliance was, the greater the deterrent effect it had. In his words, "nations form alliances because it improves the outcomes they expect to receive."[5] Certainly, this concern for physical and psychological security was influential in the burden sharing decisions of recent new NATO members. As the current Romanian President said in an interview, "with the accession to NATO, the Romanians felt safe . . . NATO meant the beginning of our road to prosperity."[6]

Finally, a rational choice explanation might emphasize the *quid pro quo* that supports burden sharing decisions of member states in NATO. Certainly, there have been side payments made by the United States to new member states in order to encourage greater levels of military spending and in order to reward contributions to NATO and U.S.-led missions in the war on terrorism. For example, Poland received a generous

$3.5 billion loan to buy F16 aircraft after committing sizable forces to Operation IRAQI FREEDOM (OIF).[7] In addition, NATO established the Joint Forces Training Centre in Poland in 2004. Both the Czech Republic and Hungary received side payments from the United States for their support in the war on terrorism.[8] In 2002, the 1999 wave of new members received a combined $35 million in Foreign Military Financing with an equal amount requested for 2003 and 2004.[9] Estonia, one of the 2004 waves of new NATO members, was scheduled to receive over $6 million per year over the same period.[10] In 2005, in addition to normal International Military Education and Training (IMET) and Foreign Military Financing (FMF) assistance, President George W. Bush requested $200 million from Congress "for coalition allies that have supported military efforts in Iraq and Afghanistan."[11] NATO also uses incentives to influence its member states. These incentives include investments in infrastructure resources by NATO common funds. For example, Poland funded most of its airfield renovation program through the NATO Security Investment Program (NSIP).[12] Romania, a big supporter of both OIF and the International Security Assistance Force (ISAF), was rewarded with the rotation of U.S. forces into Romania for training as part of Joint Task Force East.[13]

While the side payments discussed above provide some incentive, NATO has the greatest leverage over aspiring member states prior to accession through conditionality. In the case of NATO, conditionality consists of "specific conditions which an aspiring state must fulfill before accession. These conditions comprised of both adherence to the community values and the ability to contribute to the functional tasks of the organization."[14] The assessment of whether or not these conditions have been met is a subjective and very political matter. Oftentimes, geostrategic concerns can trump accomplishment of accession standards, as in the case of Georgia and the Ukraine, which have not been granted admittance into the Membership Action Plan (MAP) due to concerns over relations with Russia. Accession into NATO requires unanimous agreement by existing members and ratification by the legislatures of the member states. It is not surprising, then, that aspiring NATO members are keen to demonstrate they have not only met the intent of the conditions established, but also the objective benchmarks established by the Alliance. One of the two most recent NATO members, Albania, is a good example. In a recent visit to NATO Headquarters, Albanian representatives were "very proud to say they (were) meeting the 2% (GDP) benchmark as well as deployment and sustainability criteria."[15] These public declarations support the explanations based on conditionality and are consistent with the burden sharing behavior of new member states reviewed earlier.

Not surprisingly, conditionality was an effective tool in influencing aspiring NATO members. In Judith Kelley's study of international institutions in the early post-Cold War period, she found that membership prerequisites were an essential factor in changing state behavior.[16] Kelley also acknowledged that socialization played a role. Kelley found that while most changes in state behavior could be attributed to conditionality, "socialization-based efforts often guided them."[17] Yet, these explanations alone cannot explain why new NATO members did not free-ride once they became members of NATO. In fact, many new members increased their troop support to NATO missions after gaining membership. NATO Director of Policy

Planning Jamie Shea specifically addressed the issue of free-riding incentives after accession.

> The argument that once in the alliance, new members will slack off is not fair. For example, Romania currently has 720 (troops) deployed to Afghanistan and is trying to find another 120. That is not a bad effort for a new NATO member.[18]

However, conditionality is just one incentive to induce norm conforming behavior.

NATO has several informal mechanisms to reward states that support Alliance efforts after being granted membership. Research has shown that rewards can help states to overcome the incentives to free-ride.[19] First, NATO uses a variety of prestige rewards that are not only beneficial for domestic political use, but are sought out by both diplomatic and military bureaucrats for their own benefit. These rewards range from hosting summits, conferences, or exercises to the assignment of commands and staff positions. One example of these types of rewards is called "flags to post." A flags to post conference is convened to assign general officer billets to member states. These conferences often result in a contentious debate; these leadership positions not only yield influence in the Alliance but also prestige at home to the officers assigned to fill them.

During NATO missions, command positions are also allocated on the basis of relative troop contributions. Unless the forces are under a standing NATO Headquarters, such as the Allied Rapid Reaction Corps, then command usually goes to the state with the largest number of troops in that sector or in the overall mission. NATO also provides material incentives in the form of investments. This reward allows leaders to bring home the bacon to their national constituents and thus build support for contributions to NATO. For example, NATO investment into Poland exceeded Poland's contributions to NATO's infrastructure budget in 2004.[20] A portion of these NATO funds is being used to construct a training facility in the city of Bydgoszcz.[21] This facility will cost approximately 33 million Euros to build. Finally, individual states within NATO often provide incentives to other members to reward cooperation. As the largest and most powerful member (and leader) of the Alliance, the United States often times provides these incentives.

THE PURSUIT OF CREDIBILITY

As discussed earlier, many international relations scholars suggest that in order for states to cooperate extensively, they must first be able to make credible commitments. Typically, credibility is attributed to past behavior and a country's reputation for meeting its commitments.[22] In his book on credibility, Gideon Rose cites numerous examples of how concern for credibility influenced U. S. policy decisions in terminating conflicts, often at the expense of other national interests.[23] As in any cooperative situation, a good reputation reduces uncertainty, increases the credibility of promises, and enhances the clarity of commitments. Reputation plays an important role across issues ranging from international trade to national security. Even those scholars who argue that power and national interests are more important for credibility than reputation acknowledge that most political leaders believe in the importance of reputation for credibility.[24]

Credibility is especially important in the creation and maintenance of alliances. As Robert Keohane explains, "a good reputation makes it easier for a government to enter into advantageous, international agreements; tarnishing that reputation imposes costs by making agreements more difficult to reach."[25] Once an ally has a reputation for meeting its commitments, it is easier for that state to deepen its level of cooperation within the alliance. Reputation also strengthens the deterrence provided by an alliance. Therefore, reputations matter.

Frank Schimmelfenning also found evidence that states were concerned with reputation in his study of European Union (EU) enlargement. "In an 'institutional environment' like the EU, political actors are concerned about their reputation standing as members and about the legitimacy of their preferences and behavior."[26] This work employed a synthesis of the rational choice and sociological institutional approaches to show how rational actors (states) could be constrained by identity-based commitments to organizations. Within a security institution such as NATO, one would also expect that members are concerned about their reputations and constrained by commitments made to the Alliance.

According to this logic, new members in the NATO Alliance feel the need to establish their trustworthiness with older members. In doing so, there is a rational calculation that this credibility is essential to future transactions within both NATO and the EU. These transactions are in large measure based on trust. In addition to trust, a state's influence in an international organization or alliance is commensurate with the level of its contributions. As touched on earlier, senior officer positions in NATO are largely allocated on the basis of the size of the contributions each nation makes to the Alliance in terms of financial contributions and military forces. For example, when France decided to reenter the integrated command structure of NATO, the Alliance had to redistribute flag officer positions to ensure that France has sufficient leadership positions in NATO command and staff postings. This allocation of leadership positions is also true during NATO operations. Command and staff positions are also determined based on the size of the national contribution to the mission. That is why the United States has the overall command of the NATO mission in Afghanistan. Not only is this allocation of positions based on contributions a normal practice within the Alliance structure, it is also accepted and expected by the domestic political stakeholders. As former Senator James Talent noted, members of the NATO Alliance "should recognize that they must bear their share of the burden if they seek their share of the authority."[27]

FEAR OF ABANDONMENT

Another plausible rational explanation of burden sharing behavior by new member states is that their calculations are conditioned by their history. Most of the new member states of NATO were previously occupied by Soviet troops following World War II. These former Warsaw Pact countries consequently fear that Russia might try to reassert itself in their affairs. These states also have an historic and deep seated fear of abandonment by the West. Certainly, there is a historic legacy in states such as the Czech Republic, whose sovereignty was sacrificed to appeasement policies prior to World War II; and Poland, which was left alone to face the onslaught of Nazi Germany and the Soviet Union in 1939, despite existing security assurances from France and the United Kingdom (UK). States such as Hungary and the Czech Republic also suffered military interventions by the Soviet Union in 1956 and 1968, respectively. With their unique history, this explanation is less applicable to Albania and Croatia, since these states were outside of the Warsaw Pact.

Given this history, new member states would feel threatened by a weakened NATO or a reduced U.S. presence in NATO. Thus, there is some merit to the rationalist argument that these states retain a fear of abandonment and act accordingly.[28] Glenn Snyder's work on security dilemmas in alliances demonstrated that states' interests might converge over a fear of abandonment.[29] Therefore, new NATO members might support out of area Alliance operations, even in the absence of intrinsic national interests. In any case, the fear of abandonment, combined with a pursuit of credibility and side payments, all represent plausible explanations for norm complying behavior. However, as Alastair Johnston points out, "the presence of strategic behavior does not undermine the possibility of persuasion," nor does it rule out the impact of socialization.[30]

A SOCIOLOGICAL EXAMINATION OF BURDEN SHARING

In all of the explanations listed earlier, new members' burden sharing behavior can be interpreted as being motivated by the instrumental pursuit of state interests, whether that is to establish credibility, to garner side payments, or to mitigate fears of abandonment. However, there are equally compelling arguments that new member states are willing to bear the burdens of membership for noninstrumental reasons: persuasion and socialization. All new NATO members underwent an extensive socialization process that started with their membership in the Partnership for Peace (PfP) Program beginning in 1994. Identifying the specific socialization mechanisms found in NATO, as outlined in sociological institutionalism literature, could help explain how expectations of burden sharing were taught, monitored, and reinforced through a pre-accession screening process and the post-membership interaction with NATO headquarters and established member states. According to this logic, as the "NATO identity" takes root, new member states begin to follow the logic of appropriateness in making burden sharing commitments.[31] While burden sharing may have begun as a rational response to conditionality and a concern for establishing credibility, it became internalized over time, leading to continued burden sharing behavior based on identity as a NATO member.

Most scholars and practitioners of international relations would agree that persuasion operates in international institutions such as NATO. Oftentimes, it goes hand in hand with rational incentives such as side payments to convince actors to change their behavior. A good example might be the U.S. negotiations with Poland to convince them to host anti-missile interceptors.[32] The U.S. Government used both social pressure and potential side payments to try to convince Poland to accept U.S. anti-ballistic missiles on its territory.[33] In the end, Poland accepted this agreement in return for the Americans placing a Patriot anti-aircraft battery in Poland.[34] Social pressure and material incentives were used together to persuade Poland to accept this agreement.

Alexandra Gheciu suggests that persuasion occurs even in the absence of rewards through convincing arguments. This type of persuasion is what Thomas Risse calls the "logic of arguing."[35] Two key scope conditions for persuasion certainly existed in NATO during the pre-enlargement period: novel environment and authoritative actors.[36] Former Warsaw Pact countries were in a novel and uncertain environment during the immediate post-Cold War period when they joined NATO's PfP program. Secondly, NATO institutions and countries were seen as authoritative in light of their victory in the Cold War, highlighting their economic and political successes. As Gheciu points out in her article on NATO, persuasion usually "occurs in social interactions between actors who have drawn different conclusions regarding the nature, merits, and or implications of (an) action or Policy."[37] Yet, the success of persuasion also depends on the nature of the issue being examined. Persuasion has the greatest chance for success when the issue being socialized faces low domestic opposition.[38] For example, convincing new members to increase defense expenditures in a period of economic crisis would face a myriad of competing fiscal demands and significant political opposition and would less likely be successful when actual behavior diverges from stated Alliance norms.

SOCIALIZATION PROCESSES AND MECHANISMS WITHIN NATO

While there is some evidence that persuasion, reinforced by material incentives, was responsible for aspiring NATO members fulfilling their commitments to the Alliance, these effects are often temporary. What is more interesting is whether or not NATO's extensive socialization efforts might have led to sustained increased burden sharing behavior. Jeffrey Checkel mentioned in his study of the EU:

> socialization implies that an agent switches from following a logic of consequences to a logic of appropriateness; this adoption is sustained over time, and is quite independent from a particular structure of material incentives of sanctions.[39]

In his study of the EU's Committee of Permanent Representatives, Jeffrey Lewis also found evidence of a switch to the logic of appropriateness through a socially induced process that included "high issue density/intensity and insulation from domestic politics."[40] This switch also applies to the case regarding new NATO members' policy preferences and actions.

This transformation of norms within NATO first occurs during the Partnership and accessions process. Through their participation in NATO programs like the PfP and MAP, partners are exposed to NATO norms and procedures at their own pace. NATO commands, whether in peace time or during NATO-led missions, new member states begin to internalize the norms and procedures of the Alliance and often entrench these in their domestic, political institutions, and military bureaucracies. The longer these new members stay in the Alliance, the stronger this identity becomes and the greater their compliance with NATO norms and expectations. NATO's socialization mechanisms and programs also appear to meet the scope conditions for internalization of group norms as identified by Checkel: long and sustained interaction and intense contact.[41] As Frédéric Mérand pointed out in a 2010 study, NATO's:

various standardization and planning committees, in addition to the constant planning and conduct of operations, constitute loci of daily interaction where shared visions are produced and common professional practices reproduced.[42]

The PfP and MAP provide the mechanisms for this type of sustained and intense interaction with NATO institutions, countries, and personnel. While a major focus of these programs is on interoperability during peacekeeping missions, they also teach new members how NATO expects them to act in both the domestic arena and in regards to international obligations. In her compelling study of socialization in NATO, Gheciu found that NATO was an effective teacher of norms. She attributed NATO's success as a socializing agent to, "the parties' mutual recognition of their respective roles as 'teachers' and 'students'; the socializees' identification with the Western security community that NATO claimed to embody; and systematic interactions between teachers and students."[43] Gheciu goes on to make a strong case that the elites from the aspiring member states acknowledged and accepted the role of NATO officials and member states as legitimate teachers of democratic and Alliance norms.[44] Aspiring members of NATO were socialized through both national programs and formal NATO programs/ structures.

Socialization efforts by individual NATO countries began even prior to the fall of the Soviet Union. Individual NATO nations sought out greater contacts and cooperation with former Warsaw Pact countries. After Gorbachev announced his *perestroika* program, the United States began to gradually build bilateral diplomatic contacts with individual Warsaw Pact countries.

These relations eventually included a wide range of military to military contacts.[45] They were designed to provide dialogue, promote understanding, and foster a sense of cooperation and openness between former adversaries in light of the new strategic environment. However, they were mostly limited to senior military leadership.[46]

The urgency of these programs increased after the fall of the Soviet Union in 1991. For example, the United States initiated the European Command Co-ordination and Assistance Program in 1992 and sent contact teams to Czechoslovakia, Hungary, and Poland in May of that year.[47] Under the Joint Contact Team Program, teams were sent into former Warsaw Pact countries for 6 to 12 months at a time. These teams were specifically designed to teach their hosts the proper role of the military in a democracy. They were invited to tour U.S. military facilities. These contacts progressed into extensive bilateral exercises, port calls, and staff exchanges to help countries better understand the norms, standards, and procedures of NATO. These cooperative activities ranged from senior military leaders to small tactical units.

One such example is the State Partnership Programs (SPP), established under the auspices of the U.S. European Command in Stuttgart, Germany. The SPP began in 1993, evolving from the Joint Contact Team Program. The program paired individual states' National Guard forces with a partner nation's military units. The purpose of the SPP was two-fold: to build relationships and to increase the capacity and capability of partner countries.[48] In addition to building cooperation and interoperability, the use of reserve component forces helped to emphasize the appropriate civil-military norms within the new democracies of Central and Eastern Europe.[49] Often these relationships were established based on historical ties. For example, the Illinois National Guard paired with the Polish military. It is no coincidence that Illinois' largest city, Chicago, has one of the largest Polish populations outside of Warsaw. These cultural ties only enhanced the cooperation and understanding between these partners. Each of the 12 new NATO members had a SPP with a state National Guard that helped to socialize partner members into the norms, standards, and procedures of NATO. Many existing NATO members had similar, if less ambitious, programs. Most partner nations entered into bilateral apprenticeships with existing NATO members.

Denmark and Norway used the Nordic Council and the Baltic Security Assistance Management Group (BALTSEA) as a framework to engage and enhance cooperation with the newly independent Baltic States.[50] At their independence, the Baltic States had virtually no military capability and structure.[51] Denmark and Norway, in coordination with regional members of the EU (Sweden and Finland) worked with the Baltic States to develop the capability for defense and interoperability with NATO and EU forces. This relationship also led to a number of defense cooperation efforts between the Baltic states such as BALTBAT (a multinational peacekeeping unit established in 1994), BALTRON (a joint naval squadron focused on mine clearance and search and rescue established in 1997), and BALTNET (an airspace surveillance system established in 1996).[52] The Nordic countries also used the Nordic-Polish Battle Group to integrate partner nations into peacekeeping operations in the Balkans, starting with Poland in 1996 and Estonia, Lithuania, and Latvia in 2000.[53]

These national programs, and others, were coordinated under and reinforced by formal NATO programs. There were three main venues of socialization for aspiring NATO members through formal NATO programs/structures: the North Atlantic Cooperation Council (NACC), PfP and MAP. These programs, not only aimed at fostering greater understanding, interoperability, and cooperation with partner countries, they sought to prepare these countries for eventual membership in the Alliance. However, these tended to be more informal than other socialization tools.

The earliest formal mechanism for dialogue and cooperation with potential NATO members and other European states was the establishment of NACC. Mirrored after the North Atlantic Council (NAC), the NACC was created in December 1991 as a forum for high-level statesmen to consult and deliberate about security issues in Europe. The inaugural meeting included all 16 NATO and nine Central and Eastern European nations. This was certainly a novel time when there was a great deal of uncertainty, especially for the former members of the Soviet Union. In addition to the NATO members, nine Central and Eastern European countries, including Russia, became members of the NACC.[54] The NACC became a useful venue for consultation and support of peacekeeping efforts during the Balkan crisis.

In 1997, the NACC was replaced by the Euro-Atlantic Partnership Council (EAPC). Subsequently, some 30 partner countries joined the EAPC, 10 of which went on to become members. The EAPC offered a venue for regular consultations on relevant international political and security issues.[55]

The EAPC meets at various levels and at varying times. The EAPC meets monthly at the level of ambassadors, annually at the level of foreign and defense ministers and chiefs of defense, as well as occasionally at the summit level.[56]

These consultations cover not only short-term immediate issues, but also areas of long-term cooperation. The EAPC gives members a venue to exchange views and concerns on political and security-related issues, such as unrest in the Balkans and NATO operations in Afghanistan.

Even though these venues were useful for communicating NATO norms and procedures at the highest levels, they were not a particularly fertile setting for socialization. The NACC and EAPC meetings also lacked "authoritative actors" as each head of state had an equal opportunity to present their concerns and a political incentive to be seen as an equal partner. At the head of state level, the NACC meetings normally take place during summits. The summits are normally very public events with set agendas and a great deal of media attention.

A large part of NATO's socialization efforts can be traced to the PfP. The PfP program is more extensive than either the NACC or EAPC, and is aimed at a much broader audience. Participants in the PfP program range from national leaders to individual soldiers in staff positions or participating in NATO exercises or operations. One of the top priorities of the PfP program is to promote civilian control of the military in a democratic society. Through the PfP program, NATO makes extensive efforts to socialize new and prospective members and partners on NATO norms, standards, and procedures. PfP was designed to facilitate interoperability, promulgate civilian control over the military, and foster democratic norms and procedures. The Partnership Action Plan on Defense Institution Building (PAP-DIB) is focused on supporting democratic reforms of national defense institutions. Another component, the Partnership Action Plan against Terrorism (PAP-T), is a framework for cooperating in counterterrorism plans, information sharing, and exercises.[57] However, a large measure of the PfP program is focused on military capability.

NATO has also developed a well-defined and flexible program to build partner capabilities and interoperability with NATO forces and command structures. The Planning and Review Process (PARP) is one of the voluntary programs where partner nations negotiate force structure and readiness targets and receive feedback on their progress from NATO. Through the PARP process, NATO monitors progress, evaluates, and provides information on national forces and capabilities which might be made available for NATO training, exercises, and operations. This process mirrors NATO's own defense planning process, with the exception that PARP also encourages larger, defense-related reform efforts. Participating nations also receive feedback on their ability to meet NATO standards through the Operational Capabilities Concept (OCC).

After the NATO summit in 1994, the SACEUR, General Jowlan, created the Partnership Coordination Cell (PCC) to implement political goals established for PfP. Part of the PCC's charter was to coordinate partner participation in NATO PfP exercises. In the beginning, NATO/PfP exercises were more symbolic and politically useful than they were militarily effective. As the normal NATO exercise program was already established at this point, there was some resistance to adding ad hoc PfP exercises. In spite of these military concerns, the first NATO/PfP exercise was Cooperative Bridge held in Poland in September 1994.[58] These PfP exercises varied in scope, duration, and level, however, they all offered an opportunity for NATO and partner members to improve interoperability and teach NATO procedures, standards, and culture. In addition to learning NATO procedures, partners also were able to participate in the planning and hosting of NATO exercises.

The PCC was a particularly important and successful organization in the socialization of partner countries. The PCC set up its headquarters adjacent to SACEUR's military headquarters in Mons, Belgium. In addition to its permanent staff, the PCC also had national military representatives from the partner countries, mirroring the national military representatives across the parking lot at SHAPE. Within the PCC, NATO staff officers and partner representatives had daily interaction and worked in a cooperative atmosphere.

Partner countries were expected and encouraged to contribute to the PCC activities and decisionmaking processes and had great latitude on the density and frequency of their participation. This culture aquainted new members with the norms of NATO, where the nations are autonomous and are expected to contribute when and where they best see fit. As the PCC matured, it offered a menu of activities from which partner countries could choose activities which matched their capabilities, needs, and ambitions. Partners also developed 2-year Individual Partnership and Cooperation Programs jointly with NATO. These programs laid out the events in which partner countries could join, allowing both NATO and partner countries to program resources and begin the planning for these activities. Recently, NATO's Military Training and Exercise Program (MTEP) expanded the exercise calendar to a 5-year window.[59]

Probably the most intensive interaction comes through the NATO/PfP military program. The NATO/PfP military program has two fundamental objectives. At its most basic level, the NATO/PfP military program focuses on military interoperability. This interoperability is essential when partner forces are supporting NATO-led, peacekeeping or peace enforcement operations. The other, more political objective is to increase stability and cooperation in Europe.

The exercise program focuses on military interoperability covering some 26 broad areas, including command and control, logistics, and operations. During the exercise program, Partners are introduced to NATO Standardization Agreements (STANAGs), publications, and other standardized procedures. In fact, PfP members select specific goals in each of these areas in addition to specific exercises from the NATO/PfP Work Program, a menu of possible coordination venues.[60] At the 2002 Prague Summit, NATO also established Individual Partnership Action Plans (IPAPs).[61] In these 2-year plans, partner nations establish cooperation objectives and priorities, and NATO provides advice and political assistance in such areas as: defense, civil emergency planning, and environmental issues. Georgia was the first country to sign an IPAP with NATO in 2004.

In addition to exercises, the NATO/PfP military program also consists of two other components: education and NATO operations. Education programs focus on such fundamental skills as English language proficiency. While NATO has two official languages, French and English, English is the common language used for air traffic control and in most NATO head-quarters for day to day business. More specific NATO training opportunities are offered to partner nations through NATO schools such as the NATO Staff School in Oberammergau, Germany, and the NATO Defense College in Rome, Italy. There are also at least 20 national Partnership Training and Education Centers. In addition to NATO norms, organizations, and procedures, these schools teach students from partner countries how to build capability and interoperability while instituting broader defense and democratic reforms. There are also several national Partnership Training and Education Centers offered to civil and military representatives of partner and NATO countries.[62] NATO's Training and Education Enhancement Program (TEEP) also provides focused training for staffs participating in NATO or other multinational headquarters.

Partners gain invaluable operational experience by participating in NATO missions. At least 27 Partner nations participated in NATO Implementation Force (IFOR)/Stabilization Force (SFOR).[63] Another 17 partner nations contributed to Kosovo Forces. In December 2011, there were 21 partner nations contributing to NATO's International Security Force.[64] In these missions, partners work closely within NATO commands and with member nations. These operations allow partners to implement the NATO norms and procedures they have learned in PfP and MAP and apply them during often stressful operations. Partners work within multinational units or are attached to units from NATO member states. Guidelines for partner involvement in the planning and command and control of operations are laid out in the Political Military Framework (PMF). This effort is an attempt by NATO to link responsibility sharing to troop donations by partner nations, by giving contributors input regarding the decisionmaking process.

In addition to the military cooperation aspects, the PfP program also teaches prospective members how to adopt liberal-democratic norms.

> Joining NATO's Partnership for Peace, nations committed themselves 'to the preservation of democratic societies, their freedom from coercion and intimidation, and the maintenance of the principles of international law.[65]

Thus, many partners viewed participation in NATO-led operations in the Balkans, in support of United Nations Security Council Resolutions, as a natural extension and perhaps an objective of their participation in the PfP program.

Not only was the PfP program a venue for teaching NATO norms, rules, and decisionmaking procedures, but it also served as a platform for aspiring states to demonstrate their readiness for membership. PfP "allows partners to distinguish themselves by demonstrating their capabilities and their commitment with a view to possible NATO membership."[66] However, participation in the PfP program does not mean that a state is necessarily interested in joining NATO, nor does it mean that Alliance membership is inevitable. Of the 10 newest members of NATO, the first wave (the Czech Republic, Hungary, and Poland) entered NATO through participation in the PfP program alone. The remaining seven were subject to a much more rigorous screening process.

A program that evolved from early experience with NATO expansion is the MAP. MAP, approved at the 1999 Washington Summit, was specifically designed to better prepare candidate members for accession. It consists of various activities that an aspirant state could participate in to prepare them for accession into NATO. MAP entails more extensive reporting and feedback on progress from NATO on political and economic reform, defense reform, military resource requirements, information security, and the compatibility of domestic legislation with NATO requirements. Each MAP member is required to provide an annual national program that addresses progress on each of the chapters.[67] Compared to the PfP, MAP is a more rigorous and extensive program which serves as a necessary but not sufficient condition for admission. As the Romanian President recently stated, "MAP is an instrument that allows the Alliance to monitor the progress [of aspiring states] . . . [they] will not necessarily become members unless they meet the standards and fulfill the requirements."[68] All seven states in the most recent wave of enlargement in 2004 entered NATO through the MAP process.

States aspiring to full membership in NATO see the MAP program not only as an essential step in becoming a new NATO member, but also as a *de facto* security guarantee. Because of its reputation, there was a strong bid by Georgia and the Ukraine to receive an invitation to MAP at the Bucharest Summit, and why that move was so vehemently opposed by Russia. The MAP program also includes incentives for aspiring NATO members to reform, build capacity, and contribute to the Alliance. "MAP is more of a big stick than a big carrot," said the Estonian president, Toomas Hendrik Ilves, at a conference of the German Marshall Fund. "It forces nations to reform even when they don't want to do it."[69] Not surprisingly, there has been a difference between the first three members who entered NATO under PfP and those that entered under MAP. Under MAP, partners and aspirants must support their defense and financial data to NATO on an annual basis. This more rigorous interaction has allowed MAP members to assimilate more rapidly than the first wave of NATO members.

Clearly, through both the PfP and MAP, NATO expended a significant amount of effort to socialize new and aspiring members in the hopes of changing national preferences and institutions. Through these socialization efforts, NATO aimed to provide new members with a better understanding of their interests and obligations in relation to the Alliance. An argument can be made that persuasion and learning took place with new members in the context of PfP and MAP organizations, exercises, and activities.

Gheicu provides evidence of successful socialization and a transition to a logic of appropriateness by new NATO members.[70] Under the Warsaw Pact, these same countries acted in a purely instrumental manner. What might have appeared as burden sharing behavior was attributable to top down guidance and coercion from the Soviet Union and sometimes outright military intervention. As the Czech Deputy Defense Minister, Jiri Payne, stated, "planning security is something we never really did. It used to be made in Moscow and we only received instructions."[71] This hierarchical arrangement and absence of input by smaller members might partially explain the lack of burden sharing behavior during the Warsaw Pact. Upon gaining independence from the Soviet Union, Czechoslovakia, Hungary, and Poland reasserted their distinct individual national identities and right to sovereignty.

In contrast, NATO's consensus decisionmaking procedures and extensive socialization processes fostered a sense of "buy-in" among new members. Not surprisingly, the burden sharing behavior of these new NATO members could not be explained by instrumental decisions alone. Over time, it appeared that a new collective sense of identity evolved from participation in the PfP and membership in NATO. Domestic elites in new member states used this new sense of NATO identity to support their own domestic political positions. For example, Czech opposition member Petr Necas scolded the government, suggesting that it needed to "start acting like [a] full-fledged member of NATO."[72]

EXAMINATION OF FINDINGS: RATIONAL CHOICE VS. SOCIALIZATION

In order to evaluate the merits of these competing explanations for burden sharing behavior, this section examines the discourse used to justify burden sharing behavior during the standardized open-ended interviews. In evaluating the discourse for signs of rational logic, words whose meanings were associated with establishing or maintaining credibility or reputation were identified. Whenever an interviewee used phrases like "to demonstrate," "to show," or "to prove" in discussing the rationale for NATO contributions, this suggested a more rational logic was used to justify burden sharing. Whenever an interviewee used words like "obligation," "duty," or "appropriate" in discussing the rationale for NATO contributions, this suggested a logic of appropriateness.

As discussed earlier, standardized open-ended interviews were conducted in two different institutional settings with both military and nonmilitary elites. These different settings control for the effects of social context on the language used to justify national behavior in NATO. In the first institutional setting, interviews were conducted with International Fellows at the National Defense University in Washington, DC, and the U.S. Army War College in Carlisle, PA. Most of the officers in this setting are U.S. officers, and the curriculum is founded on U.S. military doctrine, norms, and procedures. The second set of interviews took place in Europe. The norms and procedures of NATO were the dominant feature of institutional and social context at SHAPE.

In the first setting, International Fellows were interviewed at the U.S. Army War College and the National Defense University from 2007-08. These fellows came from both new member states and from old member states. Each year, approximately 40 senior military officers are extended an invitation to attend the U.S. Army War College, and approximately 50 to attend the National Defense University. These officers are sent to these institutions as representatives of their individual governments and spend a year in Carlisle, PA, or Washington, DC, studying national strategic issues, conducting research, and learning strategic concepts and doctrine. In these settings, International Fellows constitute only 10 percent of the student body and therefore are in a minority. The International Fellows at the National Defense University represent a similar proportion of the student body. Most U.S. classmates have little familiarity with NATO norms and socialization mechanisms. In addition, the curriculum is focused on broader U.S. interests, strategy, and concepts. U.S. strategy and interests in NATO are only a small part of the curriculum. The officers interviewed from new member states were from Bulgaria, the Czech Republic, Estonia, Poland, and Romania.

The officers from the old member states were from some of the founding members of NATO: Canada, the United Kingdom (UK), and the Netherlands.

In the second institutional setting, interviews were conducted with military elites serving in both NATO and national billets at SHAPE in Mons, Belgium. SHAPE is the sole military headquarters within NATO that operates at the strategic level. SHAPE is a multi-national command that has several primary functions: assessing risks and threats, conducting military planning, and identifying and requesting forces needed to undertake Alliance missions.[73] Most of the senior military officers assigned to this headquarters work for the Alliance, not their individual countries. However, the National Military Representatives (NMRs) have a different function. The NMRs act on the instructions of their country and report back to national authorities. In sum, these NMRs retain their primary loyalty to their own countries and serve as liaisons to the Alliance. While representing their own national interests, these NMRs operate in a social environment that is dominated by NATO norms, rules, and procedures. In fact, all of the NMRs are located in the same building as the SHAPE staff.

Thus, this institutional setting differs significantly from that of either the U.S. Army War College or the National Defense University. At SHAPE, the non-U.S. officers constitute a majority of personnel assigned. Interviews were conducted with officers from six of the 10 new member states. These included the Czech Republic, Estonia, Hungary, Latvia, Lithuania, and Poland. The officers from older member states, interviewed for this project were from Spain, Portugal, and the Netherlands. Military officers from the Czech Republic, Estonia, Poland, and the Netherlands were interviewed in both settings.

To give insights on how NATO elites view burden sharing behavior of new member states, officials were interviewed from the International Staff and the International Military Staff at NATO Headquarters in Brussels, Belgium. These officials were diplomatic or foreign service personnel at the level of deputy or assistant Secretary General or were Directors within the Secretary General's private office. The norms and procedures of NATO are also the dominant feature of this institutional environment. Finally, interviews were conducted with diplomatic and military officials from the U.S. Mission to NATO. As would be expected, in all of these institutional settings, NATO norms, rules, and procedures are a significant factor shaping the social context. Interviews conducted with members of the NATO International Staff and the U.S. Mission give insights on how nonmilitary elites perceive new member burden sharing behavior.

INTERVIEWS WITH SENIOR MILITARY OFFICERS

During interviews conducted at the war colleges, senior military officers from new member countries often justified burden sharing decisions by emphasizing the need to demonstrate credibility to older members of NATO. Interviews with International Fellows at the U.S. Army War College and National Defense University representing new member states from 2007-08, used language such as "to prove" or "to demonstrate" about 40 percent of the time in their explanations of burden sharing behavior. For example, Colonel Janusz Adamczak explained that Poland contributed to NATO in order to prove that Poland was a valuable member.[74] It is possible that these responses were conditioned by the environment of the institutions where the officers were studying. It is also true that many of these International Fellows faced questions and frustration from their American counterparts as to why NATO was not doing more, specifically in Afghanistan. This social pressure might have biased the results. On the other hand, these officers mentioned their nation's obligation and duty to NATO, or the appropriateness of sharing burdens as NATO members more often than they mentioned rational incentives (e.g., credibility) in justifying burden sharing behavior. For example, the Romanian Fellow at the U.S. Army War College offered this explanation for exceeding the 2 percent standard.

> The Romanian President gave two reasons for increasing military expenditures: to replace inferior or outdated equipment for deployed troops and that Romania had a commitment to meet NATO requirements.[75]

This finding supports the argument that socialization of NATO norms has influenced the burden sharing rationale of military elites or at least that burden sharing decisions are justified using arguments based on identity and appropriateness. This data is especially surprising, given the U.S. dominated social environment at these two institutions.

As expected, language indicating the logic of consequences was less prevalent in the interviews with NMRs at SHAPE. In these interviews, all six military officers from new member states justified their state's burden sharing behaviors based on a logic of appropriateness versus a logic of consequence. NMRs more frequently mentioned their nation's obligations and duty to NATO than they mentioned the desire or need to establish credibility. In fact, appropriateness of burden sharing was mentioned nine times versus the one time concern for reputation was expressed. One NMR, Colonel Antanas Jurgatis, gave this explanation for Lithuanian support to ISAF, "Sending forces to ISAF was a hard decision because interests in Afghanistan were unclear to the Lithuanian people. But, our leaders argued that we were members of NATO and had to participate."[76] This is a stronger result than with the senior officers assigned to the U.S. Army War College and National Defense University where the rhetoric was more evenly divided between appropriateness and consequences.

It is interesting that the arguments used by officers assigned to NATO differed significantly from those of officers interviewed in a more national, institutional setting. It appears that NATO identity plays a much larger role in the rhetoric used in an institutional setting where NATO rules and procedures are the standard. This finding is in line with the socialization theories, from the international relations literature, which state that international organizations have socializing effects on the individuals participating in them.[77] More importantly for this project, these military elites explained their country's burden sharing behavior largely in term of obligations to NATO. This suggests that even rational burden sharing decisions are couched in language based on the logic of appropriateness.

Unfortunately, the number of senior military officers interviewed in both institutional settings was small. At the U.S. Army War College and the National Defense University, the interviews were limited to countries in attendance. Interviews conducted at SHAPE were constrained by the availability of the

NMRs and by the limited time and financial resources available. While the sample size was too small to make conclusive arguments, the responses suggest that both credibility and appropriateness play a role in the justification of contributions to NATO by military elites. Further studies are needed to make definitive conclusions.

Certainly, new members of NATO have both instrumental and sociological reasons for their contributions to the Alliance. As the Commander of Estonian Land Forces stated in an interview:

> Estonia supports NATO because Estonia needs NATO. Active Estonian participation in NATO missions gives weight to our voice in NATO and helps to ensure that NATO does not become marginalized as an alliance. It is also an obligation to provide forces as Estonia supported the NAC decision to initiate operations.[78]

Due to their experiences in the Cold War and position near the flanks of NATO, many new members take the territorial defense mission of NATO quite seriously. New members also appreciate their ability to influence the decisions of the Alliance, which is in stark contrast to their experience under the Warsaw Pact. This sense of ownership and security within NATO explains much of the new members' willingness to contribute to NATO's continued success. As the Romanian President reiterated in 2008:

> the alliance can rely on Romania as a partner that is always ready to be a good ally . . . we will not hesitate to respond to the policy of the alliance because we are part of it and contributing to the building of this policy.[79]

Evidence in support of the credibility concerns are also prevalent in the public discourse of government officials from new member countries that have been accused of free-riding behavior. Before and after accession to NATO, Hungary realized that its contributions to NATO would come under scrutiny. As Hungary's Ambassador to NATO stated in a 2001 speech, "only a nation that is willing and ready to take its' [sic] share of burdens can count on the support of others."[80] Domestic political actors also take advantage of these contributions or lack of contributions to gain attention or political support. In 2008, a member of the opposition Christian Democratic Party in Hungary, István Simicskó, criticized the low defense spending by the government, explaining that it hurt the international reputation of Hungary. "Embarrassingly, within NATO, only Iceland spends less on defence than Hungary."[81]

What is also interesting is that military elites from older NATO countries tend to attribute new member burden sharing behavior to instrumental concerns with credibility. This is true in both institutional settings. In interviews conducted at the U.S. Army War College, officers interviewed attributed new member burden sharing decisions to rational motivations, such as a desire to prove credibility to either the United States or NATO.

> New NATO members, especially the first three (the Czech Republic, Hungary, and Poland), joined NATO to increase security against Russia. They are willing to contribute to the Alliance just to prove to NATO, and especially to the United States, that they are worth the cost.[82]

This focus on the logic of consequences was also true in interviews of the senior political and military officials interviewed at NATO in January 2008.

Evidence in support of the credibility explanation for burden sharing is most prevalent in the language used by political and military officials assigned to NATO and the U.S. Mission to NATO. Most officials interviewed interpreted the burden sharing behavior by new member states as an attempt to demonstrate credibility and worth to the NATO Alliance. Bruce Weinrod, the Defense Advisor to the U.S. Mission to NATO, described new member burden sharing in rational terms, "New members want to show that they are serious about their commitments. . . . Their own historic experience makes them want to deal directly with security threats."[83] SACEUR's executive officer, formerly the Assistant Army Attaché to Warsaw, explained that "Poland wants to prove themselves and demonstrate that they have something to contribute to the alliance."[84] These interviews also offer insights into the perceptions of new member burden sharing.

All of the officials interviewed also stated that new members, in general, are carrying their weight in NATO burden sharing. About half of these officials attribute shortfalls in burden sharing to a lack of capability rather than a lack of willingness. In fact, NATO expects that contributions are subject to limitations of capability.[85] This expectation is reflected in the discourse of both political and military elites. According to the NATO Deputy Secretary General, "the new members have a lot of political will; their approach as new members of the club is that they want to show that they are up to the task of being members of NATO."[86] The Supreme Allied Commander, General John Craddock, specifically mentioned new members that were "carrying their weight, although they have limited capabilities. Some good examples are the Czech Republic, Estonia, Lithuania, Poland, and Romania."[87] Thus from the outside, new member burden sharing is largely viewed as a desire to demonstrate credibility and worth to the Alliance.

Another interesting finding is that this assessment of new member burden sharing was also shared by representatives of the leading country of NATO, the United States. Former United States Secretary of Defense Robert Gates told the Senate Armed Services Committee in early-2008 that he was frustrated that allies had not lived up to their commitments in ISAF. "I worry a lot about the alliance evolving into a two-tiered alliance, in which you have some allies willing to fight and die to protect people's security, and others who are not."[88] During a web chat in that same year, U.S. Ambassador to NATO, Victoria Nuland, stated that "we have been impressed by the commitment of all our new Allies to bring as much as they can to the table."[89] This characterization is interesting in that the U.S. Government's assessment of contributions from other NATO members has not been very favorable. As the theoretical "bill-payer" for free-riding behavior, one would expect the United States to be highly critical of those countries not contributing their fair share to the Alliance. In fact, the United States has been very outspoken in trying to coerce members of the Alliance to increase their contributions to both defense spending and the NATO mission in Afghanistan. Given this level of criticism by the Americans, the favorable characterization of new member burden sharing is even more convincing. In the next chapter, the context of these new member contributions is examined in a series of case studies.

CONCLUSIONS

This chapter examined issues of why states exhibit particular burden sharing behaviors. While the logic of collective action offers some insights into burden sharing decisions, it appears that multiple logics are at work. While explanations based on the logic of consequences dominate the assessment of burden sharing behavior by outside actors, new members themselves have a more complex rationale for burden sharing in NATO. Military elites from new member countries predominantly use identity-based explanations for the burden sharing behavior. The fact that most of the new member discourse examined justifies burden sharing by emphasizing appropriateness suggests that socialization may have had a positive impact in mitigating the rational incentives to free-ride. Not surprisingly, concerns for credibility also seem to inform the burden sharing decisions of new NATO members. While rational motivations (such as concerns over credibility and side payments) may drive burden sharing decisions, they are often supported using arguments based on identity.

ENDNOTES - CHAPTER 4

1. Jamie Shea, Director of Policy Planning, interviewed by author, January 31, 2008, NATO Headquarters, Brussels, Belgium.

2. Judith Kelley, "International Actors on the Domestic Scene: Membership Conditionality and Socialization by International Institutions," *International Organization*, Vol. 58, 2004.

3. James Fearon and Alexander Wendt, "Rationalism v. Constructivism: A Skeptical View," Walter Carlsnaes, Thomas Risse, and Beth Simmons, eds., *Handbook of International Relations*, London, UK: Sage Publications, 2002, p. 52.

4. Adriano Milovan, "Under the Security Umbrella: 60% of World's GDP is created," *PV International*, No. 0016, March 31, 2008, available from *www.privredni.hr/pvint/PVI0016.pdf*.

5. Alastair Smith, "Alliance Formation and War," *International Studies Quarterly*, Vol. 39, 1995, p. 419.

6. Traian Basescu, President of Romania, "Preparing for Bucharest," video interview, January 31, 2008, available from *www.nato.int/multi/2008/video.html#jan*.

7. Barre R. Seguin, "Why did Poland Choose the F-16?" Occasional Paper No. 11, Garmisch-Partenkirchen, Germany: George C. Marshall Center for Security Studies, June 2007. For further details on the loan, see the article in "Defence Budget, Poland," *Jane's Sentinel Security Assessment*, August 6, 2008, available from *www.8.janes.com*.

8. Tamás S. Kiss, "Suspend America says, 'Thank you'," *Budapest Sun Online*, October 28, 2004, available from *www.budapestsun.com/cikk.php?id=14018*.

9. "Military Assistance," undated, Washington, DC: U.S. Department of State, available from *www.state.gov/documents/organization/17783.pdf*.

10. Bureau of European and Eurasian Affairs, "Foreign Operations Appropriated Assistance: Estonia," Fact Sheet, Washington, DC: U.S. Department of State, April 28, 2008, available from *www.state.gov/p/eur/rls/fs/104123.htm*.

11. Kiss.

12. Seguin. For further details on the loan, see "Defence Budget, Poland."

13. Charlie Coon, "Military Scales Back Romania Rotation Plans," *Stars and Stripes*, February 21, 2008, available from *www.stripes.com/news/military-scales-back-romania-rotation-plans-1.75294*.

14. Frank Schimmelfenning, "International Socialization in the New Europe: Rational Action in an Institutional Environ-

ment," *European Journal of International Relations,* Vol. 6, No. 1, 2000, p. 122.

15. Anonymous Senior Diplomat and Member of the NATO International Staff, interview by author, January 31, 2008, NATO Headquarters, Brussels, Belgium.

16. Kelley, p. 425.

17. *Ibid.*

18. Shea, interview by author.

19. For example, Pamela Oliver, "Rewards and Punishments as Selective Incentives for Collective Action: Theoretical Investigations," *The American Journal of Sociology,* No. 6, 1980, pp. 1356-1375; J. Harbaugh Andreoni and L. W. Vesterlund, "The Carrot or the Stick: Rewards, Punishments and Cooperation," *American Economic Review,* No. 93, 2003, pp. 893-902; Martin Sefton, Robert Shupp, and James Walker, "The Effect of Rewards and Sanctions in Provision of Public Goods," Working Paper #2006-005, Bloomington, IL: Indiana University, Center for Applied Economics and Policy Research, August 29, 2006, available from *ssrn.com/abstract=932683*; E. Fehr and S. Gächter, "Cooperation and Punishment in Public Goods Experiments," *American Economic Review,* Vol. 90, 2000, pp. 980-994; U. Fischbacher, "Z-Tree. Zurich Toolbox for Readymade Economic Experiments," *Experimental Economics,* Vol. 10, 2007, pp. 171-178; U. Fischbacher and S. Gächter, "Social Preferences, Beliefs, and the Dynamics of Free Riding in Public Goods Experiments," *American Economic Review,* 2009.

20. "NATO—An Important Investor," *Warsaw Voice Online,* November 4, 2004, available from *www.warsawvoice.pl/view/6978.*

21. Krzysztof Sidor, "The Changing Face of NATO," *Warsaw Voice Online,* available from *www.warsawvoice.pl/view/866315 June 2005.*

22. Daryl G. Press, *Calculating Credibility,* Ithaca, NY: Cornell University Press, 2005, p. 1.

23. Gideon Rose, *How Wars End,* New York: Simon & Schuster, 2010, p. 2.

24. See Press, p. 2. He also has a good summary of the literature on "Past Action Theory."

25. Robert Keohane, *After Hegemony: Cooperation and Discord in the World Political Economy*, Princeton, NJ: Princeton University Press, 1984, pp. 105–106; Robert Keohane, "International Institutions: Can Interdependence work?" *Foreign Policy*, Vol. 110, No. 1, 1998.

26. Frank Schimmelfenning, "The Community Trap: Liberal Norms, Rhetorical Action, and the Eastern Enlargement of the European Union," *International Organization*, Vol. 55, 2001, p. 47.

27. Senator Jim Talent, "New Wine in Old Bottles: Moving Towards a Post Cold War Policy," *Forward!* Washington, DC: The Heritage Foundation, November 28, 2007, available from *www. heritage.org/press/commentary/112807a.cfm.*

28. See, for example, Glenn H. Snyder, "The Security Dilemma in Alliance Politics," *World Politics*, Vol. 36, No. 1, 1984, pp. 474-475; Kenneth A. Oye, "Explaining Cooperation under Anarchy: Hypotheses and Strategies," *World Politics*, Vol. 38, No. 1, 1985, pp. 1-24; Michael Mandelbaum, *The Fate of Nations: The Search for National Security in the Nineteenth and Twentieth Centuries,* Cambridge, UK: Cambridge University Press, 1988; Charles A. Kupchan, "NATO and the Persian Gulf: Examing Intra-Alliance Behavior." *International Organization*, Vol. 42, No. 2, 1988, pp. 317-346; and Avery Goldstein, "Discounting the Free Ride: Alliances and Security in the Postwar World," *International Organization*, Vol. 49, No. 1, 1995, pp. 39-71.

29. Glenn H. Snyder, "The Security Dilemma in Alliance Politics," *World Politics*, Vol. 36, No. 4, July 1984, p. 494.

30. Johnston, p. 1013.

31. James G. March and Johan P. Olsen, "The Institutional Dynamics of International Political Orders," *International Organization*, Vol. 52, No. 4, 1998, as cited in Thomas Risse, "Let's Argue!: Communicative Action in World Politics," *International Organization*, Vol. 54, No. 1, 2000, pp. 1-39.

32. "Poland Spurns U.S. Air Defense Offer," *Los Angeles Times*, July 5, 2008, available from *www.latimes.com/news/nationworld/world/la-fg-poland5-2008jul05,0,1045291.story?track=ntothtml*.

33. Eventually, in the face of Polish demands for *quid pro quo* and stiff Russian resistance, the United States decided to shelve these plans in 2009. See Phillip R. Cuccia, "Implications of a Changing NATO," Carlisle, PA: Strategic Studies Institute, U.S. Army War College, May 2010, p. 19, available from *www.StrategicStudiesInstitute.army.mil/*.

34. Colonel Alex Portelli, former Chief of European Division, and Political Military Affairs, United States European Command, based on interviews conducted October 2011 at the U.S. Army War College, Carlisle, PA.

35. Risse, p. 4.

36. Jeffrey Checkel, "International Institutions and Socialization in Europe: Introduction and Framework," *International Organization*, Vol. 59, No. 4, 2005.

37. Alexandra Gheciu, "Security Institutions as Agents of Socialization? NATO and the New Europe," *International Organization*, Vol. 59, No. 4, 2005, p. 981.

38. Johnston, p. 1015.

39. Checkel, p. 804.

40. Jeffrey Lewis, "The Janus Face of Brussels: Socialization and Everyday Decision Making in the European Union," *International Organization*, Vol. 59, No. 4, 2005, p. 937.

41. *Ibid.*

42. Frédéric Mérand, "Pierre Bourdieu and the Birth of European Defense," *Security Studies*, Vol. 19, No. 2, 2010, p. 342.

43. Gheciu, p. 974.

44. *Ibid.*, p. 988.

45. Robert T. Cossaboom, "The Joint Contact Team Program," Washington, DC: Joint History Office, Office of the Chairman Joint Chiefs of Staff, p. 4, available from *www.dtic.mil/doctrine/doctrine/history/jointcontactteam.pdf*.

46. *Ibid.*, p. 7.

47. *Ibid.*, p. 10.

48. "2009 State Partnership Program Fact Sheet," Stuttgart, Germany: U.S. European Command, available from *www.eucom.mil/english/spp/default.asp*.

49. Cossaboom.

50. Portelli interview.

51. *Ibid.* Also see interviews with Colonel Indrek Sirel and Colonel Antanas Jurgaitis.

52. "Baltic Defence Co-operation—Main Joint Projects," Riga, Latvia: Ministry of Foreign Affairs of the Republic of Latvia, available from *www.mfa.gov.lv/en/?id=4498*. See also NATO, "Fact Sheet: Lithuania's External Military Co-operation," available from *www.nato.int/pfp/lt/facts/fs08.html*; Portelli interview.

53. NATO, "SFOR Informer Online: NORDPOL troops working in Doboj," available from *www.nato.int/sfor/indexinf/147/p08a/t02p08a.htm*. Also Portelli interview.

54. NATO Public Diplomacy Division, *NATO Handbook*, Brussels, Belgium: NATO, 2001, available from *www.nato.int/docu/handbook/2001/hb020201.htm*.

55. NATO, "NATO 2020: Assured Security; Dynamic Engagement," May 17, 2010, p. 23.

56. NATO Public Diplomacy Division, *NATO Handbook*, p. 196.

57. NATO, "Partnership for Peace Programme," December 16, 2011, available from *www.nato.int/cps/en/natolive/topics_50349.htm?selectedLocale=en*.

58. James Sperling, Sean Kay, and S. Victor Papacosma, *Limiting institutions? The Challenge of Eurasian Security Governance,* Manchester, UK: Manchester University Press, 2003, p. 173. Also see "Partnership for Peace: Framework Document," Brussels, Belgium: NATO, January 10-11, 1994, available from *www.nato.int/cps/en/natolive/official_texts_24469.htm*.

59. "Partnership Tools," Brussels, Belgium: NATO, May 13, 2014, available from *www.nato.int/cps/en/SID-16A3E502-EF248C3B/natolive/topics_80925.htm?selectedLocale=en*.

60. Colonel (Retired) James Holcomb, former Central and Eastern European Advisor to SACEUR and Chief of the Permanent Staff, PCC, based on interviews conducted October 2011 at the U.S. Army War College, Carlisle, PA.

61. NATO, "Topic: Individual Partnership Action Plans (IPAPs)," available from *www.nato.int/cps/en/SID-8467C21F-5C8B2195/natolive/topics_49290.htm*.

62. NATO, "Partnership Tools," December 16, 2011, available from *www.nato.int/cps/en/natolive/topics_80925.htm*.

63. Jeffrey Simon, "The IFOR/SFOR Experience: Lessons Learned by PfP Partners," *Strategic Forum*, No. 120, Washington, DC: National Defense University, July 1997, available from *www.ndu/edu/inss/strforum/SF120/forum120.html*.

64. NATO, "ISAF Placemat," December 16, 2011, available from *www.nato.int/nato_static/assets/pdf/pdf_2011_12/20111214_111208-isaf-placemat.pdf*.

65. Schimmelfenning, "International Socialization in the New Europe," p. 126.

66. *Ibid.,* p. 127.

67. NATO, "Membership Action Plan," Press Release NAC-S(99)66, April 24, 1999, available from *www.fas.org/man/nato/natodocs/99042460.htm.*

68. Basescu, "Preparing for Bucharest."

69. Steven Erlanger and Steven Lee Myers, "NATO Allies Oppose Bush on Georgia and Ukraine," *The New York Times*, April 3, 2008, available from *www.nytimes.com/2008/04/03/world/europe.*

70. Gheciu, p. 976.

71. *Ibid.*, p. 986.

72. Elizabeth Weinstein, "NATO Gives New Member Mixed Review," *Prague Post Online*, June 30, 1999, available from *www.praguepost.com/P02/pp.php/?id=30507&a=3.*

73. *NATO Handbook*, 2006, p. 90.

74. Colonel Janusz Adamczak, interview by author, Carlisle, PA: U.S. Army War College, June 5, 2007.

75. Colonel Vasile Roman, interview by author, Carlisle, PA: U.S. Army War College, December 11, 2007.

76. Colonel Antanas Jurgaitis, interview by author, SHAPE Headquarters, Mons, Belgium, January 28, 2008.

77. Checkel.

78. Colonel Indrek Sirel, interview by author, Carlisle, PA: U.S. Army War College, November 6, 2008.

79. Basescu.

80. Andras Simonyi, former Hungarian Ambassador to the United States and Permanent Representative to NATO, "Hungary in NATO—after 2 Years of Membership," speech to NATO, 2001, available from *www.atlanticcommunity.org/Hungary%20in%20NATO.html.*

81. "Suspend NATO Membership," *Budapest Sun Online*, January 21, 2007, available from *www.budapestsun.com/cikk.php?id=55*.

82. Lieutenant Colonel Nicolaas Tak, interview by author, Carlisle, PA: U.S. Army War College, January 11, 2008.

83. W. Bruce Weinrod, Representative, U.S. Mission to NATO, interviewed by author, January 31, 2008, NATO Headquarters, Brussels, Belgium.

84. Colonel Tucker Mansager, Executive Officer to the Supreme Allied Commander Europe, based on interviews conducted January 28, 2008, at SHAPE Headquarters, Mons, Belgium.

85. *Troop Contributions*, Brussels, Belgium: NATO, 2011, available from *www.nato.int/cps/en/natolive/topics_50316.htm?*

86. Claudio Bisogneiro, Deputy Secretary General of NATO, interviewed by author, January 31, 2008, NATO Headquarters, Brussels, Belgium.

87. General John Craddock, Supreme Allied Commander Europe, based on interviews conducted February 1, 2008, SHAPE Headquarters, Mons, Belgium.

88. Ann Scott Tyson, and Josh White, "Gates Hits NATO Allies' Role in Afghanistan," *Washington Post.com*, February 7, 2008.

89. Victoria Nuland, U.S. Ambassador to NATO, "Ambassador Discusses Security Issues on Eve of NATO Ministerial," webchat on December 5, 2007.

CHAPTER 5

CASE STUDIES IN BURDEN SHARING
BEHAVIOR: NEW MEMBERS

ADDRESSING UNANSWERED QUESTIONS

> New members are generally doing well. However, it is
> difficult to characterize them as a group because they
> comprise a variety of states with unique institutions,
> capabilities, and history.

> General Sir John McColl
> Deputy Supreme Allied
> Commander Europe[1]

The interviews in the previous chapter provided
insight into the role of socialization in understanding
the burden sharing decisions of new North Atlantic
Treaty Organization (NATO) members. However,
greater focus on individual nations is required to understand fully the burden sharing preferences of new
members. Each state faces its own perceived threats,
domestic constraints, and "geographic burdens."[2]
Each state also has a different capacity to share the
burdens of the Alliance. If the socialization of NATO
burden sharing norms was effective, then burden sharing behavior should increase as capabilities increase.
The results of this chapter indicate that new member
contributions have risen over time as their capabilities approach their willingness to contribute. In fact,
this increased burden sharing occurred in the face of
significant fiscal, physical, and political constraints,
which are also discussed.

This chapter uses a series of short case studies to
examine burden sharing behavior of individual new

members in the context of their individual domestic and strategic environments. It begins with a brief discussion of the difference between capability and willingness, borrowing insights from the field of psychology. It is followed by a discussion of the strategic environment in which burden sharing decisions are made. The section then looks at the possible motivations and constraints in making burden sharing decisions about military expenditures and troop commitments to NATO missions. The emphasis is on the 1999 wave of new NATO members, although two member states from the 2004 and the 2009 rounds of enlargement are also examined. The cases were selected to give variation on two key independent variables: length of membership and size.

The case studies are developed around the framework of the original hypotheses and relevant independent variables derived from the theories already discussed. The case studies also provide historical context for burden sharing behavior examined in previous chapters. The case studies begin with a brief overview of the new member's history prior to joining NATO. This history includes a brief review of the pre-accession processes these states underwent prior to gaining membership in NATO and the European Union (EU). This section also reviews the decision-making processes for military expenditures and the commitment of forces to NATO missions.

Each case study looks at the physical and economic constraints facing each country. These include, but are not limited to, the key variables discussed in Chapters 2 and 3: gross domestic product (GDP), population, and geographic size, GDP growth, and threat. The case studies also examine additional fiscal and political constraints. In the face of these factors, the case studies analyze the performance of these countries on our two measures of burden sharing: defense expenditures and troop contributions. Most of the data comes from government sources and international organizations such as the Organisation for Economic Co-operation and Development (OECD), International Monetary Fund (IMF), and NATO.

The first three countries examined are the new member states from the 1999 wave of NATO enlargement (Poland, the Czech Republic, and Hungary). These states were the main focus of the previous chapters. In these case studies, the length of membership is the same, while the population size varies. All three of these members also underwent a much less rigorous accession review and formal socialization process prior to becoming members of NATO. Therefore, if socialization is the driving factor behind equitable burden sharing behavior, then these states should be more prone to free-riding behavior. The next two cases differ from the first three in that they examine two of the seven 2004 new NATO members: Romania and Estonia. These states were chosen from the other 2004 members because they represent the largest and smallest new members in that wave. They also represent one of the wealthiest (Estonia) and one of the poorest (Romania) new members. If our findings from the last chapter are correct, Romania should share a greater proportion of the burdens than a much smaller Estonia. In addition, these states should be less prone to free-riding due to the more extensive and prolonged socialization process under the Membership Action Plan (MAP). This set of cases allows for variation on the dependent variables: defense expenditures and troop contributions. The last two cases examine the two newest NATO members from the 2009 wave of enlargement: Albania and Croatia.

The case studies examine the unique histories and context within which burden sharing decisions are made by each country. The logic of collective action explains burden sharing solely in terms of outcome. Under this logic, free-riding behavior is a rational choice to minimize individual costs for Alliance members. However, burden sharing behavior is a function of two components: willingness to burden share and capability to burden share. The logic of collective action assumes that new members consciously decide to free-ride. Nonetheless, it is possible that what looks like free-riding behavior is actually a lack of capability. If limited military capability is the cause of free-riding behavior examined in the last chapters, burden sharing should increase as capability increases. These case studies look at maximum annual contributions to NATO missions as proxy measures for "deployability" and average annual contributions to NATO missions as proxy measures for "sustainability." If capability is a limiting factor on burden sharing, the observable implication is that these measures of contributions should increase over time as new members increase the number of deployable and sustainable land forces. For example, as new members improve interoperability with NATO and progress in their professionalization and modernization programs, their contributions to NATO missions should also increase. This chapter measures the willingness to contribute by looking at expenditures and troop contributions made in the face of economic or political constraints that should incentivize free-riding behavior.

CAPABILITY VERSUS WILLINGNESS

Before moving to the case studies, it would be helpful to examine the distinction between the lack of capability versus an absence of political will in evaluating burden sharing performance. Several studies in psychology have examined the difference between motivation and ability in their relation to performance. Larry Fogli, Paul Sackett, and Sheldon Zedeck suggested that motivation and ability played a different role, depending on whether the performance required a typical or maximum level of effort.[3] A maximum performance was characterized by an awareness of evaluation, acceptance of instructions to maximize efforts, and a relatively short duration. In these situations, ability was the major determinant of performance. In 2007, Neil Anderson and Ute-Christine Klehe verified this model's finding that the correlation between ability and performance increased during maximum performance.[4] Using these criteria, NATO missions receive much greater public scrutiny by NATO and the United States than other measures of burden sharing, such as defense expenditures, which take place over an extended period of time. Because of NATO's consensus procedures, changes in levels of effort during NATO missions also imply acceptance. Therefore, lessons from studying maximum performance conditions could provide insights when evaluating contributions to NATO missions.

Psychology also makes the distinction between controllability and intentionality in explaining social motivation.[5] Interpretations of behavior differ based on whether the cause of failure was controllable (actor had the ability to change the outcome) or the cause of failure was intentional (the actor willingly failed).

Not surprisingly, other people tend to respond more favorably to behavior caused by a lack of capability versus a lack of willingness. The same is true in NATO where burdens historically have been assigned based on the ability to bear them. The Alliance is tolerant of efforts constrained by a lack of capability, but not by a lack of willingness.

According to NATO's 2006 *Comprehensive Political Guidance,* capability is defined as "sufficient fully deployable and sustainable land forces."[6] If new members were in fact willing, but lacked the capability to burden share, an observable result would be that contributions to NATO missions should have increased over time as new members increased the number of deployable and sustainable land forces. By looking at case studies of individual new member countries, it is possible to determine whether or not new members' contributions have increased since gaining membership to NATO. If so, this would indicate that earlier burden sharing behavior was constrained by a lack of capability versus willingness.

OVERVIEW OF CASE STUDIES

This section looks at a select group of new NATO members to understand better the burden sharing results from previous chapters. The case studies are broken down into two parts, each related to a different dependent variable. The first part systematically looks at the independent variables (based on the model of military expenditures discussed earlier) that affect defense expenditures. For example, large states should have higher military expenditure rates as a percentage of GDP than smaller members.

Two constraints on burden sharing are also examined that were not included in the regression model: GDP per capita and debt as a percentage of GDP. States with a higher GDP per capita should be better able to afford greater military expenditures. States with higher levels of debt should have less flexibility in increasing their levels of military expenditures due in part to EU fiscal constraints.

The second part of the case study examines contributions to NATO missions. In looking at troop contributions, it is necessary first to understand the strategic context and decisionmaking process within which those decisions are made. Since the strategic context differs for each country, it is discussed briefly in the first part of each case study. The decision process to send troops to NATO missions also varies from country to country and is discussed individually for each case study.

A closer examination of contributions to NATO missions provides an opportunity to distinguish between the two components of performance: capability and willingness. If a lack of willingness is to blame for lower contributions from new members, then troop contributions should have decreased over time. However, if lagging commitments to early NATO missions were due to a lack of capability, new member contributions should have increased over time as capabilities increased. There are two main constraints to troop contributions examined in these case studies: public opinion and force size. The results would be even stronger if contributions increased in the face of domestic political opposition and reduced force structure.

All of the case studies examined share some common features: Cold War links to Russia, NATO, and

EU socialization efforts, and democratic budget processes. Most of the countries in these case studies share a common historical experience in the aftermath of World War II. All had communist governments or were ruled by a communist-led government (Croatia was a part of Yugoslavia). Five of the countries were occupied by Soviet troops, though the occupation of Romania ended in 1958. With the exceptions of Albania, Croatia, and Estonia, all of these countries were members of the Warsaw Pact. To varying degrees, the Soviet Union often interfered in the domestic politics of these nations (Estonia lost its sovereignty in 1941), though less so in Albania and the former Yugoslavia (of which Croatia was a part). This common background informs the threat perception each of these countries has of Russia today.

All of the countries also underwent NATO socialization processes. The Czech Republic, Hungary, and Poland joined the Partnership for Peace (PfP) program in 1994 and NATO in March 1999. Given their history with Russia and Germany, the NATO Article 5 guarantee meant a great deal to these countries. All three of these new NATO states joined the EU in May 2004. Albania, Estonia, and Romania also joined the PfP program in 1994. Like all new members after 1999, they had to undergo the MAP process prior to gaining entry into NATO. This was done simultaneously with their preparations for entry into the EU, which also required significant reforms and preparation. Romania joined NATO in 2004 and the EU in 2007. Unlike Romania, Estonia joined both NATO and the EU in 2004. Therefore, both Estonia and Romania were exposed to a longer and more structured socialization effort than were the nations in the 1999 wave. Like the 2004 new members, Croatia and Albania were members of PfP and went through the MAP process prior to accession in 2009. Croatia was admitted to the EU in July 2013, while Albania is still seeking entrance.

As relatively new members of the Western community, these countries face conflicting institutional pressures on defense spending. Commitments to NATO and the EU Common Security and Defense Policy (CSDP) encourage members to maintain sufficient levels of military spending and capability.[7] One of the reasons behind CSDP is an EU effort to increase the military capabilities of its members. This effort was outlined through the Helsinki Headline Goals in 1999, which were later deferred in 2004 under the Headline Goal 2010. Every 6 months, the European Council receives a progress report on military capabilities.[8] However, neither NATO nor the EU has formal mechanisms to sanction members that do not meet military spending or capability goals.

On the other hand, all new members and aspiring members of NATO are also members or candidates for the European Monetary Union (EMU). Under the EU, military expenditures are constrained by the Maastricht Criteria and the convergence criteria of the EU Stability and Growth Pact. The Stability and Growth Pact stipulates that budget deficits can be no more than 3 percent per year and government debt no more than 60 percent of GDP. Performance against these criteria is used as one of the conditions for entrance into the EMU. What is unique, though, is this Pact also empowers the European Council to penalize financially participating members failing to meet these standards.[9] Therefore, one would expect that EU fiscal pressures would constrain these states' military expenditures.

The budget process in each of these countries is similar. Every year, the military articulates its security needs to the Minister of Defense, who develops a budget proposal based on guidelines from the Minister of Finance. Once the government approves the budget proposal, it sends the consolidated budget to parliament for approval. Military budgets are relatively path dependent and can only decline incrementally from year to year, as was seen in the results from previous chapters. Much of the defense spending in Europe is nondiscretionary in the near term. These expenses include multiyear procurement contracts and on-going personnel costs. Given this constraint on budgetary flexibility, the main ways to cut spending are to cut programs, scale back operations and training, or reduce force structure.

Case Study: Poland.

Poland's strategic environment is shaped by its history and its location. Under the Nazi-Soviet Pact prior to World War II, Nazi Germany and the Soviet Union agreed to divide Poland. Poland fell to these two powers in spite of alliances with Britain and France. After World War II, Poland became a satellite state of the Soviet Union. The Soviet Union often interfered in Polish politics, especially with the rise of the Solidarity Union in the 1980s.[10] Fear of a Soviet invasion supposedly led General Wojciech Jaruzelski to impose martial law in 1981. With the fall of the Soviet Union, Russian troops finally exited the country in September 1993, exactly 54 years after the Soviet Union invaded Poland under the Nazi-Soviet Pact.[11] Given this history, Poland has been less likely to discount Russian threats. This lingering threat perception is especially true in the aftermath of the invasion of Georgia in 2008 and Crimea in 2014. Polish-Russian tensions have also been strained due to Poland's ties to the United States. On November 5, 2008, in retaliation for U.S. plans to place an anti-ballistic missile system in Poland and the Czech Republic, Russia announced plans to place short-range missiles in Kaliningrad.[12] Another important factor is Poland's position in Europe. The distance from Warsaw to Moscow is 1,149 kilometers (km), making Poland one of the closer NATO allies. Poland also shares a border with Kaliningrad, a Russian enclave between Poland and Lithuania.

As Poland approached its 10th anniversary of accession into NATO, it was not surprising that it no longer viewed itself as a "new" member of NATO. In fact, Poland has felt confident enough to make its voice heard in both the EU and NATO. For example, Poland's president was highly critical of Russia's invasion of Georgia, even as other EU members were trying to take a more neutral stand.[13] In 2008, Poland's Foreign Minister chastised other members of the NATO Alliance for lagging commitments in the International Security Assistance Force (ISAF), stating that there was "no room for free-riding" in NATO.[14]

Poland is one of the largest new member states of NATO. It has a population of over 38 million (with almost 97 percent being ethnic Poles) and a total area of over 312,679 square (sq) km. In 2013, Poland's estimated GDP purchasing power parity (PPP) equaled $817.5 billion in current prices.[15] This equates to a per capita GDP PPP of $21,214 (a little more than 66 percent of Spain's at $29,851) and makes Poland one of the poorest new members in the 1999 and 2004 waves. The good news is that Poland's GDP has grown by 29 percent since 1993 (see Figure 5-1), and it has a relatively low level of net government debt, at around 29 percent of GDP in 2013.[16]

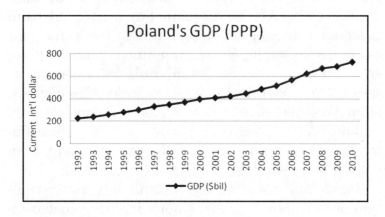

Figure 5-1. Polish GDP in Billions of Dollars.[17]

Unlike some new members, Poland was close to meeting the economic criteria for the EMU before the 2008 financial crisis. In 2008, Poland's deficit was 4.5 percent, while its public debt was around 54 percent of GDP which is below Maastricht levels.[18] Due to growing fiscal burdens resulting from the 2008 global economic downturn, Poland faced increasing pressure to cut military expenditures. While the Ministry of Defense budget increased 9.1 percent in the 1-year period between 2007 and 2008, Poland's defense expenditures only increased 23 percent from 2009 to 2013. This reflects Poland's efforts to keep its deficit level steady.[19]

In her study of burden sharing in the Warsaw Pact, Condoleezza Rice suggested that Poland was a "passive free rider" during the Cold War, due to its relatively low defense expenditures.[20] Poland has not continued this behavior since joining NATO in 1999. In fact, Poland is one of the few NATO countries to come close to meeting NATO's burden sharing target of 2 percent of GDP. A general political consensus enables Poland to maintain its relatively robust level of military spending. According to the Minister of National Defense in the current government, "all ruling parties agree on the 2 percent (level)."[21] Oftentimes, obligations to NATO are used to justify resource allocations.[22] This commitment to meeting NATO standards has been embedded into Polish law, which makes it easier for governments to fulfill NATO obligations. On May 25, 2001, the Polish Parliament (Sejm) established a 5-year defense plan "stipulating that Warsaw will spend no less than 1.95% of its gross national product on defense in an effort to bring the Polish armed forces closer to NATO military and interoperability standards."[23] Beginning in 2005, this budget was fixed at 1.95 percent of the previous year's GDP as opposed to its projected current year GDP.[24]

Given its political commitment, it is not surprising, then, that Poland's defense expenditures as a percentage of GDP have remained relatively constant, averaging 1.8 percent since 1999. This level is much higher than Spain's, which is larger (approximately 192,000-sq km), more populated (2 million people greater than Poland) and much wealthier. Spain's military expenditures have declined from 1.3 percent in 1999 to 0.9 percent of GDP in 2013. This decline is consistent with the results in previous chapters, which shows greater wealth does not necessarily equate to greater burden sharing and that new members' military expenditures would be a greater relative proportion of GDP than old members.

The second part of the case study examines the second measure of burden sharing: troop commitments. Poland has much greater flexibility in its decisions regarding troop commitments to NATO. While the separation of powers on foreign policy is somewhat unclear in the Polish Constitution,[25] the process for deploying Polish troops is straightforward. Whenever the government wishes to send Polish forces abroad, the Minister of Defense sends a proposal for commitment of forces to the Prime Minister. Under Polish law, the President (as the Commander in Chief) approves the decision to deploy troops.[26] If the President vetoes an operation, it takes a two-thirds vote to override his or her decision. The President can decide the number of troops, the equipment sent and the duration of the mission. Thus, the President has some autonomy from the pressures of public opinion in deploying troops. However, Parliament balances this power by controlling the military's budget.

Poland was generally "reluctant to become involved in the third world," under the Warsaw Pact.[27] This tendency has been reversed under NATO. Poland has shown an increasing willingness to support NATO operations. As discussed in the last chapter, Poland's relative contribution to the Stabilization Force (SFOR) (averaging 316 troops per year) roughly equaled 1.9 percent of the NATO force. Poland increased both its actual and relative contribution to Kosovo Forces (KFOR) (averaging 527 soldiers per year) to about 2.3 percent of the NATO force.

Poland was also a big supporter of the War on Terrorism. As discussed in the last chapter, Poland had one of the largest contingents in Iraq under the Multinational Forces (starting at over 2,000 troops and ending the mission with approximately 900 soldiers in 2008). Poland was also one of the earliest members of the coalition, inserting special operation forces even before the bulk of U.S. troops invaded. The decision to support OIF was made in the face of strong domestic opposition to Poland's participation, with almost 60 percent opposing participation in 2003.[28] At the request of the United States, the government twice delayed its planned withdrawal from Iraq. In the 2007 elections, the opposition party, Civic Platform, made withdrawal from Iraq one of its campaign's promises and won the election.[29] In 2008, Poland withdrew its remaining forces from OIF.

While early contributions to ISAF were constrained by commitments to OIF, Poland gradually shifted the focus of its efforts to ISAF, the NATO mission in Afghanistan. In September 2006, Poland responded to requests from NATO to fill increasing ISAF requirements. In fact, only Poland offered to send additional troops.[30] After 2007, Poland shifted additional forces from Iraq to Afghanistan. At the request of NATO, Poland again agreed to significantly increase its contributions to ISAF in 2007 and 2008. Since 2007, Poland's relative contribution to ISAF increased to 2 percent of the total NATO force (approximately 937 soldiers in 2007 and 1,130 soldiers in 2008). Poland's contribution rose to a maximum of 2,630 in 2010 before falling to 1,741 in 2013. As a point of comparison, Spain's contributions to ISAF have declined from a maximum of 1,596 soldiers in 2012 to around 863 soldiers in 2013.

Qualitatively, Polish contributions were also superior; these forces are slated for the more dangerous eastern part of Afghanistan. Polish forces were stationed in the Ghazni Province in southern Afghanistan, compared to Spanish forces that were stationed in the relatively quiet Regional Command West. In addition, Poland provided helicopters to support ISAF (a critically short item) and made these units available to other NATO forces in the south.[31] Polish officials

239

were proud to point out that their forces in ISAF had no caveats, a major point of contention within the Alliance. Poland's Foreign Minister suggested that a state which contributes "without caveats gives twice."[32] In contrast, there were some 50 national caveats imposed on NATO forces in ISAF. These caveats, though always a factor in NATO operations, inhibit the flexibility and coordination of NATO operations.[33]

Poland's decision in 2006 to increase participation in Afghanistan was made in the face of strong domestic resistance to sending Polish troops into a combat mission.[34] It was hard to justify supporting an operation some 4,000-km away from NATO's borders. In a 2007 public opinion poll, 77 percent of Polish respondents were against Polish involvement in ISAF,[35] and over 70 percent doubted whether NATO's mission to Afghanistan would contribute to peace in that country.[36] However, Polish governments held firm in their support of the NATO mission. Shortly after becoming the Minister of Defence, Bogdan Klich stated that Poland would remain committed to the NATO mission in Afghanistan "with the view to Poland's credibility in NATO."[37] In 2008, the Minister of National Defence also stated that Poland had not ruled out further extensions of the mission.[38] The United States has certainly looked favorably on Poland's contributions to Iraq and Afghanistan. The Polish Military received almost $750 billion in military aid under President George W. Bush.[39] In 2012, another $14 million for training and equipping its forces in Afghanistan had been slated.[40]

Poland's record of troop contributions is interesting because it provides insights into the willingness versus capability issue of burden sharing posed in this chapter. Since attaining membership, Poland's average and maximum troop contributions to individual

NATO and U.S.-led missions have increased steadily (see Table 5-1). In 2008, Poland had over 2,300 troops deployed between Afghanistan, Iraq, and Kosovo compared to only 1,200 in 1999. This level of support to NATO is remarkable in the face of the strong domestic opposition already mentioned and the rational incentives for Poland to free-ride. Based on the collective security guarantees of NATO, Poland shifted focus from a larger territorial defense orientation toward a more deployable crisis management force structure. During this period, the size of the Polish armed forces dropped from 205,000 in 1999 to 150,000 in 2007 and to 125,000 in 2010, a reduction of approximately 25 percent and 40 percent, respectively.[41] Concurrently, the Polish armed forces underwent an extensive modernization and transformation. In 2008, Poland announced it was ending conscription and by June of 2009, it had transitioned to a completely professional army. In addition, many missions that were not inherently military were transferred to other security agencies.

	SFOR (1999-2004)	KFOR (1999-2008)	ISAF (2003-13)	OIF (2003-10)
AVG	316	527	1,258	1700
MAX	450	763	2,630	2,300

Table 5-1. Poland's Annual Contributions to NATO/U.S.-led Missions.

With its military transformation, Poland has been able to provide a larger and more capable percentage of their armed forces to NATO missions. In 1999, the number of Polish ground forces deployed in support of NATO mission equaled 450. By 2004, 5 years after accession, it had increased forces deployed with NATO to 883 and by 2014, it had increased them to 1,405.[42] This increasing level of support, in spite of domestic opposition and declining force structure, lends credence to the explanation from the last chapter; what appeared to be free-riding behavior reflected a lack of capability versus a lack of political will. As can be seen in Table 5-1, as Poland has increased capability, it has also increased its contributions.

Case Study: Czech Republic.

While the Czech Republic shares a similar recent history with Poland, a stronger case could be made for the fear of abandonment argument in the case of the Czech Republic. In 1938, France and Great Britain signed the Munich Agreement with Germany and Italy, ceding part of Czechoslovakia to Germany in an attempt to appease Adolf Hitler, despite a previous Czechoslovakian security alliance with France signed in 1924.[43] The Munich Agreement was widely viewed as a betrayal of the Czech people. To this day, Czech Foreign policy lives under the "shadow of Munich."[44]

The Soviet Union actively intervened in Czechoslovakia twice during the Cold War. Czechoslovakia initially maintained a freely elected government, known as the National Front Government, with about half of the ministers coming from outside the Communist Party. In February 1948, a majority of noncommunist ministers became disgruntled with Communist excesses and resigned from the government in the hopes of forcing a new election. Instead, the Communist Prime Minister, with assistance from the Soviet Union, headed a coup and formed a government that was dominated by the Communist Party. The Czech population became increasingly disenchanted with the communist system in the early-1960s. In 1968, Czechoslovakia initiated a series of democratic, economic, and social reforms.[45] This liberalization movement, known in the west as Prague Spring, was threatening to Moscow. In August 1968, the Soviet Union, in conjunction with other Warsaw Pact military forces, invaded Czechoslovakia with some 400,000 to 500,000 troops. Following the invasion, some 300,000 people emigrated from Czechoslovakia.

In 1989, the Velvet Revolution toppled the communist regime in Czechoslovakia. At the request of President Václav Havel, Russian troops finally exited the country in 1991.[46] After elections in 1992, Czechoslovakia's federal government acquiesced to the requests of the Czech and Slovak Republics to separate into two distinct countries.[47] The Czech Republic is in a more benign geostrategic position than Poland. No longer in the Warsaw Pact, the Czech Republic is today surrounded by NATO members. The distance from Prague to Moscow is 1,664-km, making the Czech Republic one of the furthest new NATO members from Russia. However, the Czech Republic (like Poland) faced Russian threats in retaliation for agreeing to host radar systems in support of the U.S. missile defense system.

The Czech Republic and Hungary (like Belgium and Portugal) are about the median size of NATO members, with a population of just over 10 million (over 90 percent being ethnic Czechs).[48] Thus, they might be expected to spend a smaller percentage of their GDP on military expenditures based on the results discussed earlier. The Czech Republic's total area, at 78,866-sq km, is smaller than Poland (312,679),

Hungary (90,030), and Portugal (92,391), but larger than Belgium (30,528). Even during the Cold War, Czechoslovakia was wealthier than other Eastern European countries and had a relatively small amount of external debt.[49] The Czech Republic remains a relatively wealthy member of NATO, with an estimated GDP (PPP) of $286 billion in 2013.[50] This gives the Czech Republic a per capita GDP (PPP) of $27,200, which is less than Belgium ($37,880), but larger than both Hungary ($20,065) and Portugal ($23,068).[51] The Czech Republic experienced an annual average growth rate of almost 12 percent prior to the global financial crisis.[52]

As with all new members, the Czech Republic also faces the conflicting EU pressures on defense spending. However, the Czech Republic is in a relatively stronger position in this regard than other new EU members. In 2008, the Czech deficit was 3.1 percent, while its public debt has remained around 35 percent of GDP, well below Maastricht levels.[53] This success is partially attributable to a sound fiscal policy, including a declining level of social welfare expenditures. By 2003, social expenditures, as a percentage of GDP, had dropped from over 25 percent[54] to approximately 21 percent of GDP.[55] Given this situation, the Stability Pact imposes a less onerous constraint on the Czech Republic.

During the Cold War, Czechoslovakia generally ignored the Warsaw Pact spending targets. In fact, after 1968, the Czechoslovakian military expenditures continued to decline, as a percentage of GDP, and exceeded only those of Hungary and Romania, if measured in dollars.[56] As a member of NATO, the Czech Republic has been more willing to devote resources to support military capabilities. Czech defense expenditure, as a percentage of GDP, is below NATO's burden sharing target of 2 percent of GDP, but close to the NATO average. While the Czech Republic met or exceeded NATO standards from 1999 to 2003, its expenditures began a gradual decline coinciding with the second round of NATO expansion in 2004. This fact is interesting in that the Czech Republic is one of the wealthiest new members. Since 2011, the defense budget remained at 1.1 percent of GDP. However, the average rate of expenditures (1.8 percent between 1999 and 2009) was consistently above those of founding NATO members of comparable size (Belgium and Portugal). This average was also above that of Hungary, though slightly below that of the Czech Republic's much larger neighbor, Poland (see Figure 5-2).

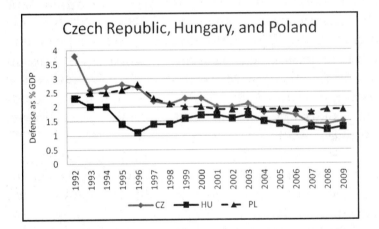

Figure 5-2. The Czech Republic's Military Expenditures versus Older Members.[57]

Having examined defense expenditures, it is now necessary to look at troop commitments. According to the Czech Constitution, the President is the commander in chief of the armed forces.[58] However, it is the Czech cabinet and Prime Minister who must first approve a mission before sending a request to Parliament for approval. Each year, the Ministry of Defence submits a list of troop and budget needs to the government, which includes planned deployments. The government submits these to Parliament for approval.[59] Decisions to send Czech military forces abroad are then included in a government resolution.[60]

However, Parliament does not always approve these requests. In 2008 the Ministry of Defence announced that it planned to pass a new resolution including an increased presence in ISAF in 2009.[61] Prime Minister Mirek Topolanek stated that the pending increases in contributions were due to "growing responsibilities in the region and obligations to our allies in NATO."[62] However, this move was opposed by the Social Democratic Party (ČSSD) and by the Communist Party.[63] According to a 2008 poll, 70 percent of Czech respondents were also against this increased commitment.[64] As a result, the Czech Parliament failed to approve this resolution by two votes in December 2009. Opposition of the ČSSD was the primary cause of this defeat.[65]

In spite of this, the Czech Republic has been an active supporter of NATO operations. As discussed in the last chapter, the Czech Republic's relative contribution to SFOR averaged 225 troops (declining from a high of 560 troops in 1999). This level of commitment represented 1.0 percent of the NATO force, while the Czech Republic comprised approximately 1.3 percent of NATO's population. The Czech Republic increased both its average and relative contribution to KFOR (averaging 365 soldiers per year from 1999 to 2008) which equaled about 2.0 percent of the NATO force. As previously mentioned, the Czech Republic committed 300 troops to OIF beginning in 2003. The decision to support OIF was made in the face of significant domestic opposition to Czech participation. With both Germany and France objecting to the invasion, the population was unsure that the Czech Republic should participate.[66] In 2007, Czech Foreign Minister Karel Schwarzenberg, from the Green Party, called for the complete withdrawal of Czech forces from OIF.[67]

Like Poland, the Czech Republic supported the U.S.-led OEF in Afghanistan prior to ISAF. Contributions to OEF continued even after ISAF was initiated. In 2008, the Czech Republic provided up to 100 Special Forces troops in the Kandahar region in support of OEF.[68] In addition, the Czech Republic also contributed to the NATO mission in ISAF. On average, the Czech Republic's annual contributions to ISAF were 395 troops, although this increased to 529 in 2012. For 3 years, the Czech Republic contributed forces to a German Provincial Reconstruction Team (PRT), and in 2008, they opened their own PRT in Logar province. The Czech Republic also provided a chemical detachment, an Operational Mentor and Liaison Team (OMLT), and air traffic control group in the capital of Kabul. At the request of the Dutch government, the Czech Republic also increased the size of its forces in southern Afghanistan.[69]

The Czech's contribution to ISAF exceeded its relative percentage of the NATO population. This level of commitment was impressive, given that the Czech government also faced domestic opposition to participation in Afghanistan, especially from the Communist Party and from the opposition party, the Social Democrats.[70] The Czech government even had to sell government bonds to fund these additional operational expenditures.[71] The Czech Republic also agreed to donate 12 critically needed helicopters to Afghanistan. In addition, the Czech government took pride in pointing out that Czech units in Afghanistan were not restricted by any caveats. [72]

A 2005 report from the Czech Minister of Foreign Affairs suggests that the Czech government was supporting NATO operations within its capability. [73] The Czech Republic's high level of support to both NATO and to U.S. operations was also rewarded by the United States. According to the U.S. State Department, "the Czech Republic has made a significant contribution to the War on Terrorism relative to its size."[74] Therefore, it is not surprising the Czech Republic, like Poland, has received side payments from the United States in return for its efforts. In 2006, total U.S. Government assistance to the Czech Republic equaled over $10 million.[75]

Since 1999, the Czech Republic steadily has increased its average troop contributions to individual NATO missions (see Table 5-2). The Czech Republic had almost 1,000 troops deployed between Afghanistan, Iraq, and Kosovo in 2008, compared to only 720 in 1999. While the number of Czech ground forces deployed to ISAF fell to around 250 in 2014, this contribution still exceeded that of both Belgium (193) and Portugal (154).[76]

This level of support is impressive in the face of a reduction in the Czech armed forces from around 73,591 professional and conscript soldiers in 1995 to 25,177 professional soldiers in 2008, a reduction of almost 70 percent.[77] Like Poland, this reduction in force structure was undertaken to meet NATO requirements. As with Poland, the Czech Republic's performance in spite of political and force structure constraints suggests that as capability increased, so did contributions to NATO missions.

	SFOR (1999-2004)	KFOR (1999-2008)	ISAF (2003-13)	OIF (2003-08)
AVG	225	365	395	124
MAX	560	553	529	300

Table 5-2. The Czech Republic's Annual Contributions to NATO/U.S.-led Missions.

Case Study: Hungary.

Hungary's World War II experience differed from Poland and Czechoslovakia in that it was an ally of Germany during the war. Hungary was finally conquered by the Soviet Union in April 1945, and a communist government was installed.[78] Following a series of democratic reforms in 1956 and a popular revolt against the Communist system, Soviet troops temporarily withdrew from Budapest. After Hungary announced its withdrawal from the Warsaw Pact on November 1, 1956, the Soviet Union invaded the country on November 3, 1956.[79] The legitimate Hungarian government was ousted, and a new Communist government installed. The Soviet Union stationed around 45,000 troops in Hungary until 1991, when they exited both Hungary and the Czech Republic.[80] Today, Hungary is surrounded by EU and NATO members and aspirants. The distance from Budapest to Moscow is 1,565-km, similar to the Czech Republic. According to its *National Security Strategy*, Hungary now faces minimal risk from traditional military aggression.[81] However, Hungary shares a border with Serbia, and remains concerned with potential ethnic conflict and instability in the Balkans.

Hungary has a slightly larger land mass than the Czech Republic and roughly the same size population, around 10 million (over 92 percent being ethnic Hungarian).[82] Historically, Hungary has had a more agriculturally based economy than Czechoslovakia. Hungary is a relatively poorer member of NATO, with an estimated GDP (PPP) of $198 billion in 2013.[83] Hungary's GDP equates to a per capita GDP (PPP) of $20,065 after dipping to $18,166 in 2009 and $18,611 in 2010. This per capita GDP is smaller than Belgium, the Czech Republic, or Portugal, and has been below that of Poland since 2010.[84]

Hungary has grown at a much slower rate than other new members, but still managed an annual average growth rate of 8.6 percent from 1993 to 2006.[85] However, this rate of growth slowed to about 2 percent in 2007 due to government programs to reduce public sector spending. The economy actually contracted in 2009 and 2010; GDP did not surpass 2008 levels until 2013.[86]

Of all of the new members of NATO, Hungary faces the most fiscal constraints resulting from the EU's Stability and Growth Pact requirements. While Hungary was aggressive in its post-Cold War economic privatization efforts, it was also saddled with an expansive social welfare system and a large amount of public debt.[87] Under economic reforms initiated by Finance Minister Lajos Bokros, Hungary was able to cut social expenditures as a percentage of GDP from 32 percent in 2000[88] to 23 percent of GDP in 2006.[89] However, it still has a long way to go. In 2008, the Hungarian deficit was 7.8 percent, while its public debt has remained around 72 percent of GDP. Both of these are well above the Stability Pact levels, as well as above those of the other new members.[90] Interestingly, only Belgium (90 percent), Greece (106 percent), and Italy (119 percent) had higher percentages of debt than Hungary. This high debt load may also contribute to Hungary's low military expenditures which, at 0.9 percent of GDP in 2013, was slightly below Belgium's at 1.1 percent.

Even as a member of the Warsaw Pact, Hungary had a reputation as a free-rider.[91] In a Cold War study on burden sharing, Bruce Russett stated that Hungary was "consistently at the bottom of the D/GNP list. . . . The need to appease Hungarian consumers, a legacy from 1956, accounts for [its] laggardness."[92] In the late-1980s, the Soviet Union and other Warsaw Pact countries attempted to pressure Hungary into increasing its defense expenditures, with little effect. During that time, Hungary had the smallest military budget in the Warsaw Pact.[93] When Hungary applied for NATO membership, it promised to keep military expenditures at a minimum between 1.7 and 1.8 percent of GDP.[94] However, Hungary found it difficult to meet this commitment. Former Hungarian defense minister Gyoergy Keleti admitted "that in order to achieve NATO membership, the country had made commitments it was not prepared to keep."[95]

Since gaining NATO membership in 1999, Hungary's defense expenditures, as a percentage of GDP, have been consistently below NATO's burden sharing target of 2 percent of GDP. In 2002, Hungary's Ambassador to NATO lamented Hungary's dismal record. "The problem is that, after getting into the club through considerable effort, we stopped caring."[96] Between 2000 and 2004, Hungarian military expenditures were, on average, 1.7 percent of GDP. This rate has steadily declined since 2003. Between 2005 and 2009, Hungary's average expenditures were below that of Portugal (1.7 percent) but above Belgium's average of 1.2 percent (see Figure 5-3).

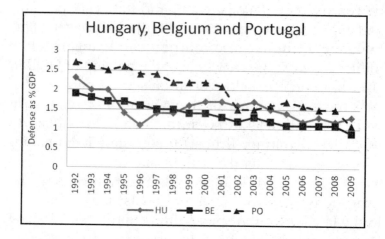

Figure 5-3. Hungary's Military Expenditures.[97]

NATO officials and other member countries have voiced their frustration with Hungary's failure to follow through on their defense spending commitments. In 2004, the NATO Secretary General chided Hungary for its low level of defense expenditures.[98] In 2007, a British Member of Parliament called for a suspension of Hungary's NATO membership. Both Hungarian political and military leaders acknowledged that Hungary had to do better. István Simicskó, a member of the Christian Democrats, suggested that his country's lackluster effort put Hungary's international reputation at stake. "Embarrassingly, within NATO, only Iceland spends less on defence than Hungary."[99] At the 2008 NATO meeting in Budapest, the Hungarian Defense Minister announced that Hungary would increase its defense expenditures by 0.2 percent in the next 5 years.[100] However, even this meager improvement was difficult to accomplish given the scope of economic issues. In 2008, Hungary was given a $25.5 billion bailout package from the IMF, EU, and World

Bank. The conditionality imposed on these loans added additional pressures on Hungary to cut its government expenditures even further in order to lower the deficit.[101]

However, a more positive picture emerges when looking at troop commitments, even though the constraints for Hungary are significant. In Hungary, the President's role in the military is more limited than in Poland. The President only controls promotions and firings of military personnel.[102] In order to deploy forces overseas, the Hungarian Parliament must first approve the operation in law. This requirement also applies to aircraft participating in military exercises. Once NATO identifies a requirement, the Military Chief of Staff submits a request to the Ministry of Defence. Once the Prime Minister and government approve the request, it is sent to Parliament for consent. Therefore these decisions are much more sensitive to public opinion.

As a member of the Warsaw Pact, Hungary was reluctant to send forces abroad to support Soviet foreign policy, unlike Czechoslovakia which was very active in the Third World.[103] Hungary has not carried this reluctance forward into NATO missions. As discussed in the last chapter, Hungary's average contribution to SFOR was 280 troops between 1999 and 2004, slightly below that of the Czech Republic (325), and well below that of Belgium (402) and Portugal (398). Like the Czech Republic, Hungary increased its average contribution to KFOR to 342 troops per year. While Hungary's average contribution was still below that of the Czech Republic (365) and Belgium (592), it exceeded that of Portugal (310) during the last 10 years of KFOR. Hungary's participation in KFOR was noteworthy, given the concern over retribution against ethnic Hungarians living in Serbia and tenuous public support.[104] Hungary provided significant logistical and transportation support, as well as critical air and land transit authority in support of NATO operations in the Balkans.[105] In fact, Hungary hosted the first NATO military base in a former Warsaw Pact country in 1995.[106] These unique contributions are hard to quantify and balance against other national contributions.

Hungary was keen to demonstrate its support to the United States during OIF. As the Hungarian National Military Representative stated in an interview, "because the U.S. was involved [in Iraq], we had to be there."[107] In fact, Hungary committed 500 troops to OIF in 2003 and approximately 290 in 2004 and 2005 before withdrawing its forces. As in the other new member countries, there was strong domestic opposition to Hungarian participation in Iraq. The Hungarian Parliament had bitter debates about extending the mandate for forces serving in Iraq, and most Hungarians were against involvement.[108] Hungary's average participation in OIF exceeded that of the Czech Republic (124 troops) and of Portugal (124 troops). Belgium did not participate in OIF.

In ISAF, Hungary's contributions increased from 130 troops in 2004 to 383 troops in 2011. This level of contribution (averaging 243 troops per year) was again below that of the Czech Republic (395), and Belgium (368), but it again exceeded that of Portugal (113). These Hungarian forces were committed to a PRT in the Baghlan Province, between Kabul and Mazar-e-Sharif in the north. Hungary also provided an OMLT and a Special Forces Team. As the Hungarian National Military representative stated in an interview with the author, "the military leadership recognizes that, once you join the alliance, you also have requirements to meet. But the difficulty is to determine how to contribute to operations while dealing with force cuts and a declining budget."[109]

That said, Hungary's contributions to NATO missions were not as strong as other new members (see Table 5-3). Unlike Poland and the Czech Republic, the total commitment from Hungary dropped from a peak in 1999 (when it had 635 troops in SFOR and KFOR) to a low point in 2008 (557 troops between KFOR and ISAF). Since Hungary has a much smaller Army than the Czech Republic, Hungary's percentage of ground forces deployed equaled about 9.6 percent of its land force.[110]

	SFOR (1999-2004)	KFOR (1999-2008)	ISAF (2003-2013)	OIF (2003-2008)
AVG	280	342	243	217
MAX	314	484	383	500

Table 5-3. Hungary's Annual Contributions to NATO/U.S.-led Missions.

Hungary's Cold War military was too large to be affordable and unsuited for interoperability with NATO.[111] Like the other new members, Hungary underwent a significant modernization and overhaul of its military forces during this period, including the switch from conscription to an all professional force by 2004.[112] Since joining NATO, the size of the Hungarian armed forces declined from 68,261 in 1999 to 20,000 in 2007, a reduction of over 70 percent.[113] While Hungary's contributions to NATO are less impressive than that of the Czech Republic, it did make a big commitment to OIF in 2003. Therefore, it is not surprising that Hungary also received side payments from the

United States. In 2006 total U.S. Government assistance to Hungary equaled approximately $15 million.[114] In 2012, Hungary received $13.3 million from the United States to support training and equipment of forces in Afghanistan.[115] Unlike Poland and the Czech Republic, it is harder to characterize Hungary's lack-luster burden sharing as a lack of capability. Rather, it appears that Hungary lacks the political willingness and fiscal discipline to fully meet its NATO obligations.

2004 Wave Case Study: Romania.

Romania is one of two countries from the 2004 wave of NATO enlargement chosen for examination. Romania, like Poland, had security guarantees from Britain and France at the beginning of World War II. After ceding territory to both Hungary and the Soviet Union under pressure, Romania joined forces with Nazi Germany.[116] Romania's pro-Axis leader, Marshal Ion Antonescu was finally overthrown by King Michael on August 23, 1944, and Romania was occupied by the Soviet Union in August 1944. Like the members of the 1999 wave, Romania was a founding member of the Warsaw Pact. However, unlike the other countries examined, Romania maintained a relatively independent foreign policy from the Soviet Union during the Cold War. At Romania's request, Soviet troops were withdrawn from Romania in 1958.[117] In addition, Romania was the only Warsaw Pact country that did not participate in the invasion of Czechoslovakia in 1968.[118]

Romania had one of the most autocratic governments in Eastern Europe during the Cold War. In 1989, Romania violently overthrew the communist government of Nicolae Ceausescu. Immediately after the revolution, the National Salvation Front (FSN) ruled Romania and won the first post-communist election in 1990.[119] The FSN became the Party for Social Democracy in Romania (PDSR), and its candidate, Ion Illiescu, won the general election in 1992. The PDSR ruled from 1992 to 1996 and again from 2000 until 2004. From November 1996 until 2000, Romania was governed by a coalition government, formed by the center-right Democratic Convention, the center-left Union of Social Democrats, and the Democratic Union of Hungarians in Romania (UDMR). In spite of this active party system, democratic institutions during this period were weak, and corruption was rampant. Therefore, Romania required significant political reform prior to entering NATO and the EU. Of the 10 new NATO members between 1999 and 2004, Romania was the only country rated by Freedom House as only partially free after 1991; it did not improve to a free rating until 1996.[120]

Romania is in a relatively secure geographic position. Romania shares a border with two NATO countries, (Hungary and Bulgaria) as well as with Serbia, Moldova, and the Ukraine. Like the Czech Republic and Hungary, Romania does not share a land border with Russia. However, both Russia and Romania are Black Sea states. The distance from Bucharest to Moscow is 1,498-km, only slightly closer than the Czech Republic or Hungary.

Romania is a medium-size NATO member, with a combined area of 237,500-sq km, it is smaller than Poland, but larger than the Czech Republic, Estonia, or Hungary. Romania has a population of approximately 22.3 million (90 percent ethnic Romanian and 7 percent ethnic Hungarians). Romania's GDP (PPP) was estimated at $285 billion in 2013, making Romania one of the poorest new members of NATO, with a per capita GDP (PPP) of $13,395.[121] Before the fiscal crisis, Romania grew at an impressive rate, its GDP increasing an average of 14.9 percent between 1993 and 2008.[122] Despite a high rate of poverty, Romania has a low level of public debt, at approximately 13 percent of GDP,[123] and a relatively low budget deficit of 2.5 percent of GDP in 2013.[124] This low level of debt again relieves Romania of some of the fiscal pressures of the Stability Pact requirements.

Because of its relatively independent foreign policy and other economic concerns, Romania was not supportive of the Warsaw Pact's spending targets during the Cold War.[125] Therefore, it spent a relatively small amount of GDP on military expenditures. After gaining NATO membership, Romania's military expenditures as a percentage of GDP have averaged 1.8 percent between 2004 and 2009 (see Figure 5-4) exceeding the NATO average.[126] The Romanian President gave two reasons for this level of military expenditures: the need to update old or inferior equipment in Iraq and Afghanistan and the commitment to fulfill Romania's obligations to NATO.[127] However, conditions attached to IMF loans, in response to the global economic crisis, might make it difficult to sustain these high levels of defense spending. In 2009, an agreement was reached to potentially give Romania a $27 billion loan package from the IMF, EU, and the World Bank.[128]

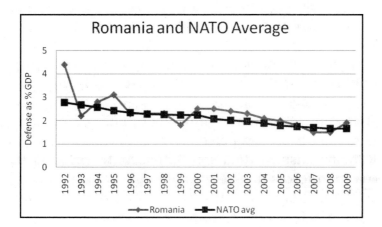

Figure 5-4. Romania's Military Expenditures versus NATO Averages.[129]

Romania has also made strong contributions to NATO missions. Like Poland, the Romanian President approves the deployment of troops to NATO missions. Article 92 of the Constitution defines the President as commander-in-chief of the country's armed forces.[130] However, Parliament has to approve any mobilization of the armed forces, after the decision is debated in the Supreme Council of National Defense. The Parliament also has to approve the budget and the number of troops being sent on any deployment. Parliamentary decisions establish the legal framework for participation in NATO operations and provide the government with the authority and resources necessary for Romanian participation.[131]

While Romania was very active in the Third World during the Cold War, its involvement was mostly through diplomatic contacts in Africa. However, unlike some Warsaw Pact countries, Romania dealt primarily with non-Warsaw Pact clients.[132] Romania has been a much more active ally under NATO. As a member of the PfP, Romania committed 200 troops to SFOR.[133] However, this project focuses on contributions since attaining membership. As in SFOR, Romania's contribution to KFOR was relatively modest at 226 troops in 2004 (averaging 180 soldiers per year between 2004 and 2008), representing about half of Romania's fair share based on percentage of NATO population. Romania also made a significant contribution to the coalition forces during U.S.-led OIF. On February 12, 2003, the Romanian Parliament voted to join OIF with around 800 troops.[134] From 2004 until 2007, Romania had, on average, over 760 troops in Iraq. These troops were withdrawn in 2009. Clearly, Romania wanted to demonstrate its commitment to the United States as a reliable partner. The decision to stay in Iraq after Spain withdrew was not an easy political decision. In 2006, Prime Minister Calin Popescu Tariceanu proposed withdrawing from Iraq in response to rising costs and falling public support. Romanian President Traian Basescu, as commander-in-chief, supported the mission and stated that the Prime Minister's comments hurt Romania's credibility. "Romania must respect its international commitments."[135] Parliament subsequently approved continuing the mission.

Romania also made a significant contribution to the U.S.-led OEF in Afghanistan and to NATO's ISAF. Retired Lieutenant General Barno, former OEF commander from October 2003 until May 2005, was especially praiseworthy of the Romanian contributions to OEF and its willingness to fight with few caveats.[136] Romania continued this robust level of contribution during NATO operations in Afghanistan with a maximum of 1,938 soldiers deployed in 2011 and averaging over 1,010 troops per year since 2004.

Secretary General Jaap de Hoop Scheffer commended Romania after the Bucharest Summit for its active participation in Afghanistan and other NATO missions.[137] Romania's participation was also qualitatively above what other allies are contributing. For example, Romania was one of the few NATO countries deploying to Afghanistan with its own strategic airlift assets. It also deployed its troops into the more dangerous southern provinces of Afghanistan (Zabul), with no national caveats. It is not surprising, then, that Romania also received side payments from the United States. American aid to Romania in Fiscal Year (FY) 2006 totaled approximately $43.55 million, of which almost $17 million was in security and law enforcement assistance.[138] More importantly, the United States maintained a training base inside of Romania that gave Romania an enhanced feeling of security in addition to increasing the capability of Romanian forces. Like Poland, Romania got a significant increase in training and equipment funding for forces in Afghanistan from the United States in 2012.[139]

The increasing level of commitment demonstrated by Romania is consistent with the earlier results in these case studies. Both Romania's average and maximum troop contributions to NATO and U.S.-led missions increased steadily since 2004 (see Table 5-4). During this same period, the size of the Romanian armed forces dropped from 217,400 in 1999 to 76,000 in 2007.[140] As part of its modernization and transformation efforts, Romania phased out conscription in 2007.[141] Romania's increasing level of support to NATO missions lends credence to the explanation that as new members increased capability, they increased their contributions to NATO missions.

	KFOR (2004-2008)	ISAF (2004-2013)	OIF (2004-2008)
AVG	180	1,010	764
MAX	226	1,938	865

**Table 5-4. Romania's Annual Contributions
to NATO/U.S.-led Missions.**

2004 Wave Case Study: Estonia.

Estonia's history certainly informs its attitude toward NATO and its larger neighbor, Russia. Estonia gained its independence from the Soviet Union in 1920. Its history of independence was rather brief. With the outbreak of World War II, Estonia was invaded by Russian troops in 1940 and incorporated into the Soviet Union. In 1941, Germany occupied Estonia and many Estonians joined the German armed forces. In 1944, the Soviet Union drove Nazi German forces from Estonia and re-established control over the country. Therefore, Estonia again lost its independence at the end of World War II. Unlike the previous case studies in this chapter, Estonia was never a member of the Warsaw Pact, nor did it have an independent army.

A symbolic start to Estonia's drive to independence began on August 23, 1989, when over one million people in the three Baltic countries formed a human chain linking Vilnius, Lithuania, to Riga, Latvia, to Tallinn, Estonia, protesting occupation by the Soviet Union.[142] This date marked the 50-year anniversary of the Nazi-Soviet Pact that divided the Eastern European and Baltic states between their larger neighbors. The following year, Estonia's Parliament declared its intention to regain independence. Estonia actually gained its independence in 1991.[143] Since gaining independence, Estonia has had a tense relationship with Russia. Russian troops were stationed in Estonia until 1994, making Estonia one of the last Eastern European countries occupied by Russian troops. Even though Estonia now falls under NATO's security umbrella, it remains in a vulnerable strategic location. The distance from Vilnius to Moscow is only 867-km, making Estonia one of the closest new NATO members to Russia. Since independence, tensions have increased over attempts to remove Soviet-era memorials and over treatment of Estonia's Russian minority which comprises over one-quarter of the total population. In 2007, Russia's major cyber attack against Estonia increased anxiety over security, as did the Russian invasion of Georgia in 2008.[144] Estonia, and other Eastern European members of NATO, place great stock in the collective defense guarantees of Article 5 and fear that the current focus on crisis management might weaken the clarity of deterrence against a resurgent Russia.[145]

Estonia is one of the smallest NATO countries and is the smallest new member state. Therefore, it should face greater incentives to free-ride within NATO than the other countries studied. Estonia has a population of approximately 1.3 million (68 percent ethnic Estonians and 26 percent ethnic Russians) and shares a border with Russia. At 26 percent of the population, Estonia's large ethnic Russian population is second in size only to Latvia's. Estonia's GDP (PPP) was estimated at $29.7 billion in 2013, increasing from the post crisis level of $23.7 billion in 2009. Estonia is one of the richest new members of NATO, with a per capita GDP (PPP) of $23,144 in 2013, increasing from $17,696 in 2009.[146] Estonia's GDP grew 8.8 percent on average from 2000 to 2007[147] and 18.5 percent from 1993 to 2007.[148] This rapid growth led to a relatively high inflation rate of 6.6 percent in 2007. Prior to the financial crisis, Estonia had an extremely low level of public debt (3.8 percent of GDP in 2007)[149] and a low deficit of 1.2 percent in 2008.[150]

Given its size and proximity to a much larger historic foe, the security guarantee from NATO is a major pillar of Estonia's *National Security Strategy*. In a government sponsored survey, over 60 percent of Estonians "named NATO membership as the key security guarantee for Estonia."[151] Estonia's political leadership also recognizes the importance of NATO. At the first year anniversary of NATO accession, Estonia's Foreign Minister stated that Estonia:

> must fulfill all the promises and commitments made when joining NATO, including the maintaining of defense expenditures at 2% of GDP. . . . We must not forget that 2% of GDP, as a reliable partner in NATO, is... a bigger security guarantee than . . . even 100% of GDP without membership in NATO![152]

As in Poland, all political parties in the Estonian parliament (Riigikogu) agree in principle on the 2 percent goal. Commitments to NATO force goals are often used as support by the MOD to justify resource allocations.[153] There is also strong domestic support for the military in Estonia. Over 76 percent of the Estonian population support maintaining or increasing military expenditures.[154]

From 2004 to 2009, Estonia maintained its defense expenditures at approximately 1.7 percent of GDP, well below NATO's burden sharing target of 2 percent of GDP, but on par with the non-U.S. NATO average, 1.7 percent (see Figure 5-5). When Estonia's expenditures as a percentage of GDP dropped below the NATO average between 2004 and 2007, this decline was largely attributed to Estonia's high economic growth rate. Between 2004 and 2007, Estonia's growth in constant prices averaged 8.2 percent.[155] In 2012 and 2013, Estonia was one of the few NATO countries at or above 2 percent.

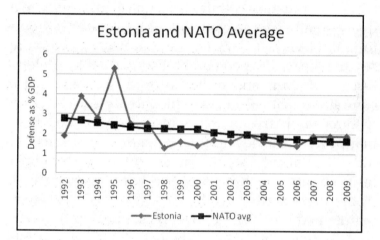

Figure 5-5. Estonia's Military Expenditures versus NATO Average.[156]

Estonia, though having a small military, has also contributed to NATO operations and the U.S. global war on terror. Prior to any involvement, though, Estonia must get the approval from its Parliament. The Minister of Defense has been delegated this authority for Article 5 missions. The Minister of Defense outlines the purpose, the troops, and the time limits. Normally, the Parliament looks for United Nations (UN) Security Council Resolutions to legitimate participation in these missions prior to approval. These mandates from parliament must be periodically renewed.

Like Romania, Estonia sent forces to SFOR under the Danish Battalion. However, this study focuses on contributions to NATO after membership. In line with other small NATO members, Estonia's relative contribution to KFOR (averaging 49 soldiers per year) roughly equaled its fair share based on percentage of NATO population. While these numbers appear relatively small, Estonia contributed a total of 500 troops to UN, NATO, or U.S.-led operations in 2007 representing nearly 8 percent of Estonia's total defense forces, which is above the European average and in compliance with NATO's deployability goals.[157] Given Estonia's military capability (especially in the area of manpower), this level of participation was at its limit.[158] Like Poland, Estonia had to contend with competing commitments for forces during this period due to troops participating in OIF. From 2004 to 2007, Estonia maintained (on average) over 36 soldiers in Iraq. This contribution was made in the face of strong domestic opposition to the Iraq war, with almost 60 percent opposing the Iraq mission in 2005. This opposition was even higher among Russian Estonians (76 percent).[159]

Similarly with Poland, Estonia had few forces in ISAF prior to 2007. At the request of NATO, Estonia sent military forces to NATO operations in Afghanistan in November 2006, and they remained there through 2008. As with Poland, this decision was made in the face of domestic doubts about the ISAF mission. In a 2007 Ministry of Defence public opinion poll, a majority of respondents supported discontinuation of Estonian involvement in missions in areas of conflict.[160] This result represented a change over previous opinion polls that favored continued involvement. Estonia saw participation in ISAF both as a national obligation and as an opportunity to increase its credibility with NATO.[161] Estonia's relative contribution to ISAF (approximately 120 soldiers per year in 2007 and 2008) was roughly double its fair share based on population. In 2008, Estonia's Parliament increased the mandate for the mission size from 150 to 180 troops.[162] In addition to the size of Estonia's commitment, these forces were stationed in the southern province of Helmand with Danish and British forces.[163] This sector was arguably one of the more dangerous sectors in Afghanistan, and two Estonian soldiers were killed there in the summer of 2007. Thus, Estonian participation was qualitatively above what many other allies are contributing.

Comparable to Poland, Estonian officials were proud to point out that their forces in ISAF have no caveats, a major point of contention within the Alliance. In an address to Parliament in 2006, the Estonian Foreign Minister justified this level of commitment in Afghanistan by stating that it strengthened Estonia's position in NATO.[164] The Deputy National Military Representative from Estonia at Supreme Headquarters Allied Powers Europe justified its commitment to ISAF using the logic of appropriateness, "We don't want to be only the security consumers when we are members of NATO."[165]

Like most of our other case studies, Estonia's contributions to NATO missions have increased over time (see Table 5-5). This level of support also lends credence to the capability argument. Unlike our other case studies, Estonia was never an independent country under the Warsaw Pact. During the post-Cold War period, Estonia had to build its armed forces from scratch. The size of the Estonian armed forces increased from 3,270 in 1999 to approximately 5,000 in 2007.[166] Estonia was the only new member examined that actually increased its force structure during this period. In spite of its small size and relative lack of military experience, Estonia increased its contributions to NATO missions after gaining membership. This burden sharing behavior supports the commitment made by Estonia's Foreign Minister during the flag raising ceremony at NATO Headquarters in 2004.

> Estonia has already demonstrated its trustworthiness as a partner in Bosnia and Herzegovina, Kosovo, Afghanistan, and also in Iraq. Now, as a full member of the Alliance, our responsibility in addressing common threats is even greater and we intend to meet our obligations as a reliable ally in the future as well.[167]

	KFOR (2004-2008)	ISAF (2004-2013)	OIF (2004-2008)
AVG	41	95	36
MAX	98	163	45

Table 5-5. Estonia's Annual Contributions to NATO/U.S.-led Missions.

2009 Wave Case Study: Albania.

Albania and Croatia are the two newest members of the NATO Alliance. Their post-World War II experience was very different from the other new members. Albania was conquered by Italy in 1939. Albanian partisans resisted first the Italian and later German occupiers, gaining control in 1944. The communist government in Albania initially had close ties to its fellow communist governments in Yugoslavia, but relations soured as Albania's Dictator, Enver Hoxha, grew wary of Marshal Josip Tito. While not a member of the Warsaw Pact, Albania aligned itself with the Soviet Union until the early-1960s when Yugoslavian and Soviet relations improved. Afterward, Albania aligned itself with Communist China over the Soviet Union until the death of Chairman Mao Zedong in 1978.[168] Under Hoxha, who ruled for 40 years after World War II, Albania was extremely isolated from other nations and extremely paranoid.[169] While suspicious of Soviet intentions throughout the Cold War, Albania also remained concerned by the harsh treatment of ethnic Albanians in Kosovo.

After the death of the communist dictator in 1985, Albania began to gradually institute more liberal policies.[170] In the aftermath of the Cold War, Albania began to open up to the West and seek further internal political reform. Albania held its first democratic elections in 1991, the same year it joined the Commission on Security and Cooperation in Europe (CSCE). It established its democracy in the midst of high levels of unemployment, corruption, and a lack of modern infrastructure. The Socialist Party (PS), successors to the communist party of Hoxha, won the first multiparty election in 1991.[171] However, they were unseated the following year in an election won by the Democratic Party (PD). Since then, the PD and PS have peacefully transferred power twice, though all of these elections had problems with fraud.[172] Like Romania, Albania required significant political reform prior to entering NATO. Albania was rated as not free by Freedom House from 1972 until 1990. Today, it is still only listed as partially free.[173]

Both Albania and Croatia are in a volatile geographic region. Albania shares a border with one NATO country (Greece) as well as with Macedonia,

Montenegro, and Kosovo. Like Croatia, Albania does not share a land border with Russia. The distance from Tirana to Moscow is 2,057-km, much further than the other cases examined in this chapter. Therefore, Albania's security threats emanate from its much closer Balkan neighbors rather than from a resurgent Russia.

Albania is a small-size NATO member by any measure. With a land area of 27,398-sq km, it is much smaller than Estonia or the other new NATO countries examined here. Albania has a population of approximately 2.9 million (95 percent ethnic Albanians) and is only the second predominantly Muslim NATO country. Albania is one of the poorest countries in Europe. As a result of Albania's closed economy during the Cold War, its GDP (PPP) was only $5.9 billion in 1992. While the transition to a market economy has been difficult, Albania's GDP (PPP) grew to an estimated $26.5 billion in 2013.[174] Albania is even poorer than Romania, with a per capita GDP (PPP) of $9,506. However, it was able to maintain a 6 percent average growth rate from 2004 to 2008 while keeping inflation around 3 percent. In fact, Albania was one of the few European countries to have positive growth in 2009, and its GDP has grown by 16 percent between 2009 and 2013.[175] Albania also has a moderate level of public debt, at approximately 70.4 percent of GDP in 2013.[176]

Due to its extreme paranoia, Albania maintained a relatively large military force during the Cold War. While exact details are difficult to determine due to a lack of transparency during Communist rule, it is estimated that Albania spent about 5 percent of its GDP on military expenditures in the late-Cold War period.[177] Given its small size and poverty, Albania would be expected to spend much less relative to other allies in the post-Cold War period. However, like most new member countries examined here, its defense expenditures have gradually converged on the NATO average. In fact, at 1.8 percent, it exceeded the NATO average in 2009 (see Figure 5-6). This finding is not consistent with the findings that wealth was correlated with military expenditures as a percentage of GDP. However, it does support the argument that new members spend relatively more than older members.

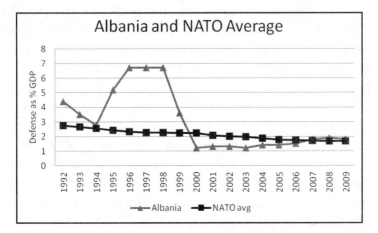

Figure 5-6. Albania's Military Expenditures versus NATO Average.[178]

As a member of NATO's MAP, Albania began to institute many democratic and institutional reforms, such as reducing corruption, judicial reform, improving public administration and improving relations with neighboring countries. This undertaking was a difficult task for a country lacking transparency and trust. In fact, the country underwent months of riots and civil unrest after the collapse of a pyramid investment scheme in 1997. This crisis resulted in a UN mission, Operation ALBA, to restore calm and deliver humanitarian aid under UN Security Council Resolution

1011.[179] In 2011, there were, again, riots over election results which threatened Albania's near-term chances for membership in the EU.[180]

Under the current constitution, Parliament has to approve any mobilization of the armed forces or use of Albanian territory after the President makes the proposal.[181] During the Kosovo crisis, the Parliament quickly approved the use of Albanian sea and air ports by NATO. In fact, Albania transferred a great deal of its sovereignty to the United States and NATO during Kosovo due to concern over the 700,000 Kosovar-Albanian refugees.[182] The Parliament also has to approve the military budget. The Ministry of Defense establishes priorities and negotiates a budget with the Ministry of Finance, which is then sent to Parliament for approval. Politicians often justify their budget requests "because of our commitments to NATO."[183]

Albania became involved in supporting NATO at the same time it was opening up to the outside world. Starting in 1996, Albania contributed a platoon to SFOR. This platoon first served in Croatia and then in Bosnia and Herzegovina as guards for a German logistics base.[184] Albanian troop commitments to SFOR increased to 100 soldiers in 1998 and were approximately 70 when the EU replaced the NATO-led force. While not directly contributing ground forces, Albania also played a critical role during KFOR. As mentioned above, Albania sacrificed much of its sovereignty in support of NATO operations during KFOR. In addition to hosting Task Force Apache, a major combat force whose presence helped coerce Serbia into halting hostilities, Albania hosted over 2,400 logistics support troops and turned over domestic air traffic control to the United States. That logistics support command became a regional military headquarters, NATO HQ Tirana, in 2002.[185]

Albania supported coalition forces in Iraq, under OIF, and in Afghanistan under ISAF. Between 2004 and 2008, Albania averaged around 93 soldiers in Iraq. Albania increased its contributions to ISAF from 30 troops in 2007 to a maximum 333 troops in 2012. This increasing level of commitment is consistent with the earlier results in these case studies. Both Albania's average and maximum troop contributions to NATO and U.S.-led missions have increased steadily (see Table 5-6). During this same period, the size of the Albanian armed forces dropped from 73,000 in 1992 to 14,000 in 2010.[186] Again, as Albania increased capability, it increased its contributions to NATO missions.

	SFOR (1997-2007)	ISAF (2007-2013)	OIF (2004-2008)
AVG	78	218	93
MAX	100	333	81

Table 5-6. Albania's Contributions to NATO/U.S.-led Missions.

2009 Wave Case Study: Croatia.

The Kingdom of Yugoslavia was created after World War I from parts of the Austro-Hungarian Empire. After Yugoslavia was conquered by Axis forces during World War II, Croatia was set-up by Germany and Italy as a puppet state. However, many partisan groups continued to resist the Nazi occupation. After the war, Yugoslavia became an independent Communist state under dictator Marshall Tito, who was a Croat. Croatia was just one republic within the federation that comprised Yugoslavia. Although Soviet troops were allowed to enter a portion of the country, Yugoslavia had liberated itself from the Axis forces. While Yugoslavia was initially aligned with the Soviet Union after the war, Tito split with Stalin and his country remained in a nonaligned status for most of the Cold War.

While still a republic under Yugoslavia, Croatia conducted elections in 1990. This election brought the Croatian Democratic Union (HDZ) under Communist Franjo Tudjman to power.[187] He and his party remained in power through the tumultuous decade that followed. Croatia declared its independence in 1991, but faced 4 years of conflict with its neighbors before stability began to set in.[188] Only in 1998 did Serbia return all occupied territory to Croatia. While Croatia expressed an early interest in NATO's PfP, it did not join until 2000. It joined the MAP in 2002, hosting a NATO civil emergency response exercise that same year. The following year, it hosted NATO's bi-annual PfP naval exercise, "Cooperative Engagement." Since then it has been an active participant in MAP and initiated the required reforms of both its political and military institutions.

The former Republic of Yugoslavia was rated as not free by Freedom House from 1972 until 1980. However, Croatia has had an easier time with democratization than some of the other new NATO members, or the other five republics that were a part of Yugoslavia. After gaining independence, Croatia improved from partially free in 1991 to free in 2000.[189] Croatia had a peaceful transition from the HDZ to the Social Democratic Party (SDP) in the 2000 parliamentary elections, though the HDZ regained power in 2003. Croatia has also faced the trial of several political and military figures for war crimes during its struggle for independence.

Croatia shares a border with two NATO countries, Hungary and Slovenia, as well as with Bosnia and Herzegovina, Serbia, and Montenegro. Like Albania, Croatia does not share a land border with Russia and the distance from Zagreb to Moscow is 1,866-km. Therefore, Croatia's security threats are much closer than Russia. In fact, Croatia had armed conflicts with three of its neighbors in the 1990s (Bosnia and Herzegovina, Serbia, and Slovenia). There are still lingering ethnic tensions resulting from these wars.

By any measure, Croatia is a small country. With a land area of 55,974-sq km, it is smaller than the Czech Republic, but almost twice the size of Albania. It has a population of approximately 4.4 million (90 percent ethnic Croatians).[190] As a result of the warfare during the 1990s, Croatia's economy struggled initially after declaring independence. In 1992, its GDP (PPP) was approximately $7.2 billion. However, after the 2000 elections, Croatia's economy began to grow at a rate of between 6 percent and 8 percent annually.[191] With an estimated 2013 GDP (PPP) of $77.8 billion, Croatia has a per capita GDP of $18,190, which ranks it below Estonia, Hungary, and Poland, but above Romania and Albania. However, Croatia has been plagued by high unemployment, over 17 percent in 2010, and a level of public debt at around 55 percent of GDP.

Because Croatia was a part of Yugoslavia during the Cold War, it is impossible to compare its current spending with that during the Cold War. Like all of the republics of the former Yugoslavia, Croatia's military was armed primarily with Soviet equipment and has therefore had to focus its efforts on modernization and standardization with its NATO allies. Croatia had a large defense budget during the early-1990s due to the on-going conflicts with its neighbors. Since

1999, Croatia's defense expenditures, as a percentage of GDP, have dropped steadily. Given its small size, Croatia, too, would be expected to spend much less relative to other allies in the post-Cold War period. Like most new member countries examined here, its defense expenditures have gradually converged on the NATO average. In fact, at 1.6 percent in 2009, it was slightly below the NATO average of 1.7 percent. Since the size of the Croatian military is limited by the arms limitations of the Dayton Peace accords, which NATO brokered, this shortfall cannot be attributed to free-riding behavior. (See Figure 5-7.)

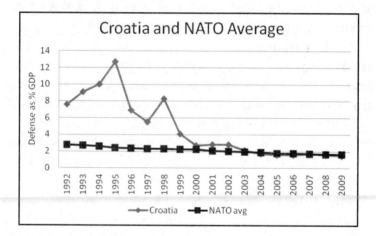

Figure 5-7. Croatia's Military Expenditures versus NATO Average.[192]

Having examined defense expenditures, it is now necessary to look at troop commitments. Due to its involvement in the Balkan conflicts, Croatia did not contribute troops to SFOR in Bosnia and Herzegovina. However, it did allow the UN and NATO use of its territory. Croatia leased a helicopter base to the United Kingdom (UK) in support of the UN Protection Force in the former Yugoslavia (UNPROFOR) and hosted a logistical support headquarters for NATO.[193] The same is true for NATO operations in Kosovo. Croatia has provided invaluable access to port facilities, military installations, in addition to over flight rights. Croatia has made increasing military contributions to the ISAF in Afghanistan since 2003. This commitment included a team deployed to Ghor Province as a part of the Lithuanian PRT.[194] In fact, Croatia's commitment of forces continued to grow after achieving NATO membership. As a symbol of its increasing capability and willingness to support its European partners, Croatia also committed to supporting an EU battle group under Germany in 2012. Like the other case studies in this chapter, the size of the Croatian armed forces has dropped from 100,000 in 1992 to 18,600 in 2010. As mentioned, the size of Croatia's armed forces is constrained by the terms of the Dayton Peace accords.[195]

	ISAF (2007-2013)
AVG	252
MAX	320

Table 5-7. Croatia's Annual Contributions.

Summary of Case Studies.

The cases studies examined in this section are generally consistent with the results from earlier chapters: the largest new member states had higher levels of military expenditure rates as a percentage of GDP than two of the smaller members. This result is consistent with the expectations of the collective action literature and Olson's "exploitation of the great" hypothesis. That said, the Czech Republic, characterized as a small NATO state in Chapter 4, also had a relatively high average expenditure rate in comparison with Hungary (also from the 1999 wave) and with two original members of similar size: Belgium and Portugal.

In all seven cases, military expenditures, as a percentage of GDP decreased from 1992 to 2009, in concert with the collective action predictions of increased free-riding behavior as the group size increases. For Albania and Croatia, it is too early to see if their defense expenditures decrease as their length of membership increases. This decline is also in line with the findings of previous chapters that suggested burden sharing decreased with age.

When looking at the additional constraints on military expenditures, states with a higher GDP per capita did not necessarily have greater military expenditures. It is interesting to note that two of the three highest average military expenditures, as a percentage of GDP, came from Romania and Poland, two of the poorest new member countries in terms of GDP per capita. The findings suggest that pressure from the EU might have been a constraint on military expenditures. Hungary's level of debt (72 percent of GDP) and deficits (7.8 percent) were the highest of any of the case studies examined. In consideration of the EU Stability Pact incentives, perhaps there is a tipping point after which a large government debt inhibits military expenditures. While outside the purview of this project, further study is required on the impact of high levels of debt on military expenditures.

The second part of the case study examined contributions to NATO missions. In this issue area, the logic of collective action and rational choice predictions of decreasing contributions were not supported. Rather, contributions increased as the capabilities of new member states increased. As discussed earlier, burden sharing behavior is a function of two components: willingness to burden share and capability to burden share. In the case of military expenditures, new members' burden sharing behavior varied based on the level of political willingness and possibly the level of debt. The results of the case study suggest that limited military capability constrained early contributions to NATO missions. However, six out of the seven case studies showed increasing average annual contributions to NATO missions over time (sustainability), and three had increasing maximum levels of contribution (deployability). Thus, contributions to ISAF exceeded those to KFOR, which exceeded those made to SFOR. These results support the argument that as capability increased, new member burden sharing levels increased.

This chapter also analyzed the constraints facing these countries in making decisions to support NATO operations. One major constraint to burden sharing examined was domestic political opposition. In many of the case studies, increased contributions to NATO missions were made in the face of significant political opposition. This finding reinforces the results of interviews of NATO officials examined earlier in the chapter. These officials all suggested that new members had the willingness to share in the Alliance burden, but often lacked capability. The other major constraint was the declining force size in the new member countries. Six of seven new members experienced significant reductions in force structure. Yet, most states actually increased their contributions to NATO missions over time. The other case, Estonia, was building a military force from scratch and therefore had increasing force levels and increasing contributions.

In only one case do the results support the collective action or rational choice predictions of declining contributions after membership: Hungary. Of all the new members since 1999, Hungary had the lowest military expenditures as a percentage of GDP. Hungary was also the only country studied that had an absolute decrease in average and maximum contributions to NATO missions. However, here too, Hungary did improve its relative contributions over time from SFOR to ISAF in relation to older NATO states of comparable size (Belgium and Portugal).

CONCLUSIONS

This chapter examined the context of contributions by individual new members and how these contributions were related to capability and political will. Based on the results of the case studies, it appears that new NATO members generally have the political will to bear their fair share of NATO burdens. This willingness is evident in both the assessment of NATO officials in the previous chapter and in the examination of new member contributions to NATO missions. The results also indicate that, contrary to hypothesis H3, new member contributions have risen over time as their capabilities improved. This result can be attributed to both a concern for credibility and effective socialization by NATO. As a former U.S. European Command official explained, new members "want to be seen as security providers."[196]

Even where there have been legitimate concerns over free-riding by new members, as in Hungary, the Alliance appears willing to accept less than optimal burden sharing in return for Alliance solidarity and democratic governance. This has long been a feature of NATO. As James Golden pointed out in his study of NATO in the 1980s:

> The long-run advantages of the alliance—democratic processes, consensual decision making, relatively free and efficient economic markets—frequently translate into short-run problems in building consensus and sustaining defense commitments.[197]

However, the increasing pressures of the ongoing operations in Afghanistan may change this dynamic within NATO.

NATO officials realize that the magnitude of changes since the end of the Cold War necessarily constrained new member contributions to NATO missions. As a senior NATO official stated, "all former Warsaw Pact countries had to establish new governance institutions and reform their militaries at the same time. We wanted them to become a more democratic, not necessarily a more capable force."[198] In spite of these major challenges, the case studies demonstrate that new member contributions to NATO missions have generally increased in the years after attaining membership. Therefore, despite facing differing strategic environments and international and domestic constraints, new members seem to share the burdens of NATO within the limits of their capability.

ENDNOTES -CHAPTER 5

1. General Sir John McColl, Deputy Supreme Allied Commander Europe, interview by author, February 1, 2008, SHAPE Headquarters, Mons, Belgium.

2. Simon Duke, *The Burdensharing Debate*, New York: Saint Martin's Press, 1993, p. 1.

3. Larry Fogli, Paul R. Sackett, and Sheldon Zedeck, "Relations Between Measures of Typical and Maximum Job Performance," *Journal of Applied Psychology*, Vol. 73, No. 3, 1988, pp. 482-486.

4. Neil Anderson and Ute-Christine Klehe, "Working Hard and Working Smart: Motivation and Ability during Typical and Maximum Performance," *Journal of Applied Psychology*, Vol. 92, No. 4, 2007, p. 978.

5. Friedrich Forsterling, *Attribution: An Introduction to Theories, Research and Applications*, East Sussex, UK: Psychology Press, 2001, pp. 150-151.

6. NATO, "Comprehensive Political Guidance," *NATO Online Library*, November 29, 2006, available from *www.nato.int/docu/basictxt/b061129e.htm*.

7. European Union, "Europa Glossary," undated, available from *europa.eu*.

8. European Union, "Capabilities Improvement chart II/2005," Press Release 14729/05 (Presse 307), Brussels, Belgium, November 21, 2005, available from *europa.eu*.

9. European Union, "Europa Glossary."

10. Glenn E. Curtis, "Poland: A Country Study," U.S. Library of Congress, Washington, DC: U.S. Government Printing Office (GPO), 1992, available from *countrystudies.us/poland/89.htm*.

11. Major Generals ING. Svetozar Nadovic, Hartmut Foertsch, Imre Karacsony, and Zdzislaw Ostrowski, *The Great Withdrawal*, Bratislava, Slovakia: Slovak Republic Ministry of Defence, 2005, p. 237.

12. "Europe Uneasy over Russian Plans to Deploy Missiles," *Deutsche-Welte*, November 6, 2008, available from *www.dw-world.de/dw/article/0,2144,3768711,00.html*.

13. Andrew Curry, "Will Poland Split EU over Russia Policy?" *Spiegel Online International*, August 18, 2008, available from *www.spiegel.de/international/europe/0,1518,572105,00.html*.

14. David Ljunggren, "Poland Raps NATO Members over Afghan Commitments," *Reuters*, February 4, 2008, available from *www.reuters.com/article/topNews/idUSN0458791220080204*.

15. International Monetary Fund, "Reports for Selected Countries and Subjects," World Economic Outlook Database, available from *www.imf.org/external/data.htm*.

16. *Ibid.*

17. *Ibid.*

18. Organization for Economic Co-Operation and Development (OECD), "Country statistical profiles 2008," Statistical Extracts, available from *stats.oecd.org/wbos/viewhtml.aspx?queryname =460&querytype=view&lang=en*.

19. See IMF reports above as well as "Poland Revising Budget, But Holding Planned Deficit Steady," *The Warsaw Voice Online*, November 20, 2008, available from *www.warsawvoice.pl/newsX. php/7311/254901709*.

20. Condoleezza Rice, "Defense Burden-Sharing," David Holloway and Jane M. O. Sharp, eds., *The Warsaw Pact: Alliance in Transition*, Ithaca, NY: Cornell University Press, 1984, p. 64.

21. Bogdan Klich, Polish Minister of National Defence, "Europe-NATO-American Perspectives of Partnership," speech given at the Forum on Euro-Atlantic Security, Krakow, Poland, October 23-24, 2008. Recording provided by Nathan Harig, Jagiellonian University.

22. Colonel Slawomir Wojciechowski, interviews conducted December 11, 2007, at the U.S. Army War College, Carlisle, PA.

23. International Institute for Strategic Studies, *The Military Balance*, London, UK: Routledge, 2003, p. 36. Also found in "Basic Information on the MOND Budget for 2007," Warsaw, Poland:

Polish Ministry of National Defence, available from *www.wp.mil. pl/en/strona/126/LG_89*.

24. "Defence Budget, Poland," *Jane's Sentinel Security Assessment*, August 6, 2008, available from *www8.janes.com*.

25. "President And Prime Minister bickering again over foreign policy," *The Warsaw Voice Online*, December 12, 2007, available from *www.warsawvoice.pl/newsX.php/5359/2549017099/ printVer/*.

26. Bogdan Zaryn, "New Defense Minister Promises to Pull Out Polish Troops from Iraq in 2008," Polish Radio, November 19, 2007, available from *www.polskieradio.pl/zagranica/news/print. aspx?id=69776*.

27. Rice, p. 81.

28. Slawomir Majman, "Why Poland Is in Iraq," *The Warsaw Voice Online*, September 11, 2003, available from *www.warsawvoice. pl/printArticle.php?a=3423*.

29. Zaryn.

30. Molly Moore and John Anderson, "NATO Faces Growing Hurdle as Call for Troops Falls Short," *The Washington Post*, September 18, 2006, available from *www.washingtonpost.com/wp-dyn/ content/article/2006/09/17/AR2006091700570.html*.

31. Klich.

32. Ljunggren.

33. Stephen Fidler and Jon Boone, "Fields of Little Glory: NATO Begins to Scale Back Its Afghan Ambitions," *Financial Times*, November 18, 2007, p. 10.

34. Slawek Szefs, "Poles Not Pleased with Decision to send 1,000 Troops to Afghanistan," *Network Europe*, September 22, 2006, available from *networkeurope.radio.cz/feature/poles-not-pleased-with-decion-to-send-1000-troops-to-afghanistan*.

35. "Military Involvement in Iraq and Afghanistan, October 2007," *World Opinion Update*, Vol. 32, No. 1, 2008, p. 2.

36. "Iraq and Afghanistan: Involvement of the Polish Military, June 2007," *World Opinion Update*, Vol. 31, No. 5, September/ October 2007, p. 100.

37. Gabriela Baczynska, "Polish Troops May Train, not Fight in Iraq," *Reuters*, November 19, 2007, available from *www.reuters. com/articlePrint?articleID=USL1964979720071119*.

38. Klich.

39. Nicholas Kralev and Andrew Borowiec, "Warsaw Ups Ante for U.S. Shield," *The Washington Times*, January 16, 2008, available from *www.washingtontimes.com/news/2008/jan/16/warsaw-ups-ante-for-us-shield/*.

40. Viola Gienger, "Pentagon Steers More Money to Eastern European Allies as West Cuts Budgets," *Bloomberg.com*, January 19, 2012.

41. Jeffrey Simon, "NATO Expeditionary Operations: Impacts Upon New Members and Partners," occasional paper, Washington, DC: National Defense University, March 2005. For data from 2007, see NATO, "NATO-Russia Compendium of Financial and Economic Data Relating to Defence," information for press, NATO Headquarters, December 20, 2007, available from *www. nato.int/issues/defence_expenditures/index.html*.

42. International Institute for Strategic Studies, *The Military Balance*, London, UK: Routledge, 1999, 2004, and 2014.

43. Ihor Gawdiak, ed., *Czechoslovakia: A Country Study*, Library of Congress, Washington: GPO, 1987, available from *country studies.us/czech-republic/*.

44. Dominik Jun, "The Long Shadow of the Munich Agreement," Radio Praha, September 30, 2008, available from *www. radio.cz/en/article/108781*.

45. Stephen F. Larrabee, "Soviet Crisis Management in Eastern Europe," David Holloway and Jane M. O. Sharp, eds., *The Warsaw Pact: Alliance in Transition*, Ithaca, NY: Cornell University Press, 1984, pp. 122–123.

46. *Ibid.*, p. 89.

47. Central Intelligence Agency (CIA), "World Factbook," Washington, DC: CIA, undated, available from *https://www.cia. gov/library/publications/the-world-factbook/geos/ez.html*, Czech Republic.

48. *Ibid.*

49. Robert, R. Kaufman, "Market Reform and Social Protection: Lessons from the Czech Republic, Hungary, and Poland," *East European Politics and Societies*, Vol. 21, No. 1, 2007, p. 115.

50. International Monetary Fund, "Reports for Selected Countries and Subjects," *World Economic Outlook Database*, available from *www.imf.org/external/data.htm*.

51. CIA, "World Factbook," Czech Republic.

52. International Monetary Fund, "Reports for Selected Countries and Subjects."

53. OECD, "Country statistical profiles 2008."

54. *Ibid.*

55. Organization for Economic Co-Operation and Development (OECD), "Society at a Glance," 2007, available from *www. oecd.org/dataoecd/12/7/38138100.xls*.

56. Rice, pp. 60–64.

57. NATO, "NATO-Russia Compendium of Financial and Economic Data Relating to Defence."

58. Czech Ministry of Defence, "General Information for Visiting this Website," available from *www.army.cz/scripts/detail. php?pgid=122*.

59. Major General Josef Sedlak, Czech National Military Representative, interviews conducted January 28, 2008, at the SHAPE Headquarters, Mons, Belgium.

60. Czech Ministry of Defence, "NATO Operation 'Joint Enterprise' in Kosovo," available from *www.army.cz/scripts/detail. php?id=6527.*

61. Colonel Josef Kopecky, interview by author, November 6, 2008, at the National Defense University, Ft. McNair, Washington, DC.

62. Ondrej Bouda, "Politicians Debate Foreign Missions," *The Prague Post*, October 15, 2008, available from *www.praguepost.com/ articles/2008/10/15/politicians-debate-foreign-missions.php.*

63. *Ibid.*

64. "Czech Oppose More Afghan Deployments," *Angus Reid Global Monitor*, October 12, 2008, available from *www.angus-reid. com/polls/view/31995.*

65. Karel Janicek, "Czech Lawmakers Do Not Extend Afghanistan Mission," *The Miami Herald*, December 19, 2008, available from *www.miamiherald.com/news/world/AP/story/819725.html.*

66. Kopecky.

67. Kimberly Ashton, "Czech Troops to Remain in Iraq," *The Prague Post Online*, October 17, 2007, available from *www.praguepost.com/articles/2007/10/17/czech-troops-to-remain-in-iraq/print.*

68. Czech Ministry of Defence, "Current Deployments," available from *www.army.cz/scripts/detail.php?id=6568.*

69. *Ibid.*

70. Jan Velinger, "Czech Government to Send Troops to Counter Al-Qaeda in Afghanistan," Radio Prague, January 15, 2004, available from *www.radio.cz/en/article/49458.*

71. Simon, "NATO Expeditionary Operations," p. 17.

72. Cyril Svoboda, Minister of Foreign Affairs, "Report on the Foreign Policy of the Czech Republic 2005," 2005, p. 12, available from *www.mzv.cz/wwwo/mzv/default.asp?ido=19275&idj=2&amb=1 &ikony=&trid=1&prsl=&poccl*.

73. *Ibid.*

74. Bureau of European and Eurasian Affairs, "Background Note: Czech Republic," Washington, DC: U.S. Department of State, available from *www.state.gov/r/pa/ei/bgn/3237.htm*.

75. Bureau of European and Eurasian Affairs, "U.S. Government Assistance to Eastern Europe under the Support for East European Democracy (SEED) Act," Washington, DC: U.S. Department of State, January 2006, available from *www.state.gov/p/eur/ rls/rpt/64007.htm*.

76. For ISAF contributions, see NATO, ISAF, "Troop numbers and contributions," Brussels, Belgium: June 2014. For size of Czech Army, see International Institute for Strategic Studies, *The Military Balance*, 1999, 2004, 2014.

77. Czech Ministry of Defence, "Personnel Size in 1993-2008," undated, available from *www.army.cz/scripts/detail.php?id=5770*. Also see Simon, "NATO Expeditionary Operations." See also NATO, "NATO 2020: Assured Security; Dynamic Engagement," May 17, 2010, p. 37. This target was subsequently raised to 10 percent.

78. Stephan R. Burant, *Hungary: A Country Study*, U.S. Library of Congress, Washington, DC: GPO, 1989 available from *countrystudies.us/hungary/35.htm*.

79. Larrabee, pp. 118–119.

80. Nadovic *et al.*, pp. 213, 228.

81. Hungarian Ministry for Foreign Affairs, *The National Security Strategy of the Republic of Hungary*, Budapest, Hungary: Ministry for Foreign Affairs, undated, available from *www. mfa.gov.hu/kum/en/bal/foreign_policy/security_policy/national_sec_ strategy_of_hun.htm*.

82. CIA, "World Factbook," Washington, DC: CIA, Hungary.

83. International Monetary Fund, "Reports for Selected Countries and Subjects."

84. CIA, "World Factbook," Washington, DC: CIA, Poland.

85. International Monetary Fund, "Reports for Selected Countries and Subjects."

86. CIA, "World Factbook," Hungary.

87. Kaufman, p. 119.

88. *Ibid.*

89. OECD, "Society at a Glance."

90. OECD, "Country statistical profiles 2008."

91. Anonymous (NATO official speaking on background), interviews conducted February 1, 2008, at SHAPE Headquarters, Mons, Belgium. Also see Rice, p. 64.

92. Bruce M. Russett, *What Price Vigilance?: The Burdens of National Defense*, New Haven, CT: Yale University Press, 1970, p. 114.

93. Kenneth E. Nyirády, *Hungary: A Country Study*, U.S. Library of Congress, Washington: GPO, 1989, available from *lcweb2. loc.gov/cgi-bin/query/r?frd/cstdy:@field(DOCID+hu0195.*

94. Lieutenant Colonel István Biró, "The National Security Strategy and Transformation of the Hungarian Defense Forces," U.S. Army War College Strategy Research Paper, 2005, available from *handle.dtic.mil/100.2/ADA432740.*

95. Celeste A. Wallander, "NATO's Price," *Foreign Affairs*, Vol. 81, No. 6, 2002, pp. 2-8, available from *proquest.umi.com/pqdw eb?did=276842621&sid=1&Fmt=3&clientId=20167&RQT=309&VN ame=PQD.*

96. András Simonyi, formerly Hungarian Ambassador to the U.S. and Permanent Representative to NATO, "Our three wasted years," *Budapest Sun Online*, June 6, 2002, available from *www. budapestsun.com/cikk.php?id=16652.*

97. NATO, "NATO-Russia Compendium of Financial and Economic Data Relating to Defence."

98. Tamas S. Kiss, "NATO and PM in Talks over Funding," *Budapest Sun Online*, October 28, 2004, available from *www. budapestsun.com/cikk.php?id=14018.*

99. "Suspend NATO Membership."

100. "Hungary Ups Defence Expenses," *Budapest Sun Online*, October 15, 2008, available from *www.budapestsun.com/cikk. php?id=28870.*

101. Zoltan Simon, "Hungary Pays with Growth Prospects for IMF–led Bailout Package," *Bloomberg.com*, October 29, 2008, available from *www.bloomberg.com/apps/news?pid=20670001&refer=&si d=aFkdVbffn19k.*

102. Brigadier General Csaba Ujfalusi, Hungarian National Military Representative, interviews conducted January 28, 2008, at SHAPE Headquarters, Mons, Belgium.

103. Rice, pp. 80–81.

104. Simon, "NATO Expeditionary Operations," p. 11.

105. Colonel Tibor Benko, *Hungary: From Warsaw Pact to NATO*, Strategy Research Project, Carlisle, PA: U.S. Army War College, 2001, p. 11.

106. Rick Rozoff, "U.S. Employs Afghan War to Build Global NATO," *Global Research*, January 6, 2011, available from *www. globalresearch.ca/index.php?context=va&aid=22673.*

107. Ujfalusi.

108. "Suspend NATO Membership," *Budapest Sun Online,* January 21, 2007, available from *www.budapestsun.com/cikk. php?id=55.*

109. Ujfalusi.

110. NATO, "National Commitments to Operations and Missions," Hungary, available from *www.nato.int/issues/commitment/ docs/080325-hungary.pdf.*

111. Colonel Tibor Bozo, *Hungary A Member of NATO,* Strategy Research Project, Carlisle, PA: U.S. Army War College, 2003, p. 6.

112. Cindy Williams, "From Conscripts to Volunteers: NATO's Transitions to All-Volunteer Forces," *Naval War College Review,* 2005, p. 12.

113. Simon, "NATO Expeditionary Operations." For data from 2007, see NATO, "NATO-Russia Compendium of Financial and Economic Data Relating to Defence."

114. Bureau of European and Eurasian Affairs, "U.S. Government Assistance to Eastern Europe under the Support of East European Democracy (SEED) Act."

115. Gienger.

116. Ronald D. Bachman, ed., *Romania: A Country Study,* Library of Congress, Washington, DC: GPO, 1989 available from *countrystudies.us/romania/.*

117. *Ibid.*

118. Larrabee, p. 126.

119. "Romania," London, UK: Foreign and Commonwealth Office, May 22, 2007, available from *www.fco.gov.uk/en/about-the-fco/country-profiles/europe/romania?profile=history&pg=3.*

120. "Comparative Scores for All Countries from 1973 to 2008," Washington, DC: Freedom House, 2008, available from *www.freedomhouse.org/template.cfm?page=15.*

121. International Monetary Fund "Reports for Selected Countries and Subjects."

122. *Ibid.*

123. *Ibid.*

124. *Ibid.*

125. Rice, p. 61.

126. In 2003, the Romanian Government made a commitment to spend a minimum of 2.38 percent of GDP for defense from 2003 to 2006. However, it was unable to maintain that commitment. See Lieutenant Colonel Nicolae-Stefan Z. Ciocoiu, *Romanian Armed Forces Transformation Process – The Core Issue of the National Military Strategy Towards NATO Integration,* Carlisle, PA: U.S. Army War College, 2004, available from *www.dtic.mil.*

127. Roman.

128. "Romania Gets IMF Emergency Loan," BBC News Online, March 25, 2009, available from *news.bbc.co.uk/2/hi/business/7962897.stm.*

129. NATO, "NATO-Russia Compendium of Financial and Economic Data Relating to Defence."

130. Claudia Degeratu, "Civil-Military Relations in Romania," Plamen Pantev, ed., *Civil-Military Relations in South Eastern Europe,* Sofia, Bulgaria: Institute for Security and International Studies, 2001, p. 160, available from *www.isn.ethz.ch/isn/Digital-Library/Publications/Detail/?ord516=OrgaGrp&ots591=0C54E3B3-1E9C-BE1E-2C24-A6A8C7060233&lng=en&id=131.*

131. "Romania: An Active Ally within an Active and Solid Alliance," Bucharest, Romania: Ministry of Foreign Affairs, undated, available from *www.mae.ro/index.php?unde=doc&id=4995&idlnk=1&cat=3.*

132. Thomas P. M. Barnett, *Romanian and East German Policies in the Third World,* London, UK: Praeger Publishing, 1992, pp. 23–30.

133. Jeffrey Simon, "The IFOR/SFOR Experience: Lessons Learned by PFP Partners," Institute for National Strategic Studies Strategic Forum, No. 120, Washington, DC: National Defense University, July 1997, available from *www.ndu.edu/inss/strforum/ SF120/forum120.html*.

134. Roman, *From Partner to Ally — Romania's Interest and War on Terrorism*, Carlisle, PA: U.S. Army War College, 2004, available from *www.dtic.mil/cgi-bin/GetTRDoc?AD=ADA478505&Location= U2&doc=GetTRDoc.pdf*.

135. Alison Mutler, "Romanian PM Proposes Pulling Iraq Troops," *The Washington Post*, June 29, 2006.

136. Lieutenant General David Barno, interview by author, Carlisle, PA: U.S. Army War College, January 25, 2008.

137. Secretary General Jaap de Hoop Scheffer, "Romanian President Visit," NATOchannel.tv, June 3, 2008, available from *www.natochannel.tv/default.aspx?aid=2645&lid=315*.

138. Bureau of European and Eurasian Affairs, "U.S. Government Assistance to and Cooperative Activities with Central and Eastern Europe," Washington, DC: U.S. State Department, January 2007, available from *www.state.gov/p/eur/rls/rpt/92682.htm*.

139. Gienger. Romania will get $14.3 million as opposed to $7.3 million in 2011.

140. Simon, "NATO Expeditionary Operations." For data from 2007, see NATO, "NATO-Russia Compendium of Financial and Economic Data Relating to Defence."

141. "Briefing of highest-ranked authorities of MoND and Polish Armed Forces," Warsaw, Poland: Polish Ministry of National Defence, April 2, 2008, available from *www.wp.mil.pl/en/ artyku/4601*.

142. Steven Paulikas, "Balts Remember the 'Glorious Way'," *The Baltic Times*, August 26, 2004, available from *www.baltictimes. com/news/articles/10738/*.

143. CIA, "World Factbook," Washington, DC: CIA, Estonia.

144. "Estonian President Visits NATO," NATO News, February 4, 2008, available from *152.152.94.201/docu/update/2008/02-february/e0204a.html.*

145. Maria Mälksoo, "NATO's New Strategic Concept: What is at Stake for Estonia?" Policy Paper, Tallin, Estonia, November 2008, Part II. Referenced in Phillip R. Cuccia, "Implications of a Changing NATO," Carlisle, PA: Strategic Studies Institute, U.S. Army War College, May 2010, available from *www.StrategicStudiesInstitute.army.mil/.*

146. International Monetary Fund, "Reports for Selected Countries and Subjects."

147. "Economy at a Glance," Tallinn, Estonia: Estonian Ministry of Foreign Affairs, October 10, 2008, available from *www.vm.ee/estonia/kat_398/pea_172/281.html.*

148. International Monetary Fund, "Reports for Selected Countries and Subjects."

149. "Estonia Public debt," *Index Mundi,* undated, available from *www.indexmundi.com/estonia/public_debt.html.*

150. "Estonian Central Bank Announces Budget Deficit," *The Baltic Times,* October 23, 2008, available from *www.baltictimes.com/news/articles/21624/.*

151. Estonian Ministry of Foreign Affairs, "Support for NATO Membership," *Estonia in NATO,* December 15, 2005, available from *www.vm.ee/eng/nato/kat_359/1007.html.*

152. Rein Lang, Estonian Foreign Minister, "Address by Foreign Minister Rein Lang at the celebrating of the first anniversary of Estonia's NATO accession," Tallinn, Estonia, April 4, 2005, available from *www.vm.ee/eng/nato/aken_prindi/5363.html.*

153. Colonel Indrek Sirel, interviews conducted at Carlisle Barracks, PA, U.S. Army War College, November 6, 2008.

154. Tonis Ormisson, "Public Opinion and National Defence, July 2007," Tallinn, Estonia: Estonian Ministry of Defence, 2008, available from *www.mod.gov.ee/static/sisu/files/ENG_NATO_ report_2007_06-summary.pdf.*

155. International Monetary Fund (IMF), "Estonia—2007 Article IV Consultation Concluding Statement of the IMF Mission," May 14, 2007, available from *www.imf.org/external/np/ ms/2007/051407.htm.*

156. International Monetary Fund "Reports for Selected Countries and Subjects."

157. *Ibid.*

158. Sirel, interview.

159. Estonian Ministry of Defence, "Public Opinion and National Defence, March 2005," Tallinn, Estonia: Research Centre Faktum, March 2005, available from *www.kmin.ee/static/sisu/ files/2005-04-25_Kmin_eng_parandatud.pdf.*

160. Ormisson.

161. Sirel, interview.

162. *Ibid.*

163. Urmas Paet, Estonian Foreign Minister, "Estonia's contribution to rebuilding Afghanistan," speech to Riigikogu, Tallinn, Estonia, November 15, 2006, available from *www.vm.ee/eng/nato/ aken_prindi/7913.html.*

164. *Ibid.*

165. Lieutenant Colonel Kaoidume, Deputy NMR, based on interviews conducted at the SHAPE Headquarters, Mons, Belgium, January 28, 2008.

166. Simon, "NATO Expeditionary Operations." For data from 2007, see NATO, "NATO-Russia Compendium of Financial and Economic Data Relating to Defence."

167. Kristiina Ojuland, Estonian Foreign Minister, "Address by Foreign Minister at the flag-raising ceremony at NATO Headquarters," April 2, 2004, available from *www.vm.ee/eng/nato/ kat_360/4385.html*.

168. "Albania," London, UK: Foreign and Commonwealth Office, July 14, 2010, available from *www.fco.gov.uk/en/about-the-fco/country-profiles/europe/albania*.

169. "Comparative Scores for All Countries from 1973 to 2008."

170. *Ibid*.

171. "Albania," Foreign and Commonwealth Office.

172. "Country Reports," Washington, DC: Freedom House, available from *www.freedomhouse.org/template.cfm?page=363&year =2010&country=7766*.

173. "Comparative Scores for All Countries from 1973 to 2009."

174. International Monetary Fund "Reports for Selected Countries and Subjects."

175. "Albania."

176. International Monetary Fund "Reports for Selected Countries and Subjects."

177. "Military Spending," Global Security Organization, available from *www.globalsecurity.org/military/world/europe/al-budget.htm*.

178. NATO, "NATO-Russia Compendium of Financial and Economic Data Relating to Defence."

179. Colonel Riccardo Marchio, "'Operation Alba': A European Approach to Peace Support Operations in the Balkans," Strategic Research Paper, Carlisle, PA: U.S. Army War College, available from *oai.dtic.mil/oai/oai?verb=getRecord&metadataPrefix= html&identifier=ADA378201*.

180. "Q&A: Political Unrest Threatening Albania," Reuters, January 25, 2011, available from *www.reuters.com/article/idUSTRE 70O2JW20110125?pageNumber=1.*

181. International Institute for Strategic Studies, *The Military Balance,* London, UK: Routledge, 2010.

182. Colonel Vladimir Avdiaj, interview, Carlisle, PA, U.S. Army War College, January 28, 2010.

183. *Ibid.*

184. "Peacekeeping Missions," Tirana, Albania: Ministry of Defence, available from *www.mod.gov.al/index.php?option=com_ content&view=article&id=33.*

185. "NATO Relations with Albania," Brussels, Belgium: NATO Headquarters, available from *www.nato.int/cps/en/SID-BC485EEB-70ABEBFB/natolive/topics_48891.htm?selectedLocale=en.*

186. International Institute for Strategic Studies, *The Military Balance,* London, UK: Routledge, 1991-2010.

187. "Country Reports," Freedom House.

188. CIA, "World Factbook," Croatia.

189. "Comparative Scores for All Countries from 1973 to 2008."

190. CIA, "World Factbook," Croatia.

191. *Ibid.*

192. NATO, "NATO-Russia Compendium of Financial and Economic Data Relating to Defence."

193. International Institute for Strategic Studies, *The Military Balance,* 1997, pp. 28-100.

194. NATO, "NATO relations with Croatia," available from *www.nato.int/cps/en/natolive/topics_31803.htm.*

195. *The Military Balance*, 1997, pp. 28-100.

196. Colonel Alex Portelli, former Chief of European Division, and Political Military Affairs, United States European Command, interviews conducted October 2011, Carlisle, PA, U.S. Army War College.

197. James R. Golden, *The Dynamics of Change in NATO: A Burden-Sharing Perspective*, New York: Praeger Publishing, 1983, p. vii.

198. NATO official speaking on background, interviews conducted at SHAPE on February 1, 2008.

CHAPTER 6

CONCLUSIONS AND THE WAY FORWARD

INSIGHTS INTO BURDEN SHARING IN THE NORTH ATLANTIC TREATY ORGANIZATION

As we go forward, U.S. defense strategy demands even closer partnership with our European allies.

Chuck Hagel,
Secretary of Defense[1]

Summary of Key Findings.

While facing continued challenges and public scrutiny, the North Atlantic Treaty Organization (NATO) has successfully negotiated major transitions, including the fall of the Soviet Union, enlargement from 16 to 28 members, and a protracted conflict in Afghanistan. While this resilience can be partially explained by NATO's unique position as an alliance of democracies, it is also attributable to NATO's norms of shared burdens and risks.[2] This book set out to answer some fundamental questions about burden sharing in NATO. While much has been written about burden sharing, this work has focused on the three less-studied components of burden sharing: the variations in burden sharing within Europe, the burden sharing behavior of new members, and the impact of enlargement on burden sharing. Building upon the previous body of work—in particular the logic of collective action, rational choice, and the socialization literature—this report yields some new and important insights into burden sharing behavior within NATO.

After extensive research, this analysis confirms that the collective action literature is still a useful framework for analyzing burden sharing. Specifically, the findings that larger NATO states often shoulder a disproportionate share of the Alliance's financial burdens are consistent with the logic of collective action. Larger European states (as defined by gross domestic product [GDP] and population size) tend to be closer to the NATO guidelines on defense expenditures (2 percent of GDP) than smaller states. This expectation is especially true for the United States. Specifically, Mansur Olson's writing concerning the "exploitation of the great" hypothesis suggests that smaller states would not be willing to fully contribute to public goods (like defense), since larger states would provide more than enough security for all.[3] The notion of a public good is central to this argument. A public good is any item or service that has two distinct qualities: nonexcludability and nonrival consumption. Nonexcludability refers to those who do not contribute to the provision of a particular good or service cannot feasibly be kept from benefiting from it. For example, every state in NATO benefits from U.S. nuclear deterrent, whether or not they contribute to those forces. Nonrival consumption means that consumption of the good or service by one actor does not diminish the amount available to others. Again, nuclear deterrence is an ideal example of a public defense good.

However, as the benefits of conventional military goods become less public in nature (rival consumption and excludability), Todd Sandler and Keith Hartley's joint product model becomes a better lens through which to view state behavior.[4] For example, conventional troops deployed in other theaters are not readily available for Alliance use (rival consumption).

Thus, the finding that larger states tend to have higher military expenditures as a percentage of GDP is better attributed to the fact that larger states derive a greater proportion of private benefits from these defense expenditures. U.S. global responsibilities and broader national interests require additional military capacity beyond the requirements of the Alliance. At the same time, the United States reaps the private benefits of global influence and leadership. When other NATO states derive private benefits from joint Alliance products, they too can be expected to share a greater portion of the burden. As Simon Duke pointed out in his 1993 study of NATO burden sharing, "calls for the U.S. allies to contribute to their defence expenditures have been heeded where it is in the interests of that country to do so."[5]

Also consistent with the predictions of the joint product model, larger states provide a significantly greater proportion of the air power during NATO missions. This phenomenon was true in Bosnia, Kosovo, Afghanistan, and most recently in Libya. This disparity not only reflects the nonpublic nature of air power, but also an implicit division of labor within the Alliance. NATO has deliberately attempted to maximize the comparative advantages of individual members during force planning and generation processes. Smaller members are routinely discouraged from pursuing autarky and encouraged to find niche capabilities.[6] For example, the Baltic states were discouraged from developing fully capable and independent air forces. The required expenditures needed to develop these skilled armed forces would have diverted resources from other military operations that these countries were better suited to provide.[7] Instead, they rely on other NATO countries to provide this security.

301

Perhaps the most significant contribution of this project concerns the burden sharing behavior of new members. The findings suggest that, on average, new members burden share at a relatively higher level than older members, *ceteris paribus*. This result was especially true for military expenditures immediately after gaining membership and for troop contributions to NATO's International Security Assistance Force (ISAF) mission and the U.S.-led Operation IRAQI FREEDOM (OIF). The logic of collective action cannot explain this result. Interviews with senior NATO officials and quotes from national political leaders expressed concerns for reputation and the desire to comply with NATO burden sharing norms. This sentiment may have contributed to the ability of new members to overcome the rational incentives to free-ride. The contributions to out of area missions, in particular, suggest the successful socialization of new NATO members into NATO burden sharing norms. In fact, they suggest a transition to a logic of appropriateness as Alexandria Gheichu's earlier studies suggest.[8] They also answer the puzzle of why these states, which are more focused on territorial defense than their older NATO counterparts, were willing to deploy their most capable forces thousands of miles from their homeland in support of missions that did not provide a direct security benefit to them.

As with the larger NATO states, the relative burden sharing levels between new and old NATO members varied depending on the degree of private benefits attributable to a particular mission and the capability of the states to contribute. Immediately after enlargement, older members' troop contributions to the NATO missions, Stabilization Force (SFOR) in Bosnia and the Kosovo Force (KFOR), exceeded those of new members as a percentage of population. This disparity was largely attributable to the greater military capability of older members at that time; new members were transitioning to democratic political systems and western-style military systems. However, as the military capabilities of the new members increased, they were more willing and able to assume greater Alliance burdens. This ability was demonstrated as new members contributed at a higher level to both OIF and ISAF in Afghanistan.

Scope Conditions: Identities, Socialization, and Norms.

After the fall of the Soviet Union, many European nations found themselves in an unfamiliar, ambiguous, and volatile environment. In this context, new NATO members pursued greater security and increased prosperity while establishing their role as reliable members of the western community. These new identities were constructed gradually over time through NATO's socialization processes in both the Partnership for Peace (PfP) and Membership Action Plan (MAP). These identities were further reinforced through participation in NATO's command structure and in numerous NATO operations. Identification as a NATO member helped shape new member preferences and behavior. This change was especially true when burden sharing norms matched accepted practice by older NATO members, or where new members were trying to build their credibility by committing to NATO missions. Socialization efforts were less successful when the actions of existing NATO members did not conform to the espoused norms of burden sharing (e.g., NATO's target of military expenditures at 2 percent of GDP). In this case, the joint product model and the logic of collective action proved to be a better predictor of state behavior.

The constructivist literature suggests that "identities are acquired by socialization into the intersubjective structures of the international system."[9] PfP and MAP socialized new members into an ideal conception of membership and burden sharing behavior. NATO members monitored the behavior of aspiring members during participation in these two programs and provided routine feedback and assistance. As a result, participation in these programs gradually changed both new member self-conception (as members of the West) and their preferences for burden sharing. As their identification with NATO grew over time, new members were more willing to accept the burdens imposed by membership. The strong identification with NATO led to "sharing, cooperation, perceived mutuality of interests, and the willingness to sacrifice personal interests for group interests," under the conditions at the end of the Cold War.[10] This finding was not consistent with the expectations of either the logic of collective action or other rationality based theories.

The argument that new members internalized the norms of burden sharing is strongest regarding contributions to NATO missions. It is in the area of contributions to NATO missions that the NATO norms of equitable burdens, espoused by NATO, most closely matched actual performance among existing NATO members. The findings also demonstrate that new members were concerned with their ability to make credible commitments, especially regarding future consideration for membership in the European Union (EU) and to fostering a closer relationship with the United States. New members were keen to build and maintain their reputations by supporting NATO missions abroad. Yet, these new NATO members also rationalized their contributions to these missions in terms of appropriateness versus pure self-interest. This finding is in line with constructivist expectations that, as new members construct new identities, free-riding would be discouraged.[11]

Rational Choice and the Problem of Free-Riding.

At first look, the results of this report conformed with the rational choice predictions that new member free-riding would increase once the incentives of membership conditionality were removed. New member military expenditures, as a percentage of GDP, did decline after they gained membership.[12] While new members had a relatively greater level of defense expenditures than did older members, this divergence was short lived. Over time, the new members' willingness to devote a greater proportion of GDP to defense expenditures waned. This result was consistent with Judith Kelley's findings on conditionality; once states were members of NATO, there was no rational reason for them to continue the higher levels of military expenditures.[13] New members also faced competing demands from their desire to gain EU membership, which required greater fiscal controls, lower deficit, and debt levels.

Yet, there is another equally compelling explanation for declining military expenditures after accession. In the area of military expenditures, the formal NATO norms of burden sharing and actual behavior of NATO members have long diverged. New members had little incentive to maintain higher levels of defense expenditures given the lack of compliance by other NATO members. As the case studies show, in an era of low conventional threats and competing domestic demands for funds, increasing defense expenditures to meet NATO goals was difficult. Without formal sanctioning mechanisms within NATO, new members gradually converged on the NATO averages of defense spending. After the Cold War, the average NATO military expenditures were well below the level agreed to by NATO as an Alliance norm of 2 percent of GDP.

Declining overall levels of military expenditures after NATO enlargement also appear to be consistent with the predictions of the collective action literature. According to Olson, collective action problems are magnified in larger groups. Thus, as NATO expanded, free-riding behavior should have also increased. This report revealed that declining levels of military expenditures did not begin with NATO enlargement; they merely continued after NATO enlargement. Declining NATO defense expenditures were largely the result of a changed strategic environment. As the Soviet Union disintegrated, the perception of threat diminished and military expenditures declined.[14] This result is consistent with Stephen Walt's balance of threat theory[15] and Peter Forster and Stephen Cimbala's correlation between perceived threats and burden sharing.[16] One of the reasons the United States did not follow suit is that it was pursuing the private benefits of global leadership as well as the war in Iraq. While declining NATO military expenditures remain a major concern for the United States, this trend is unlikely to change in the near future given the difficult fiscal realities faced by Western nations.

The joint product model provides a good framework for understanding troop contributions to NATO peacekeeping missions. Where European interests were more clearly at risk, such as in the Balkans and in operations in Libya, European members increased their relative share of the NATO force. Where U.S. interests were dominant, as in Afghanistan, the reverse was true. These findings suggest that the difference between private and public benefits was a better predictor of burden sharing than GDP or population size during the missions examined.

A novel finding from this report was that the expansion of NATO membership did not result in declining troop contributions to NATO missions, contrary to the expectations from the logic of collective action. In the missions examined, non-U.S. NATO members, both small and large, maintained or increased their relative levels of troop contributions after both waves of enlargement in 1999 and 2004. The next section reviews the key findings from the previous chapters by hypothesis. These hypotheses were derived from multiple theoretical approaches as shown in Table 6-1. Where the findings are consistent with specific theoretical claims, those theories are indicated in parentheses.

		Findings
H-1:	Large states will share greater relative proportion of burdens than small states	Supported for: - military expenditures, if size is measured by GDP and population. - air contributions. (Logic of Collective Action/ Joint Product Model). Not supported for troop contributions. (Joint Product Model)
H-2:	New members will share greater relative proportion of burdens than old members	Supported for military expenditures. (Socialization and credibility literature) Supported for OIF & ISAF. Not supported for SFOR and KFOR (due to a lack of capability).

Table 6-1. Summary of Findings.

		Findings
H-3:	New member burden sharing declines after accession into NATO.	Supported for military expenditures in absolute terms. (Logic of Collective Action). Not Supported for: - military expenditures in relative terms -troop contributions to KFOR or ISAF. (Socialization and credibility literature)
H-4:	The defense expenditures of NATO members, as percent of GDP, should increase as states are physically closer to Russia, or as Russian military expenditures increase.	Not Supported.
H-5:	Free-riding behavior should increase with NATO enlargement.	Not Supported for: - military expenditures. - troop contributions. (Joint Product Model, Socialization and credibility literature)

Table 6-2. Summary of Findings Continued.

DETAILED REVIEW OF FINDINGS
BY HYPOTHESIS

Hypothesis 1: Large states will share greater relative proportion of burdens than small states.

This analysis validated the collective action prediction that large states would share a greater relative proportion of burdens than small states. Large states have greater capabilities, global responsibilities, and broader interests, allowing for a larger benefit from common defense than smaller NATO nations. The results were strongest when using military expenditures as a percentage of GDP. This traditional measure of burden sharing was derived from Olson's logic of collective action and subsequent works, such as those by Sandler and Hartley. Two measures of size (GDP and population) were positive and statistically significant during both the Cold War and post-Cold War periods.[17] The results were most robust for economic size (GDP), which was statistically significant with and without the United States included in the data set. This finding suggests that, on average, larger countries (as measured by GDP and population) had higher military expenditures as a percentage of GDP. This finding is in line with the "exploitation of the great" hypothesis from the logic of collective action. During the late-Cold War period, country size (as measured by the amount of land area a state had to defend) was also statistically significant. This result was not surprising, given the conventional nature of the threat during that period.

The findings on air power contributions to NATO missions also support the "exploitation of the great" hypothesis from the logic of collective action. This result was true in all of the case studies of NATO missions. Larger NATO states consistently provided a greater relative proportion of the air power during NATO missions. However, there are several explanations for this result, not related to intentional free- riding. First, this disparity reflects a de facto division of labor within NATO. Small countries are actively discouraged by the Alliance from developing redundant military capabilities, such as air superiority, where the Alliance has surplus capability. Second, the provision of air power by larger states utilizes their comparative advantage in technology and greater economies scale and is usually reciprocated by greater relative troop contributions from smaller allies.

An interesting finding of this report was that large states did not always share a greater relative proportion of troop contributions to NATO missions than small states. This finding is particularly important as troop contributions reflect the willingness of NATO states to assume political risks in pursuit of Alliance-wide benefits. When looking at troop contributions to NATO peacekeeping missions, the joint product model provides the best insight into burden sharing behavior. The United States, as the largest and wealthiest NATO state, did not always contribute a larger or even proportionate share of ground troops to NATO missions. Much depended upon the perceived private benefits and risks associated with a particular mission as predicted by the joint product model. When it did contribute a larger relative percentage of the force, as in ISAF, the United States was pursuing private benefits, such as the Global War on Terror. The same is true of the Big Four European members of NATO. In the two operations in the Balkans, SFOR and KFOR, and in Libya, the European members had more to lose from failure (i.e., illegal immigration and the spread of ethnic conflict) and therefore provided more than their fair share of troops. On the other hand, the smaller NATO countries, on average, provided an appropriate number of troops to the NATO missions examined. These findings suggest that the difference between private and public benefits was a better predictor of burden sharing during the missions examined.

Hypothesis 2: New members will share greater relative proportion of burdens than old members.

The findings also support the second hypothesis that new members would burden share at a relatively higher level than older members, which was consistent with both the socialization literature and the literature concerning credibility. This finding was true for both Alliance inputs (defense expenditures as a percentage of GDP) and Alliance outputs (troop contributions). Regarding inputs, the statistical analysis suggested that as the length of membership increased, military expenditures as a percentage of GDP decreased. To validate the results of the regression equation, additional comparisons were made between the new members that entered NATO in 1999 (the Czech Republic, Hungary, and Poland) and the older members of similar population size (Belgium, Portugal, and Spain). Unlike during the Cold War period, these findings were conclusive; new members spent a greater percentage of GDP, *ceteris paribus*, than older members.

A comparison was also made between new member spending and Russian military expenditures. This test helped to control for the alternative explanation that perceived threat was responsible for greater military spending levels by new members. Many new members are geographically closer to Russia than other NATO members and had been occupied and/or invaded by the Soviet Union after World War II. Changes in the average military expenditure levels of the new members were inversely correlated with Russian military expenditures after 1999. The study found that as Russian military expenditures rose, new members' defense spending decreased as a percentage of GDP. This is consistent with the regression findings that conventional threat perception was not a significant predictor of military expenditures during this period. However, this does not suggest that Eastern European states no longer felt threatened by Russia, rather they were more sensitive to alliance spending than to Russian spending.

The examination of Alliance outputs (troop contributions) also supported the hypothesis that new members would burden share at a relatively higher level than older members. New NATO members were willing and eager to become security providers and carry their fair share of NATO burdens.[18] While their contributions were initially hindered by a lack of military capability in the midst of NATO reforms, they increased as their capacity increased. This willingness to burden share can be attributed to both a desire for credibility and to the successful socialization efforts of NATO.

During the humanitarian mission by the NATO Response Force (NRF) to Pakistan in 2005, the Czech Republic and Hungary contributed a greater percentage of forces than did their counterparts of equal size, Belgium and Portugal.[19] The Czech Republic and Hungary also contributed a greater proportion of forces to the ISAF in Afghanistan. Poland's contributions to ISAF also exceeded Spain's contributions from 2007 through 2011. While Spain's troop contributions exceeded those of Poland early on in ISAF, Polish contributions before 2007 were constrained by a large commitment of troops to the U.S.-led OIF. As OIF troop levels fell, Poland increased its contributions to ISAF.

The contributions of new member states also came with fewer restrictions than those of the older members. While older members contributed more troops to the earlier NATO missions, such as Bosnia and Kosovo, this disparity reflected the limited capacity of new member nations as they entered the Alliance rather than a lack of willingness to pull their weight. As the capability of new members increased due to NATO reforms, greater operational experience and training efforts, so too did their contributions. The interviews and case studies of new member countries support this assertion.

From a collective action perspective, it is surprising that new members have contributed as much as they have to NATO missions. Even when the operations had little direct linkage to their traditional security concerns or direct national interests, new members contributed to NATO operations within their means. In the interviews conducted as a part of this book, officials from these countries primarily used the logic of appropriateness to explain their contributions to NATO. These interviews also revealed that the pursuit of private benefits, such as establishing credibility with the United States and NATO, certainly played a factor in the burden sharing decisions of new members. This result suggests that the socialization of NATO burden sharing norms and the concerns with establishing credibility influenced new members' willingness to contribute.

Hypothesis 3: New member burden sharing declines after accession into NATO.

As predicted by the conditionality literature, new members' burden sharing did decline in absolute terms after accession into NATO. However, while new members' military expenditures as a percentage of GDP declined after accession, expenditures did not decline on a relative basis compared to older members. This finding is counter to the expectations from the conditionality literature. New members' military expenditures as a percentage of GDP remained at or above the average of non-U.S. NATO military expenditures after enlargement. These findings were true for both the 1999 and 2004 wave of new members. It is too soon to make any judgments about whether this holds true for the 2009 wave.

Declining military expenditures, as a percentage of GDP, reflect a broader trend of declining military expenditures in non-U.S. NATO allies. Some of this decline can be attributed to more rapid economic growth by new members after 1999. On average, new members had an average growth rate of 6.9 percent compared to 2.27 percent for the United States during this period. Thus, while absolute spending increased, military spending as a percentage of GDP decreased. New members also felt a greater sense of security once inside NATO, though that sense of security has been under pressure since Russia's invasion of Georgia in 2008 and Crimea in 2014. Finally, declining military expenditures as a percentage of GDP reflected the fiscal realities in the wake of the global economic crisis as many NATO countries came to grips with their rising levels of debt. This decline is especially true for Hungary, which has a very high level of debt. While the United States faces similar fiscal pressure, it is unlikely that its level of military spending will drop below 2 percent of GDP any time soon.

The case studies revealed that, on average, new members' contributions to NATO missions increased in the years after attaining membership. In general, as military capability increased, relative contributions to NATO missions increased. This increase was true in all three NATO missions examined in detail: SFOR, KFOR, and ISAF. While there were individual cases where absolute troop contributions declined, these were usually in concert with a reduction in the size of the total NATO force due to decreasing mission requirements. In ISAF, where mission requirements increased every year, the average troop contributions from new members increased.

Hypothesis 4: The defense expenditures of NATO members should increase as states are physically closer to Russia, or as Russian military expenditures increase.

This book yielded some interesting insights regarding the perception of threat. Not surprising, threat perceptions differ between the Cold War period and the post-Cold War period. During the statistical analysis of the Cold War period, Russian military expenditures were positively related to non-U.S. military expenditures as a percentage of GDP. This result was statistically significant and robust using three different statistical methods. As Russian spending increased, so too did non-U.S. NATO spending.[20] During the Cold War, increases in Russian military expenditures seemed to follow increases in U.S. military expenditures as a percentage of GDP, although they were only moderately correlated. However, not surprising, non-U.S. NATO military expenditures as a percentage of GDP were strongly correlated with Russian military expenditures.

In the post-Cold War period, U.S. and Russian military expenditures were also correlated. Again, Russian military expenditures seemed to follow increases in U.S. military expenditures as a percentage of GDP. However, Russian military expenditures explained only 5 percent of the variance in non-U.S. NATO defense expenditures after the Cold War. As the Supreme Allied Commander Europe said, "After the Cold War ended, many believed that Europe and Eurasia were no longer at threat of being invaded."[21] More importantly, the military expenditures of the new member states were not responsive to increases in Russian military expenditures. At least until the Russian invasion of Georgia in 2008 and Crimea in 2014, many NATO allies no longer saw Russia as a conventional security threat. Even then, there was no decline in contributions to ISAF after the Russian invasion of Georgia. Instead, new members actually increased their participation in ISAF.

Hypothesis 5: Free-riding behavior should increase with NATO enlargement.

The test results for the fifth hypothesis were also mixed, but suggest that overall free-riding behavior did not increase after NATO enlargement as predicted by the logic of collective action. In all three peacekeeping operations, the findings did not support the hypothesis that free-riding behavior would increase with NATO enlargement. After NATO expanded in 1999 and again in 2004, the average annual contribution of small NATO countries increased during SFOR, KFOR, and ISAF. Had NATO expansion led to greater free-riding, these levels of contributions should have declined after enlargement. This result suggests that future rounds of enlargement may not lead to increased free-riding behavior as suggested by the logic of collective action.

At first glance, the findings regarding military expenditures are consistent with a linkage between enlargement and free-riding behavior. Average non-U.S. military expenditures did decrease as a percentage of GDP after both waves of enlargement. However, this correlation does not suggest causation. There are three alternative explanations for this phenomenon. While non-U.S. military expenditures as a percentage of GDP declined after enlargement, some of this was attributable to economic growth which was inversely related to military expenditures in the regression models. Non-U.S. NATO members had a slightly higher growth rate than the United States during this period. Most importantly, rising levels of U.S. military expenditures after 2001 were largely related to the U.S. war in Iraq. This conflict, which several key NATO allies objected to, was responsible for a large portion of the increase in U.S. military expenditures during this period. Thus, this increase could be better explained by the U.S. pursuit of private benefits. Of note, even accounting for the Iraqi war, the gap between U.S. and non-U.S. NATO military expenditures in 2006 was still less than in 1992. Finally, declining military expenditures can also be explained by a declining conventional threat perception in Europe. With perceived declining regional threats to their national interests, NATO members could be expected to reduce their military expenditures.[22] Yet, with their global interests, the United States, France, and the United Kingdom (UK) would not necessarily follow suit.

HOW BURDEN SHARING DECISIONS ARE MADE

This project also revealed some important findings that were not included in the initial hypotheses, such as how burden sharing decisions are made and the components of burden sharing. Burden sharing is a complex process that consists of weighing national interests, alliance commitments, and domestic political considerations. The decisionmaking process is dynamic and unique to each country. However, there are some patterns that seem to emerge. While rational motivations (such as concerns over credibility and side payments) may drive burden sharing decisions, those decisions are often supported publically using arguments based on identity as suggested by Judith Kelly in her study on conditionality. Politicians and leaders often cite obligations to the Alliance when trying to increase military expenditures or justify troop contributions. This language, which suggests a logic of appropriateness, was also used by new members in explaining their contributions to NATO during the interviews.[23]

This book also examined the distinction between willingness and capability in burden sharing, borrowing insights from such fields as psychology. The focus of the burden sharing literature has been on willful free-riding as rational behavior. Often what appears to be free-riding behavior actually reflects a lack of capability rather than a lack of willingness to contribute. This distinction is important in that the remedies for lagging contributions differ based on the root cause. In this project, new members increasingly contributed to the Alliance in the face of significant fiscal, physical, and political constraints. While most new members were unable to sustain their military expenditures at the NATO standard of 2 percent of GDP, they did relatively better than their older counterparts. Some have also locked in their contribution levels by passing binding domestic legislation. Poland, for example, enacted new laws to peg its defense budget to the NATO standard.

The examination of troop contributions to NATO missions yielded a similar finding. Early shortfalls in troop contributions reflected a lack of capability at the time of entry into NATO. As new members changed their military organizations, procedures, and equipment in order to meet NATO standards, their military capabilities increased, as well as their contributions to NATO missions. In Afghanistan, new members have provided more troops, with fewer restrictions, than their older NATO counterparts of similar size. Often, this was done in the face of stiff domestic opposition and declining force structure.

Using complementary methodological approaches to study burden sharing in NATO, this project sought to answer not only what was happening in NATO, but why it was happening.[24] The quantitative techniques best explained burden sharing behavior of NATO states in their contributions to defense expenditures. The former suggests that defense expenditures are more readily explained by a more rationalist approach (e.g., the joint product model) than by a more sociological explanation. The interviews and case studies provided a better method to understand clearly the meaning of those empirical results, especially when looking at contributions to NATO missions.[25] This analysis not only increased our knowledge of burden sharing and NATO, but hopefully advanced the dialogue between rationalist approaches, such as the logic of collective action, and more sociological approaches.[26] The results should also inform future policy decisions related to NATO.

FUTURE POLICY CONSIDERATIONS

The results of this analysis provide insights that could help strengthen the Alliance and the U.S. position as a global and alliance leader. NATO has been a reliable security partner of the United States for over 60 years. As Secretary Hillary Clinton mentioned during the 2012 Munich Security Conference, Europe remains the "partner of first resort."[27] In the 2010

National Security Strategy, the United States reiterated its desire to seek multilateral approaches and to share the burdens of security. "Our national security goals can only be reached if we make hard choices and work with international partners to share burdens."[28] NATO has many mechanisms that facilitate cooperation and security in the trans-Atlantic region. These need to be sustained. However, there is more that could be done to enhance Alliance capabilities and lead to more equitable burden sharing within the Alliance.

NATO should expand mechanisms to institutionalize burden sharing, such as its common funding budget. NATO should increase the common fund budget to cover needed Alliance capabilities and expenses such as NRF deployment costs. This could help mitigate the disparity of military contributions in areas such as airlift, precision munitions, and intelligence, surveillance, and reconnaissance. Common funding tends to bind states, enabling them to more easily justify their NATO commitments domestically. Because each NATO nation has an established cost-share for NATO common funds, these increased costs could be distributed within an established burden sharing framework and justified domestically as a duty of membership (see Table 6-3).

	Civil Budget	Military Budget	NATO Security Investment Program
United States	21.7%	22.5%	21.7%
Big 4 (UK, Germany, France, and Italy)	49.8%	48.9%	49.3%
Smaller members	28.5%	28.6%	29.0%

Table 6-3. NATO Common Budget Cost Shares.

NATO common funds already pay for selected Alliance-wide facilities and capabilities. For example, NATO owns a fleet of airborne surveillance and early warning aircraft. NATO could add a limited amount of common funded strategic airlift assets to help share the burdens of supporting NATO missions and minimize the domestic repercussions of increasing national defense spending. NATO should also move to expand common funding for the NATO Reaction Force. This development would make it easier for new and old members to commit forces to the NRF and to follow through when the NRF is activated.

In addition to the common funding budget, NATO has to look for ways to develop capability in the face of increasing economic pressures. While nations should be held accountable for meeting NATO commitments, it may not be realistic to expect that European nations will be willing and able to meet the 2 percent GDP standard in the face of the current global economic crisis. Therefore, NATO should increase capability by promoting a further division of labor both externally (in coordination with the EU) and internally (during established NATO force planning processes). The EU has developed substantial peacekeeping capabilities that could alleviate some of the stress on NATO and the United States. The EU is already moving in this direction in Bosnia, Kosovo, and Africa. NATO must continue to work with the EU to develop complementary capabilities. Within the Alliance, NATO would be wise to continue to encourage smaller members to develop niche capabilities. By maximizing each institution and nation's comparative advantage, the Alliance will get more proficiency at a lower cost.

Another such way to build NATO's abilities is to fully implement the Smart Defense concept, adopted at the 2012 summit. Smart Defense was envisioned to improve cooperation in the development and sharing of capabilities as outlined in the 2010 Strategic Concept. Therefore, the Alliance should expand collective capabilities such as the Alliance Ground Surveillance system and Airborne Warning and Control System, as well as other cooperative programs such as the C-17 program and the Strategic Airlift Interim Solution.

NATO also needs to continue to support the EU Common Security and Defense Policy (CSDP) and European Defense Agency (EDA). The CSDP gives the EU a mechanism to launch both civilian and military missions independently of NATO, thus easing the burdens on the Alliance. The EDA provides a parallel mechanism to the NATO Smart Defense initiative by providing incentives for members to increase their cooperation in the development of military capabilities. Because EU requirements are often easier to justify domestically than are NATO requirements, this complementary program offers both organizations another opportunity to increase cooperation.

While the United States and NATO should continue to hold allies accountable for meeting their Alliance commitments (both expenditures and contributions to NATO missions), they also need to recognize the constraints faced by allies and work with them in increasing their military capability. Vilifying Alliance partners for domestic political gain is counterproductive.[29] The United States and other major European powers should continue to promote the development of military capabilities in new NATO members and other international partners. While the 2010 U.S. *National Security Strategy* made a commitment to use training and assistance programs to increase capabilities and improve burden sharing, these programs must be protected from cuts as the United States and Europe deal with trimming national debt.[30]

Finally, the United States must keep its remaining forces in Europe to facilitate joint training and exercise programs, especially with newer NATO members. The United States announced in January 2012 that it was going to reduce the number of Army brigades stationed in Europe from four to two.[31] While these reductions are manageable, further reductions would leave just a token force in place, reducing U.S. influence and increasing security concerns of new members. The United States must also continue to reaffirm its commitment to NATO's Article 5 mission. This issue was a key recommendation of the Group of Experts (led by former Secretary of State Madeleine Albright) in 2010. Secretary Clinton and Secretary Leon Panetta sought to reassure NATO allies of the U.S. commitment to Europe during the 2012 Munich Security Conference.[32] The U.S. provision of Patriot missiles to Turkey during the Syrian crisis is a good start to reaffirming that commitment to NATO.

The United States needs to recognize publicly the contributions made by new members and continue its efforts to enhance new member capabilities. The focus should be on building capability in the new NATO members and sustaining their willingness to contribute through military assistance, bilateral cooperation, and continued public recognition. As time goes on, new members may feel less compelled to live up to their commitments if other NATO members free-ride. To address burden sharing issues with older members, the United States must look for ways to increase their willingness to contribute more to the Alliance and to justify the importance of the Alliance contributions to their constituents.

NATO remains one of the most successful alliances in history. This book demonstrates that, although burden sharing is a dynamic process, most allies have continued to contribute to the Alliance in the face of significant constraints. Shared risk and responsibility is a founding principle of NATO and the glue that holds it together. NATO enlargement has not led to greater free-riding behavior, but rather added vitality to burden sharing efforts in NATO. This is important as NATO remains open to future expansion in accordance with Article 10 of the North Atlantic Treaty, though it is unlikely that the next wave of NATO enlargement will come anytime soon.[33]

Grousing over lagging allied contributions will not go away. Nor will enormous strains on the Alliance lessen in the near future. The NATO mission in Afghanistan is anticipated to persist through 2014 as currently scheduled. The United States and the EU also continue to face significant economic challenges. Based on the analysis in this project, it is reasonable to expect that the leaders of the Alliance, especially the United States, will continue to bear a larger proportion of the burdens, especially in areas where they have a comparative advantage: air and sea power, precision munitions, and other high technologically advanced capabilities (NATO's operation in Libya in 2011 is a case in point.). That said, smaller members can and should be expected to provide commensurate contributions in areas such as ground forces and niche capabilities. By maximizing each nation's comparative advantage, all NATO members can benefit.

Whenever NATO does decide to further expand, new and future member states can be expected to contribute to the Alliance, though they may be constrained by political and military capability shortfalls. NATO's newest members, admitted on April 1, 2009, have validated that new members can prove their reliability by contributing to NATO missions. For example, Albania and Croatia's 2010-11 contributions to Afghanistan were significant and proportionate to their population (Albania, 295/260 troops and Croatia, 295/320, respectively).[34] Croatia's Ambassador to the United States made a telling statement on April 1, 2009, the day Croatia was accepted into NATO: ". . . and let me reassure you that you can continue to count on Croatia as a responsible and a reliable ally."[35] This sentiment reflects a commitment to NATO norms that has been expressed by the previous waves of new members.

While leaving the door open to future enlargement, NATO should focus its efforts on consolidation for the near future. NATO membership for Georgia and the Ukraine face an uphill battle due to stiff Russian resistance and domestic political disarray. Other European states, such as Bosnia and Herzegovina, Former Yugoslav Republic of Macedonia, Montenegro, and Serbia aspire to become members.[36] However, these states face much greater obstacles to integration than did the earlier waves of new NATO members. All three will require significant economic and political reforms to meet Alliance standards. Bosnia and Herzegovina faces increasing instability as ethnic and political issues resurface. The former Yugoslav Republic of Macedonia faces the continued resistance of Greece to its membership in NATO. Bosnia and Herzegovina and Macedonia are also relatively less wealthy than other NATO members, with an estimated 2010 per capita GDP of $7,751 and $9,350. With the exception of the former Yugoslav Republic of Macedonia, which joined PfP in 1995, most of these countries have not had the extensive socialization experiences of the 2004 and 2009 waves of NATO enlargement. Bosnia and Herzegovina, Montenegro, and Serbia only joined the PfP program in 2006. There appears to be little appetite for further NATO expansion given the current fiscal crisis in Europe.

When NATO does expand again, as discussed by the Group of Experts in 2010, it can expect its new members to demonstrate their credibility to NATO as did previous new members.[37] Participation in PfP, MAP, and NATO missions abroad will enhance the interoperability and military capability of new members and other partners alike. While contributions to NATO missions will be constrained by military and economic factors, this analysis has shown that new members can be expected to contribute their fair share.

FUTURE RESEARCH

One of the important findings from this project concerns the impact of threat on burden sharing decisions. In the post-Cold War period, NATO states have become less sensitive to increased military expenditures by Russia. With the recent deterioration of NATO-Russian relations, especially after the invasion of Crimea, this phenomenon may change. The impact of a more assertive Russian foreign policy and a smaller U.S. foot print on burden sharing decisions in NATO needs further examination. Two possible outcomes are foreseeable. First, as insecurity increases, NATO states may reverse the trend of declining levels of military expenditures. This reaction would be more pronounced in those NATO countries closest to Russia. Second, NATO members might shift their focus toward territorial defense. For example, the former Warsaw Pact countries which are physically closer to Russia might eschew the development of expeditionary and niche capabilities to focus on more conventional deterrent forces.

Another interesting area requiring further research is the impact of the global financial crisis on relative levels of military expenditures in NATO. The United States has announced a $1 trillion cut in its defense budget over the next 10 years, with the potential for even further reductions as the United States withdraws forces from Afghanistan in 2014.[38] If NATO is a uniquely privileged group, the relative decline in U.S. economic power, as well as declining mission requirements, should lead to a decline in U.S. military expenditures relative to NATO. If so, NATO allies should increase their levels of burden sharing in response to these changes.

At the same time, the greater fiscal demands facing all NATO allies will most likely constrain any net growth in military expenditures. These economic pressures might also lead to reduced support to NATO peacekeeping operations.[39] These fiscal constraints are exacerbated by an aging population in many Western European nations, especially the older, more prosperous members of NATO.

The growing involvement of both NATO and the EU in peacekeeping operations provides another interesting research question. Does burden sharing behavior differ substantially between NATO and the EU? While NATO is primarily a military/political alliance, EU is a political/legal institution historically focused on economic and social issues. Yet, both NATO and the EU have recent experiences in undertaking peacekeeping missions in Europe and abroad. Both NATO and the EU recently underwent enlargement, which largely consisted of the same countries. Two of the major differences between these institutions are the more extensive, legal requirements of the EU (e.g., *acquis communitaires*) and the absence of the United States in the EU. With the inclusion of the United States, NATO has been characterized as a uniquely privileged group. As a uniquely privileged group, NATO should be more prone to free-riding behavior than the EU. It would be interesting to see if this hypothesis bears out in contributions to EU missions. Another area to study would be to examine whether or not the "exploitation of the great" occurs in the EU, where there is not one dominant actor.

NATO's new Strategic Concept, approved by the Alliance at the Lisbon Summit in 2010, provides another interesting topic for further study. NATO has laid out its ambition to be a global security provider. In a 2010 U.S. Army War College publication, it was noted that NATO is "no longer simply a trans-Atlantic alliance. The new Strategic Concept also implies that NATO will work with other security organizations in a global effort."[40] As it does so, NATO will find its limited resources stretched even further. Therefore, burden sharing issues will remain salient and recurring topics of discussion and debate within the Alliance.

NATO has been one of the most resilient and successful alliances in history. Undergoing significant changes in the past 20 years, NATO still faces a future full of volatility and uncertainty. Despite this turmoil, one feature that has consistently sustained the Alliance has been its ability and willingness to collectively share burdens and risk. This is not to imply that all members share the same burdens and risk. Rather,

NATO has developed a dynamic burden sharing culture where there is a de facto division of labor. As in any organization, the more powerful members often have to assume greater responsibility and costs. However, other members often pick up the slack when required and able to do so.

This project has focused on updating the literature on burden sharing in NATO in the context of current NATO issues. The United States and its NATO allies will likely continue to face difficult issues in the near future. Certainly burden sharing debates will remain a salient feature of NATO and a topic of interest for both academics and policy makers. As Kori Schake, a Professor of Security Studies at the United States Military Academy and Hoover Fellow, stated immediately prior the 60th Anniversary of NATO, "the fundamental bargain [in NATO] is sound; and while it's often frustrating that Europeans won't do more, without NATO they would do much less."[41]

ENDNOTES - CHAPTER 6

1. Chuck Hagel, Secretary of Defense, Press Briefing at NATO Headquarters, Brussels, Belgium, February 27, 2014, available from *www.defense.gov/transcripts*.

2. Wallace J. Thies, *Why NATO Endures*, Washington DC: Catholic University of America, 2009.

3. Mancur Olson, Jr., The *Logic of Collective Action: Public Goods and the Theory of Groups*, Rev. Ed., New York: Schocken Books, 1971, pp. 3, 29.

4. Keith Hartley and Todd Sandler, *The Political Economy of NATO*, New York: Cambridge University Press, 1999, pp. 34-37.

5. Simon Duke, *The Burdensharing Debate*, New York: Saint Martin's Press, 1993, p. 232.

6. This is in line with Boyer's findings on comparative advantage in the provision of public goods. Mark A. Boyer, "Trading Public Goods in the Western Alliance System," *Journal of Conflict Resolution*, No. 33, 1989, pp. 700-727. Also see Mark A. Boyer, *International Cooperation and Public Goods*, London, UK: Johns Hopkins University Press, 1993.

7. NATO nations have committed to providing air defense for the Baltic States, on a 4-month rotational basis, while the Baltic states have developed niche capabilities in areas such as cyber warfare and countermine operations.

8. Alexandria Ghiecu, "Security Institutions as Agents of Socialization? NATO and the New Europe," *International Organization*, Vol. 59, No. 4, 2005.

9. Andreas Hasenclever, Peter Mayer, and Volker Rittberger, *Theories of International Regimes*" Oxford, UK: Cambridge University Press, 1997, p. 189.

10. Jonathan Mercer, "Rationality and Psychology in International Politics," *International Organization*, Vol. 59, Winter 2005, p. 96.

11. Alexander Wendt proposed that "increasing diffuse reciprocity and the willingness to bear costs without selective incentives," helped explain why new NATO members did not free-ride as expected. See Alexander Wendt, "Collective Identity Formation and the International State," *American Political Science Review*, Vol. 88, 1994, p. 386. Also see Hasenclever, Mayer, and Rittberger.

12. Judith Kelley, "International Actors on the Domestic Scene: Membership Conditionality and Socialization by International Institutions," *International Organization*, Vol. 58, 2004.

13. *Ibid.*; and Alastair Iain Johnston, "Conclusions and Extensions: Toward Mid-Range Theorizing and Beyond Europe," *International Organization*, Vol. 59, 2005, p. 1015.

14. A small portion of the drop in military expenditures as a percentage of GDP is partially due to increasing prosperity on the part of non-U.S. allies. As the denominator increased (GDP), the ratio of military expenditures to GDP necessarily declined.

15. Stephen M. Walt, "Alliance Formation and the Balance of World Power," *International Security*, Vol. 9, No. 4, Spring 1985, p. 9.

16. Peter K. Forster, and Stephen J. Cimbala, *Multinational Military Intervention: NATO Policy, Strategy and Burden-Sharing*, Burlington, UK: Ashgate, 2010, p. 206.

17. Fixed Effects Vector Decomposition (FEVD).

18. Where political will might be seen as lacking, as in Hungary, free-riding behavior was more prevalent. Even then, Hungary made a considerable effort to contribute and bear some of the risks involved.

19. While Spain's level of contributions exceeded that of Poland, this was largely due to Spain's role as the land component headquarters during NRF 5. However, since the NRF responsibilities rotate with each NRF, caution should be used when generalizing the findings from this case.

20. In the post-Cold War period, the threat variable was still positively correlated to non-U.S. military expenditures, but was only statistically significant using one of the three statistical methods found in Appendix B.

21. "Obama Voices Support for NATO Expansion Despite Russian Qualms," *Deutsche Welle*, March 25, 2009, available from *www.dw-world.de/dw/article/0,,3894552,00.html*.

22. At the end of the day, defense expenditures are zero-sum, domestic political issue. Resources spent on defense are not available for other programs like social welfare programs which have strong domestic constituents.

23. For a critique of these explanations, there is an extensive literature on "cheap talk." For example, see James Johnson, "Is Talk Really Cheap? Prompting Conversation between Critical Theory and Rational Choice," *The American Political Science Review*, Vol. 87, No. 1, March 1993, pp. 74-86.

24. Joseph Jupille, James A. Caporaso, and Jeffrey T. Checkel, *Comparative Political Studies*, Vol. 36, No. 1/2, February-March 2003, p. 21.

25. This study used the domain of application model, as discussed by Jupille, Caporaso, and Checkel to determine the best approach to the research question at hand. See *ibid*.

26. *Ibid.*, p. 8.

27. "NATO—Information, News, and Pictures," *The Wall Street Journal Online*, February 6, 2012, available from *online.wsj.com/article*.

28. "National Security Strategy," Washington, DC: The White House, May 2010, p. 34.

29. Jamie Shea, Director of Policy Planning, interview by author, January 31, 2008, NATO Headquarters, Brussels, Belgium.

30. "National Security Strategy," p. 47.

31. Julian E. Barnes, "U.S. to Cut Forces in Europe," *The Wall Street Journal*, January 13, 2012, available from *online.wsj.com/article*.

32. "NATO 2020: Assured Security; Dynamic Engagement," Brussels, Belgium: NATO, May 17, 2010, p. 8.

33. *Ibid.*, p. 10.

34. "ISAF Placement," Brussels, Belgium: NATO, June 6, 2011.

35. Kolinda Grabar-Kitarovic,Croatia's Ambassador to the United States, "Remarks at the acceptance of the Instruments of Accession to the North Atlantic Treaty," April 1, 2009, available from *www.state.gov/s/d/2009/121233.htm*.

36. Phillip R. Cuccia, *Implications of a Changing NATO*, Carlisle, PA: Strategic Studies Institute, U.S. Army War College, May 2010, p. 6, available from *www.StrategicStudiesInstitute.army.mil/*.

37. "NATO 2020," p. 10.

38. Elisabeth Bumiller and Thom Shanker, "Panetta to Offer Strategy for Cutting Military Budget," *The New York Times*, January 2, 2012, available from *www.nytimes.com*.

39. Some nations are already scaling down non-NATO contributions. For example, Poland's Defense Minister Bogdan Klich announced on February 4, 2009, that Poland would "end its military missions in Lebanon, the Golan Heights, and Chad as part of the government's plan to cut spending in response to the global economic crisis." See "Poland to End Three Military Missions," *The Warsaw Voice Online*, February 5, 2009, available from *www.warsawvoice.pl/newsX.php/6999/2549017099/printVer/*.

40. Cuccia, p. 6.

41. Kori Schake, posting on the Expert Blogs, "NATO at 60: Birthday Party or Funeral," *National Journal*, March 30, 2009, available from *security.nationaljournal.com/2009/03/nato-at-60-birthday-party-or-f.php*.

CHAPTER 7

SELECTED BIBLIOGRAPHY

Joel R. Hillison

Adamczak, Colonel Janusz. Interview by author, June 5, 2007, U.S. Army War College, Carlisle Barracks, PA.

AFSOUTH. "SFOR Air Component," AFSOUTH Fact Sheets, NATO, August 18, 2003. Available from *www.afsouth.nato.int/factsheets/SFORAirComponent.htm* (accessed on January 7, 2008).

_____. "Operation Deliberate Force." AFSOUTH Fact Sheets, NATO, August 18, 2003. Available from *www.afsouth.nato.int/factsheets/DeliberateForceFactSheet.htm* (accessed on January 7, 2008).

_____. "Operation Deny Flight." AFSOUTH Fact Sheets, NATO, July 18, 2003. Available from *www.afsouth.nato.int/operations/denyflight/DenyFlightFactSheet.htm* (accessed on January 7, 2008).

Anderson, Neil, and Ute-Christine Klehe. "Working Hard and Working Smart: Motivation and Ability during Typical and Maximum Performance." *Journal of Applied Psychology*, Vol. 92, No. 4, 2007, p. 978.

Anonymous (NATO official speaking on background). Based on interviews conducted February 1, 2008, at SHAPE Headquarters, Mons, Belgium.

Anonymous (Senior Diplomat and Member of the NATO International Staff). Interview by author, January 31, 2008, NATO Headquarters, Brussels, Belgium.

Ashton, Kimberly. "Czech Troops to remain in Iraq." *The Prague Post Online*, October 17, 2007. Available from *www.praguepost.com/articles/2007/10/17/czech-troops-to-remain-in-iraq/print* (accessed January 24, 2008).

Asiedu, Dita. "NATO's Six Years of Dramatic Change—How Has the Czech Republic Fared?" *Český rozhlas 7* (Radio Praha), March 11, 2005. Available from *www.radio.cz/en/article/64286* (accessed March 25, 2009).

Avdiaj, Colonel Vladimir. Interview by author, January 28, 2010, U.S. Army War College, Carlisle Barracks, PA.

Axelrod, Robert. *The Evolution of Cooperation.* New York: Basic Books, 1984.

Axelrod, Robert, and Robert O. Keohane. "Achieving Cooperation under Anarchy." In *Cooperation under Anarchy*, edited by Kenneth A. Oye, Princeton, NJ: Princeton University Press, 1986.

Bachman, Ronald D. *Romania: A Country Study.* Washington, DC: Government Printing Office (GPO) for the Library of Congress, 1989. Available from *countrystudies.us/romania/* (accessed November 11, 2008).

Baczynska, Gabriela. "Polish Troops May Train, Not Fight in Iraq." *Reuters*, November 19, 2007. Available from *www.reuters. com/articlePrint?articleID=USL1964979720071119* (accessed November 19, 2007).

Banks, Arthur, William Overstreet, and Thomas Muller, *Political Handbook of the World 2007*, Washington, DC: CQ Press, 2007.

Barnett, Thomas P. M. *Romanian and East German Policies in the Third World.* London, UK: Praeger Publishing, 1992.

Barno, Lieutenant General (Retired) David W. (former Commander, Operation Enduring Freedom and Director, NESA Center at National Defense University). Interview by author at Carlisle Barracks, PA, on January 25, 2008.

Benko, Colonel Tibor. *Hungary: From Warsaw Pact to NATO.* Strategy Research Project, Carlisle Barracks, PA: U.S. Army War College, 2001.

Bisogneiro, Claudio, Deputy Secretary General of NATO. Interview by author, January 31, 2008, Brussels, Belgium.

Biró, István. "The National Security Strategy and Transformation of the Hungarian Defense Forces," U.S. Army War College Strategy Research Paper, 2005. Available from *handle.dtic. mil/100.2/ADA432740* (accessed November 12, 2008).

Boyer, Mark A. ""Trading Public Goods in the Western Alliance System," *Journal of Conflict Resolution*, No. 33, 1989.

_____.*International Cooperation and Public Goods*, London, UK: Johns Hopkins University Press, 1993.

Bozo, Colonel Tibor. "Hungary a Member of NATO," Strategy Research Project, Carlisle Barracks, PA: U.S. Army War College, 2003.

Bräuninger, Thomas. "A Partisan Model of Government Expenditure." *Public Choice* 125, No. 3-4, 2005, pp. 409-429.

_____."Partisan Veto players, Party Preferences, and the Composition of Government Expenditures." *Annual meeting of Public Choice Society.* Nashville, TN, 2002.

Breunig, Christian. "The More Things Change, the More Things Stay the Same: A Comparative Analysis of Budget Punctuations." *Journal of European Public Policy*, Vol. 13, No. 7, 2006.

Burant, Stephan R. *Hungary: A Country Study.* (Washington, DC: GPO, the U.S. Library of Congress, 1989). Available from *countrystudies.us/hungary/35.htm* (accessed November 11, 2008).

Central Intelligence Agency. "World Factboook," 2008. Available from *https://www.cia.gov/library/publications/the-world-factbook/index.html.*

Checkel, Jeffrey. "International Institutions and Socialization in Europe: Introduction and Framework." *International Organization*, Vol. 59, No. 4, 2005.

Ciocoiu, Lieutenant Colonel Nicolae-Stefan Z. *Romanian Armed Forces Transformation Process – The Core Issue of the National Military Strategy Towards NATO Integration,* Strategic Research Project, Carlisle Barracks, PA: U.S. Army War College, 2004. Available from *www.dtic.mil* (accessed November 14, 2008).

Clark, General Wesley K. *Waging Modern War.* New York: Public Affairs, 2001.

Congressional Budget Office. "NATO Burdensharing after Enlargement." Washington, DC: Congress of the United States, August 2001. Available from *www.cbo.gov/showdoc.cfm?index=297 6&sequence=2&from=0* (accessed November 13, 2006).

Congressional Research Service (CRS), Report RL33110. "The Cost of Iraq, Afghanistan, and Other Global War on Terror Operations since 9/11," July 14, 2008. Available from *www.fas.org/sgp/ crs/natsec/RL33110.pdf* (accessed August 11, 2008).

Conybeare, John. "Public Goods, Prisoners' Dilemmas and the International Political Economy." *International Studies Quarterly,* 1984.

Council on Foreign Relations, *Political Handbook of the World,* New York: McGraw-Hill, 1975-2007.

Craddock, General John (Supreme Allied Commander Europe). Interview by author, SHAPE Headquarters, Mons, Belgium, 1 February 2008.

Crawley, Vince. "NATO Faces Challenge in Pakistan Earthquake Response." Bureau of International Information Programs. *The Washington File,* Washington, DC: U.S. Department of State, November 16, 2005. Available from *www.globalsecurity. org/military/library/news/2005/11/mil-051116-usia03.htm* (accessed September 21, 2008).

Curry, Andrew. "Will Poland Split EU over Russia Policy?" *Spiegel Online International,* August 18, 2008. Available from *www.spiegel.de/international/europe/0,1518,572105,00.html* (accessed December 14, 2008).

Curtis, Glenn E. "Poland: A Country Study," Washington, DC: GPO, the U.S. Library of Congress, 1992. Available from *countrystudies.us/poland/89.htm* (accessed November 11, 2008).

Czech Ministry of Defense. "Current Deployments." Available from *www.army.cz/scripts/detail.php?id=6527* (accessed January 6, 2009).

_____. "General Information for Visiting this Website." Available from *www.army.cz/scripts/detail.php?pgid=122* (accessed November 12, 2008).

_____. "MOD History of Czech Military Operations Abroad (1990-2007)." Available from *www.army.cz/scripts/detail.php?id=5717* (accessed September 21, 2008).

_____. "NATO Operation 'Joint Enterprise' in Kosovo." Available from *www.army.cz/scripts/detail.php?id=6527* (accessed November 12, 2008).

_____. "Personnel Size in 1993-2008," undated. Available from *www.army.cz/scripts/detail.php?id=5770* (accessed December 15, 2008.)

"Czech Oppose More Afghan Deployments." *Angus Reid Global Monitor*, October 12, 2008. Available from *www.angus-reid.com/polls/view/31995* (accessed November 21, 2008).

"Defence Budget, Poland." *Jane's Sentinel Security Assessment*, August 6, 2008. Available from *www8.janes.com* (accessed November 5, 2008).

Degeratu, Claudia. "Civil-Military Relations in Romania," In *Civil-Military Relations in South Eastern Europe*, edited by Plamen Pantev, Sofia, Bulgaria: Institute for Security and International Studies, 2001.

Deni, John R., *The Future of American Landpower: Does Forward Presence Still Matter? The Case of the Army in Europe.* Monograph, Carlisle, PA: Strategic Studies Institute, U.S. Army War College, October 2012.

Downs, Anthony. *An Economic Theory of Democracy*. Boston, MA: Addison-Wesley, 1957.

Economist.com. "Country Briefings," undated. Available from *www.economist.com/countries/* (accessed 21 August 2007).

Erlanger, Steven and Steven Lee Myers. "NATO Allies Oppose Bush on Georgia and Ukraine." *New York Times*, April 3, 2008. Available from *www.nytimes.com/2008/04/03/world/europe/03nato. html?8au&emc=au* (accessed April 3, 2008).

"Estonian Central Bank Announces Budget Deficit." *The Baltic Times*, October 23, 2008. Available from *www.baltictimes. com/news/articles/21624/* (accessed November 20, 2008)

Estonian Ministry of Defense. "Public Opinion and National Defence, March 2005." Research Centre Faktum, Tallinn, Estonia: March 2005. Available from *www.kmin.ee/static/sisu/ files/2005-04-25_Kmin_eng_parandatud.pdf* (accessed November 5, 2008).

_____. "Support for NATO Membership." Tallinn, Estonia: December 15, 2005. Available from *www.vm.ee/eng/nato/ kat_359/1007.html* (accessed November 5, 2008).

Estonian Ministry of Foreign Affiars, "Economy at a Glance," Tallinn, Estonia: October 10, 2008. Available from *www.vm.ee/ estonia/kat_398/pea_172/281.html* (accessed November 5, 2008).

"Estonia Public debt." *Index Mundi*, undated. Available from *www.indexmundi.com/estonia/public_debt.html* (accessed November 20, 2008).

Europa. "The History of the European Union." undated. Available from *europa.eu/abc/history/2000_today/index_en.htm* (accessed November 20, 2008).

Europa Publications. *Western Europe*, London, UK: Routledge, 1989-2009.

_____. *Central and South Eastern Europe*, London, UK: Routledge, 2001-09.

"Europe Uneasy over Russian Plans to Deploy Missiles." *Deutsche-Welte*, November 6, 2008. Available from *www.dw-world.de/dw/article/0,2144,3768711,00.html* (accessed November 14, 2008).

European Union. "Capabilities Improvement chart II/2005." Press Release 14729/05 (Presse 307), Brussels, Belgium, November 21, 2005. Available from *europa.eu* (accessed November 5, 2008).

_____. "Europa Glossary," Brussels, Belgium, undated. Available from *europa.eu/scadplus/glossary/european_security_ defence_policy_en.htm* (accessed November 5, 2008).

Fearon, James, and Alexander Wendt. "Rationalism v. Constructivism: A Skeptical View." In *Handbook of International Relations*, edited by Walter Carlsnaes, Thomas Risse, and Beth Simmons, London, UK: Sage Publications, 2002.

Fidler, Stephen, and Boone, Jon. "Fields of Little Glory: NATO Begins to Scale Back Its Afghan Ambitions." *Financial Times*, November 18, 2007.

Flowers, Sergeant Claude. "CENTCOM Public Affairs 2006-07-27." Ministry of National Defense: Warsaw, Republic of Poland, July 27, 2006. Available from *www.mon.gov.pl/en/artykul/2100* (accessed January 18, 2008).

Foertsch, Hartmut; Imre Karacsony; Svetozar Nadovic; and Zdzislaw Ostrowski, *The Great Withdrawal*. Bratislava, Slovak Republic: Ministry of Defence, 2005.

Fogli, Larry, Paul R. Sackett, and Sheldon Zedeck. "Relations Between Measures of Typical and Maximum Job Performance." *Journal of Applied Psychology*, Vol. 73, No. 3 (1988), pp. 482-486.

Forster, Peter K., and Stephen J. Cimbala. *The US, NATO and Military Burden-Sharing*. New York: Frank Cass, 2005.

Forsterling, Friedrich. *Attribution: An Introduction to Theories, Research and Applications*. East Sussex, UK: Psychology Press, 2001.

Freedom House. "Comparative Scores for All Countries from 1973 to 2008." 2008. Available from *www.freedomhouse.org/template.cfm?page=15* (accessed November 15, 2008).

Fritz-Assmus, Dieter, and Klaus Zimmermann. "West German Demand for Defence Spending," In *The Economics of Defense Spending*, edited by Keith Hartley and Todd Sandler, London, UK: Routledge, 1990.

Gallis, Paul. "NATO in Afghanistan: A Test of the Transatlantic Alliance." Washington, DC: Congressional Research Service, July 16, 2007.

Gates, William R., and Katsuaki L. Terasawa, "Reconsidering Publicness in Alliance Defence Expenditures: NATO Expansion and Burden Sharing," *Journal of Defence and Peace Economics*, October 2003.

Gawdiak, Ihor, ed. *Czechoslovakia: A Country Study*. Washington, DC: GPO, the Library of Congress, 1987. Available from *countrystudies.us/czech-republic/* (accessed November 11, 2008).

General Accounting Office, Report GAO/NSIAD-98-172,"NATO: History of Common Funded Cost Shares." May 1998. Available from *www.gao.gov/archive/1998/ns98172.pdf* (accessed May 13, 2010).

_____. Report GAO-08-423R, "Global War on Terrorism: Reported Obligations for the Department of Defense," January 30, 2008. Available from *www.gao.gov/new.items/d08423r.pdf* (accessed August 11, 2008).

German Marshall Fund of the United States and the Compagnia di San Paolo. "Transatlantic Trends 2003: Key Findings." 2003. Available from *www.transatlantictrends.org/trends/doc/2003_english_key.pdf* (accessed November 11, 2008).

Gheciu, Alexandra. "Security Institutions as Agents of Socialization? NATO and the New Europe." *International Organization*, Vol. 59, 2005.

Global Security. "Iraq Coalition Troops, February 2007." Available from *www.globalsecurity.org/military/ops/iraq_orbat_coalition.htm* (accessed September 21, 2008).

_____. "Russian Military Budget Expenditures." Available from *www.globalsecurity.org/military/world/russia/mo-budget-expenditures.htm* (accessed September 21, 2008).

Golden, James R. *The Dynamics of Change in NATO: A Burden-Sharing Perspective.* New York: Praeger Publishing, 1983.

Goldsmith, Benjamin E. "Bearing the Defense of Burden, 1886-1989," *Journal of Conflict Resolution*, Vol. 47, No. 5, (2003).

Goldstein, Avery. "Discounting the Free Ride: Alliances and Security in the Postwar World." *International Organization*, Vol. 49, No. 1 (1995).

Gordon, Lincoln, "Economic Aspects of Coalition Diplomacy—The NATO Experience." *International Organization*, Vol. 10 (1956).

Gordon, Michael R. "The 2000 Campaign: The Military; Bush Would Stop U.S. Peacekeeping in Balkan Fights." *New York Times*, October 21, 2000, Available from *query.nytimes.com* (accessed January 18, 2008).

Grabar-Kitarovic, Kolinda (Croatia's Ambassador to the United States), "Remarks at the Acceptance of the Instruments of Accession to the North Atlantic Treaty," April 1, 2009. Available from *www.state.gov/s/d/2009/121233.htm* (accessed April 3, 2009).

Hallams, Ellen. *A Transatlantic Bargain for the 21st Century: The United States, Europe, and the Transatlantic Alliance.* Monograph, Carlisle, PA: Strategic Studies Institute, U.S. Army War College, September 2013.

Hartley, Keith, and Todd Sandler. *The Economics of Defense.* London, UK: Routledge, 1995.

_____. *The Political Economy of NATO.* New York: Cambridge University Press, 1999.

Hasenclever, Andreas, Peter Mayer, and Volker Rittberger. *Theories of International Regimes.* Cambridge, UK: Cambridge University Press, 1997.

Hendrickson, Ryan C. "The Miscalculation of NATO's Death." *Parameters* (Spring 2007).

Hibbs, Douglas. "Political Parties and Macroeconomic Policy." *American Political Science Review,* Vol. 71 (1977).

Hillison, Joel R., *New NATO Members: Security Consumers or Producers?* Monograph, , Carlisle, PA: Strategic Studies Institute, U.S. Army War College, April 2009.

Hooper, John and Ian Black. "Anger at Rumsfeld Attack on 'Old Europe'." *The Guardian,* January 24, 2003. Available from *www.guardian.co.uk/world/2003/jan/24/germany.france* (accessed January 16, 2009).

de Hoop Scheffer, Jaap (Secretary General of NATO). "Romanian President Visit." *NATOchannel.tv,* June 3, 2008. Available from *www.natochannel.tv/default.aspx?aid=2645&lid=315* (accessed November 18, 2008).

_____. "Statement by the Secretary General on enhanced NATO assistance for Pakistan." NATO Press Release 2005(134), October 21, 2005. Available from *www.nato.int/docu/pr/2005/p05-134e.htm* (accessed September 21, 2008).

Hungarian Ministry for Foreign Affairs. *The National Security Strategy of the Republic of Hungary.* Budapest, Hungary, undated. Available from *www.mfa.gov.hu/kum/en/bal/foreign_policy/security_policy/national_sec_strategy_of_hun.htm* (accessed December 15, 2008).

"Hungary Ups Defence Expenses," *Budapest Sun Online,* October 15, 2008. Available from *www.budapestsun.com/cikk.php?id=28870* (accessed November 5, 2008).

International Institute for Strategic Studies. *The Military Balance.* London, UK: Routledge, 1977-2007.

International Monetary Fund. "Reports for Selected Countries and Subjects." *World Economic Outlook Database*, (April 2008), Available from *www.imf.org* (accessed November 5, 2008).

_____. "Estonia-2007 Article IV Consultation Concluding Statement of the IMF Mission." May 14, 2007. Available from *www.imf.org/external/np/ms/2007/051407.htm* (accessed November 6, 2008).

"Iraq and Afghanistan: Involvement of the Polish Military, June 2007." *World Opinion Update*, Vol. 31, No. 5 (2007).

Islamic Republic News Agency (IRNA). "Pakistan: Italian Engineers to Join NATO Forces in Kashmir." Available on *Relief Web*, December 2, 2005. Available from *www.reliefweb.int/rw/rwb.nsf/db900sid/VBOL-6JPE8W?OpenDocument* (accessed March 25, 2009).

Janes. "Defence Budget, Poland." *Jane's Sentinel Security Assessment*, August 6, 2008. Available from *www8.janes.com* (accessed November 5, 2008).

Janicek, Karel."Czech Lawmakers Do Not Extend Afghanistan Mission." *Miami Herald*, December 19, 2008. Available from *www.miamiherald.com/news/world/AP/story/819725.html* (accessed December 29, 2008). Article is no longer available on Miami Herald website.

Johnston, Alastair Iain. "Conclusions and Extensions: Toward Mid-Range Theorizing and Beyond Europe." *International Organization*, Vol. 59 (2005).

_____. "Treating International Institutions as Social Environments." *International Studies Quarterly*, Vol. 45, No. 1 (2001).

Jun, Dominik. "The Long Shadow of the Munich Agreement." *Radio Praha*, September 30, 2008. Available from *www.radio.cz/en/article/108781* (accessed November 11, 2008).

Jupille, Joseph, James A. Caporaso, and Jeffrey T. Checkel. "Integrating Institutions: Rationalism, Constructivism, and the Study of the European Union." *Comparative Political Studies*, Vol. 36, No. 1 (2003).

Jurgaitis, Colonel Antanas. Interview by author, January 28 2008, Supreme Headquarters Allied Powers Europe (SHAPE), Mons, Belgium.

Kaoidume, Lieutenant Colonel Kalev Interview by author, January 28, 2008, SHAPE Headquarters, Mons, Belgium.

Kaufman, Robert, R., "Market Reform and Social Protection: Lessons from the Czech Republic, Hungary, and Poland," *East European Politics and Societies*, Vol. 21, No. 1 (2007).

Kelley, Judith. "International Actors on the Domestic Scene: Membership Conditionality and Socialization by International Institutions." *International Organization*, Vol. 58 (2004).

Keohane, Robert O. *After Hegemony: Cooperation and Discord in the World Political Economy*. Princeton, NJ: Princeton University Press, 1984.

_____. "International Institutions: Can Interdependence work?" *Foreign Policy*, No. 110 (Spring 1998) pp. 82-96.

King, Gary, Robert O. Keohane, and Sidney Verba. *Designing Social Inquiry*. Princeton, NJ: Princeton University Press, 1994.

Kiss, Tamás S. "NATO and PM in Talks Over Funding." *Budapest Sun Online*, October 28, 2004. Available from *www.budapest-sun.com/cikk.php?id=14018* (accessed November 12, 2008).

_____. "Suspend America Says, 'Thank you'." *Budapest Sun Online*, October 28, 2004. Available from *www.budapest-sun.com/cikk.php?id=14018* (accessed on March 28, 2008).

Klich, Bogdan (Polish Minister of National Defence). "Europe-NATO-American Perspectives of Partnership." Speech given at the Forum on Euro-Atlantic Security, Krakow, October 23-24, 2008. Recording provided by Nathan Harig, Jagiellonian University, Krakow, Poland.

Klingemann, Hans-dieter, Richard I. Hofferbert, and Ian Budge. *Parties, Policies, and Democracy.* Oxford, UK: Westview Press, 1994.

Kopecky, Colonel Josef. Interview by author, November 6, 2008, Washington, DC: National Defense University, Ft. McNair.

Kosovo Force (KFOR). NATO graphic available from *www. nato.int/kfor/structur/nations/placemap/kfor_placemat.pdf* (accessed September 21, 2008).

Kr[alev, Nicholas and Borowiec, Andrew. "Warsaw Ups Ante for U.S. Shield." *Washington Times,* January 16, 2008. Available from *www.washingtontimes.com/news/2008/jan/16/warsaw-ups-ante-for-us-shield/* (accessed January 16, 2008).

Krebs, Ronald. "Perverse Institutionalism: NATO and the Greco-Turkish Conflict," *International Organization*, Vol. 53, No. 2 (1999).

Kupchan, Charles A. "NATO and the Persian Gulf: Examing Intra-Alliance Behavior." *International Organization*, Vol. 42, No. 2 (1988).

Lang, Rein (Estonian Foreign Minister). "Address by Foreign Minister Rein Lang at the celebration of the first anniversary of Estonia's NATO accession." Tallinn, Estonia, April 4, 2005. Available from *www.vm.ee/eng/nato/aken_prindi/5363.html* (accessed November 5, 2008).

Larrabee, Stephen F. "Soviet Crisis Management in Eastern Europe." In *The Warsaw Pact: Alliance in Transition,* edited by David Holloway and Jane M. O. Sharp. Ithaca, NY: Cornell University Press, 1984.

Lepgold, Joseph. "NATO's Post-Cold War Collective Action Problem." *International Security,* Vol. 23, No. 1 (1998).

Lipson, Charles. "Why are some International Agreements Informal." *International Organization*, Vol. 45, No. 4 (1991).

Ljunggren, David. "Poland Raps NATO Members Over Afghan Commitments." *Reuters,* February 4, 2008. Available from *www.reuters.com/article/topNews/idUSN0458791220080204* (accessed February 13, 2008).

Looney, Robert E. and Stephen L. Mehay. "United States Defence Expenditures: Trends and Analysis." In *The Economics of Defense Spending,* edited by Keith Hartley and Todd Sandler, London, UK: Routledge, 1990.

Mandelbaum, Michael. *The Fate of Nations: The Search for National Security in the Nineteenth and Twentieth Centuries,* Cambridge, UK: Cambridge University Press, 1988.

Mansager, Colonel Tucker (Executive Officer to the Supreme Allied Commander Europe). Based on interviews conducted January 28, 2008, at SHAPE Headquarters, Mons, Belgium.

March, James G. and Johan P. Olsen. "The Institutional Dynamics of International Political Orders." *International Organization,* Vol. 52, No. 4, (1998). As cited in Thomas Risse, "Let's Argue!: Communicative Action in World Politics," *International Organization,* Vol. 54, No. 1 (2000) pp. 1-39.

Majman, Slawomir. "Why Poland is in Iraq." *The Warsaw Voice Online.* September 11, 2003. Available from *www.warsawvoice.pl/printArticle.php?a=3423* (accessed January 4, 2008).

McColl, General Sir John (Deputy Supreme Allied Commander Europe). Interview by author, February 1 2008, SHAPE Headquarters, Mons, Belgium.

"Military Involvement in Iraq and Afghanistan, October 2007." *World Opinion Update* Vol. 32, No. 1 (2008).

Milovan, Adriano. "Under the Security Umbrella: 60% of World's GDP is created." *PV International,* No. 0016 (March 31, 2008). Available from *www.privredni.hr/pvint/PVI0016.pdf* (accessed April 10, 2008).

Milner, Helen V., and Robert O. Keohane. *Internatinalization and Domestic Politics.* Cambridge, UK: Cambridge University Press, 1996.

Mirr, Colonel (Ret.) Steven, former military aide to General Jones and Director of the Defense Operations Division, U.S. Delegation to NATO. Based on interviews conducted on January 31, 2008, at NATO Headquarters, Brussels, Belgium.

"Misiones Internacionales." *Revista Espanola de Defensa*, Vol. 18, No. 214 (December 2005).

Moravcsik, Andrew. "Taking Preferences Seriously: A Liberal Theory of International Politics." *International Organization*, Vol. 51 (1997).

Mosley, Layna. "Private Governance for the Public Good? Exploring Private Sector Participation in Global Financial Regulation." Paper prepared for a Festschrift in Honor of Robert O. Keohane Conference at Princeton University, Princeton, NJ, 2005.

Murdoch, James C., and Todd Sandler. "Controversy: Alternative Approaches to the Study of Alliance Burden Sharing. "*International Studies Quarterly*, Vol. 35 (1991).

_____. "Nash-Cournot or Lindahl Behavior? An Empirical Test for the NATO Allies." *Quarterly Journal of Economics*, Vol. 105 (1990).

_____. "NATO Burden Sharing and the Forces of Change." *International Studies Quarterly*, Vol. 25 (1991).

NATO. "Comprehensive Political Guidance." *NATO Online Library*, November 29, 2006. Available from *www.nato.int/docu/basictxt/b061129e.htm* (accessed December 6, 2008).

NATO. "Membership Action Plan." Press Release NAC-S(99)66, April 24, 1999. Available from *www.fas.org/man/nato/natodocs/99042460.htm* (accessed November 5, 2008).

_____. "National Commitments to Operations and Missions." Czech Republic, Available from *www.nato.int/issues/commitment/docs/080730-czech.pdf* (accessed November 21, 2008).

_____. "National Commitments to operations and missions." Hungary, Available from *www.nato.int/issues/commitment/docs/080325-hungary.pdf* (accessed November 21, 2008).

_____. "National Commitments to operations and missions." Poland, Available from *www.nato.int/issues/commitment/docs/080730-czech.pdf* (accessed November 21, 2008).

_____. "NATO-Russia Compendium of Financial and Economic Data Relating to Defence." Iinformation for press, NATO Headquarters, December 20, 2007. Available from *www.nato.int/issues/defence_expenditures/index.html* (accessed November 11, 2008).

NATO Allied Command Operations. "All NATO Countries Contribute to Pakistan Relief." February 28, 2006. Available from *www.nato.int/shape/news/2005/pakistan_contributions.htm* (accessed September 21, 2008).

_____. "The Last NATO Cargo Shipment Arrived in the United States," *SHAPE News.* October 4, 2005. Available from *www.nato.int/SHAPE/news/2005/10/051005b.htm* (accessed October 23, 2008).

_____. "NATO Launches Response Force." October 15, 2003. Available from *www.nato.int/shape/news/2003/10/i031015.htm* (accessed January 27, 2009).

_____. "The NATO Response Force." Available from *www.nato.int/shape/issues/shape_nrf/nrf_intro.htm* (accessed September 21, 2008).

_____. "NATO Response Force Continues Relief Effort," *SHAPE News.* September 6, 2005. Available from *www.nato.int/SHAPE/news/2005/09/050914a.htm* (accessed October 23, 2008).

_____. "NATO Response Force Q & A's." Available from *www.nato.int/shape/issues/shape_nrf/nrf_q_a.htm* (accessed September 21, 2008).

NATO Euro-Atlantic Disaster Response Coordination Center (EADRCC), Daily Situation Reports. *Earthquake Pakistan, Final Sit-*

uation Report No. 23. Brussels, Belgium: NATO, February 15, 2006. Available from *www.nato.int/eadrcc/2005/pakistan/060215-final.pdf* (accessed on March 25, 2009).

NATO Information for Press, "NATO-Russia Compendium of Financial and Economic Data Relating to Defence," 1977-2013. Available from *www.nato.int/issues/defence_expenditures/index.html* (accessed May 2, 2014).

_____. Press Release NAC-S(99)66, "Membership Action Plan," NATO. April 24, 1999. Available from *www.fas.org/man/nato/natodocs/99042460.htm* (accessed November 5, 2008).

_____. "National Commitments to Operations and Missions." Available from *www.nato.int/issues/commitment/docs/080730-czech.pdf* (accessed November 21, 2008).

_____. NATO News, "Estonian President Visits NATO," February 4 2008. Available from *152.152.94.201/docu/update/2008/02-february/e0204a.html* (accessed November 21, 2008).

NATO, ISAF. "International Security Assistance Force and Afghan National Army strength & laydown." 2006-2008. Available from *www.nato.int/isaf/docu/epub/pdf/isaf_placemat.pdf* (accessed September 21, 2008).

NATO Public Diplomacy Division. *NATO Handbook.* Brussels, Belgium: NATO, 2001. Available from *www.nato.int/docu/handbook/2001/hb020201.htm* (accessed September 21, 2008).

_____. Public Diplomacy Division, *NATO Handbook* (Brussels, Belgium: NATO, 2006).

Nuland, Victoria (U.S. Ambassador to NATO). "Ambassador Discusses Security Issues on Eve of NATO Ministerial." Webchat on December 5, 2007. Available from *www.america.gov/st/wash file-english/2007/December/20071205163651eaifas0.8371393.html* (accessed on February 27, 2008).

Nyirády, Kenneth E., *Hungary: A Country Study.* Washington, DC: GPO, the Library of Congress, 1989. Available from *lcweb2.loc.gov/cgi-bin/query/r?frd/cstdy:@field(DOCID+hu0195).*

Ojuland, Kristiina (Estonian Foreign Minister). "Address by Foreign Minister at the flag-raising ceremony at NATO Headquarters." April 2, 2004. Available from *www.vm.ee/eng/nato/kat_360/4385.html* (accessed November 5, 2008).

Olson, Mancur, Jr., *The Logic of Collective Action: Public Goods and the Theory of Groups.* Rev. Ed. New York: Schocken Books, 1971.

Olson, Mancur, Jr., and Richard Zeckhauser. "An Economic Theory of Alliances." *Review of Economics and Statistics*, Vol. 38 (1966), pp. 266-279.

Oneal, John R. "The Theory of Collective Action and Burden Sharing in NATO." *International Organization*, Vol. 44, No. 3 (1990).

Oneal, John R., and Mark A. Elrod. "NATO Burden Sharing and the Forces of Change." *International Studies Quarterly*, Vol. 33 (1989).

Ormisson, Tonis. "Public Opinion and National Defence, July 2007." Tallinn, Estonia: Ministry of Defence, 2008. Available from *www.mod.gov.ee/static/sisu/files/ENG_NATO_report_2007_06-summary.pdf* (accessed November 5, 2008).

Organization for Economic Co-Operation and Development. Stat Extracts, "Country Statistical Profiles," Available from *stats.oecd.org/wbos/viewhtml.aspx?queryname=460&querytype=view&lang=en* (accessed November 5, 2008).

_____. "Society at a Glance," 2007. Available from www.oecd.org/dataoecd/12/7/38138100.xls (accessed 5 November 2008).

_____. "Conference on Security and Co-operation in Europe Final Act,"1975. Available from *www.osce.org/documents/mcs/1975/08/4044_en.pdf* (accessed July 30, 2008).

_____. "History of the OSCE," *OSCE Handbook*, October 11, 2007. Available from *www.osce.org/publications/sg/2007/10/22286_955_en.pdf* (accessed July 30, 2008).

Oye, Kenneth A. "Explaining Cooperation under Anarchy: Hypotheses and Strategies." *World Politics*, Vol. 38, No. 1, 1985.

"Pakistan Earthquake Relief Operations: MOD Assistance Provided to the Relief Effort." Fact sheet, undated. London, UK: Ministry of Defence. Available from *www.mod.uk/DefenceInternet/ FactSheets/OperationsFactsheets/PakistanEarthquakeReliefOperation- sModAssistanceProvidedToTheReliefEffort.htm* (accessed September 21, 2008).

"Poland Withdraws Troops from Iraq." *The Warsaw Voice On- line*, October 6 2008. Available from *www.warsawvoice.pl/newsX. php/6999/2549017099/printVer/* (accessed October 7, 2008).

Romanian Ministry of National Defense, "Briefing of Highest- Ranked Authorities of MoND and Polish Armed Forces," Avail- able from *www.wp.mil.pl/en/artyku/4601* (accessed November 18, 2008).

Paet, Urmas (Estonian Foreign Minister). "Estonia's Contri- bution to Rebuilding Afghanistan." Speech to Riigikogu, Tallinn, Estonia, November 15, 2006. Available from *www.vm.ee/eng/nato/ aken_prindi/7913.html* (accessed November 5, 2008).

"Poland Revising Budget, But Holding Planned Deficit Steady." *The Warsaw Voice Online*, November 20, 2008. Available from *www.warsawvoice.pl/newsX.php/7311/2549017099* (accessed November 20, 2008).

"Poland Spurns U.S. Air Defense Offer." *Los Angeles Times*. July 5, 2008. Available from *www.latimes.com/news/nationworld/ world/la-fg-poland5-2008jul05,0,1045291.story?track=ntothtml* (accessed March 25, 2009).

"Poland Withdraws Troops from Iraq." *The Warsaw Voice On- line*, October 6, 2008. Available from *www.warsawvoice.pl/newsX. php/6999/2549017099/printVer/* (accessed October 7, 2008).

Polish Ministry for National Defense. "Basic Information on the MOND Budget for 2007," Available from *www.wp.mil.pl/en/ strona/126/LG_89* (accessed on November 4, 2008).

_____. "Briefing of Highest-Ranked Authorities of MoND and Polish Armed Forces." April 2, 2008. Available from *www.wp.mil.pl/en/artyku/4601* (accessed November 18, 2008).

Polish Press Agency. "Polish Premier Starts Visit to Afghanistan." August 22, 2008. U.S. Open Source Center. Available from *https://www.opensource.gov* (accessed November 4, 2008).

_____. Poland Sends First Two Helicopters for Afghan Contingent." August 4, 2008. U.S. Open Source Center. Available from *https://www.opensource.gov* (accessed November 4, 2008).

"President and Prime Minister Bickering Again over Foreign Policy." *The Warsaw Voice Online*, 12 December 2007. Available from *www.warsawvoice.pl/newsX.php/5359/2549017099/printVer/* (accessed January 4, 2008).

Rice, Condoleezza., *"Defense Burden-Sharing,"* In *The Warsaw Pact: Alliance in Transition*, edited by David Holloway and Jane M. O. Sharp. Ithaca, NY: Cornell University Press, 1984.

Risse, Thomas. "Let's Argue!: Communicative Action in World Politics." *International Organization*, Vol. 54, No. 1, 2000.

Roman, Colonel Vasile V. Interview by author, December 11, 2007. Carlisle Barracks, PA: U.S. Army War College.

Roman, Colonel Vasile V. "From Partner to Ally — Romania's Interest and War on Terrorism." Strategy Research Project (Carlisle Barracks: U.S. Army War College, 2008). Available from *www. dtic.mil/cgi-bin/GetTRDoc?AD=ADA478505&Location=U2&doc=Ge tTRDoc.pdf* (accessed November 5, 2008).

"Romania." London, UK: Foreign and Commonwealth Office. May 22, 2007. Available from *www.fco.gov.uk/en/about-the-fco/country-profiles/europe/romania?profile=history&pg=3* (accessed November 5, 2008).

"Romania gets IMF emergency loan." *BBC News Online*, March 25, 2009. Available from *news.bbc.co.uk/2/hi/business/7962897.stm* (accessed March 25, 2009).

Romanian Ministry of Foreign Affairs, "Romania: An Active Ally within an Active and Solid Alliance," Available from *www.mae.ro/index.php?unde=doc&id=4995&idlnk=1&cat=3* (accessed November 5, 2008).

Romanian Ministry of National Defense. "Briefing of Highest-Ranked Authorities of MoND and Polish Armed Forces." Available from *www.wp.mil.pl/en/artyku/4601* (accessed November 18, 2008).

"Romania's Budget Deficit at 2.6 pct/GDP in 2007." *Romania News Watch*, February 29, 2008. Available from *www.romanianewswatch.com/2008/02/romanias-budget-deficit-at-26-pctgdp-in.html* (accessed November 5, 2008).

Russett, Bruce M. *What Price Vigilance? The Burdens of National Defense*. New Haven, CT: Yale University Press, 1970.

Sandler, Todd. "The Economic Theory of Alliances: A Survey." *Journal of Conflict Resolution*, 1993.

_____. "Impurity of Defense: An Application to the Economics of Alliances." *KYKLOS*, 1977.

_____. "NATO Burden Sharing: Rules or Reality?" In *Peace, Defence, and Economic Analysis*, edited by Christian Schmidt and Frank Backaby, London, UK: Macmillan, 1987.

Sandler, Todd, and John F. Forbes. "Burden Sharing, Strategy, and the Design of NATO." *Economic Inquiry*, Vol. 18, 1980.

Schake, Kori. posting on the Expert Blogs, "NATO at 60: Birthday Party or Funeral," *National Journal*, March 30, 2009. Available from *security.nationaljournal.com/2009/03/nato-at-60-birthday-party-or-f.php* (accessed April 1, 2009).

Schimmelfenning, Frank. "International Socialization in the New Europe: Rational Action in an Institutional Environment." *European Journal of International Relations*, Vol. 6, No. 1, 2000.

_____. "The Community Trap: Liberal Norms, Rhetorical Action, and the Eastern Enlargement of the European Union," *International Organization*, Vol. 55, 2001.

Sedlak, Major General Josef (Czech National Military Representative). Based on interviews conducted January 28, 2008, at the SHAPE Headquarters, Mons, Belgium.

Seguin, Barre R. "Why did Poland Choose the F-16?" Occasional Paper No. 11, Garmisch, Germany: George C. Marshall Center for Security Studies, June 2007.

Shea, Jamie, Director of Policy Planning NATO. Interview by author, January 31, 2008. Brussels, Belgium.

_____. "A NATO for the 21ST Century: Toward a New Strategic Concept," *Fletcher Forum World Affairs*, Vol. 31, No. 2 (Summer, 2007).

Sidor, Krzysztof. "The Changing Face of NATO." *Warsaw Voice Online*, June 15 2005. Available from *www.warsawvoice.pl/view/8663* (accessed on April 1, 2008).

Simonyi, Ambassador Andras. "Hungary in NATO—after Two Years of Membership." Speech to NATO, 2001. Available from *www.atlanticcommunity.org/Hungary%20in%20NATO.html* (accessed December 5, 2006).

Simon, Jeffrey. "The IFOR/SFOR Experience: Lessons Learned by PFP Partners." Institute for National Strategic Studies Strategic Forum, No. 120, Washington, DC: National Defense University, July 1997. Available from *www.ndu.edu/inss/strforum/SF120/forum120.html* (accessed November 18, 2008).

_____. "The New NATO Members: Will they contribute?" *Strategic Forum*, No. 160, Institute for National Strategic Studies, Washington, DC: National Defense University, April 1999. Available from *www.ndu.edu/inss/strforum/SF120/forum120.html* (accessed May 9, 2007).

_____. "NATO Expeditionary Operations: Impacts upon New Members and Partners." Occasional paper, Strategic Studies Institute, Washington, DC: National Defense University, March 2005.

Simon, Zoltan. "Hungary Pays with Growth Prospects for IMF–led Bailout Package." *Bloomberg.com*, October 29, 2008. Available from *www.bloomberg.com/apps/news?pid=20670001&refe r=&sid=aFkdVbffn19k* (accessed October 30, 2008).

Sirel, Colonel Indrek. Interview by author, Carlisle Barracks, PA, U.S. Army War College, November 6, 2008.

Smith, Alastair. "Alliance Formation and War." *International Studies Quarterly*, Vol. 39, 1995.

Smith, Craig S. "Threats and Responses: Brussels; Chirac Scolding Angers Nations that Back U.S." *New York Times*, February 19, 2003. Available from *query.nytimes.com* (accessed November 7, 2008).

Smith, R. P. "Models of Military Expenditure," *Journal of Applied Econometrics*, Vol. 4, No. 4, 1989.

Snidal, Duncan. "Rational choice and International Relations," In *Handbook of International Relations*, edited by W. Carlnaes, B. Simmons, and T. Risse, New York: Sage Publishing, 2002.

Snyder, Glenn H. "The Security Dilemma in Alliance Politics." *World Politics*, Vol. 36, No. 1, 1984.

Soroka, Stuart, and Christopher Wlezien. "Opinion-Policy Dynamics: Public Preferences and Public Expenditure in the UK." *British Journal of Political Science*, Vol. 35, 2005.

Stabilization Force (SFOR). "History of the NATO-led Stabilisation Force (SFOR) in Bosnia and Herzegovina." NATO, undated. Available from *www.nato.int/sfor/docu/d981116a.htm* (accessed July 5, 2008).

Sullivan, Vice Admiral William D., Military Representative of the U.S. to NATO. Interview by author, February 1, 2008, Brussels, Belgium.

"Suspend NATO Membership," *Budapest Sun Online*, January 21, 2007. Available from *www.budapestsun.com/cikk.php?id=55* (accessed on March 28, 2008).

Svoboda, Cyril (Minister of Foreign Affairs). "Report on the Foreign Policy of the Czech Republic 2005." Available from *www.mzv.cz/wwwo/mzv/default.asp?ido=19275&idj=2&amb=1&ikony=&trid=1&prsl=&poccl* (accessed April 2, 2008).

Szefs, Slawek. "Poles Not Pleased with Decision to Send 1,000 Troops to Afghanistan." *Network Europe*, September 22, 2006. Available from *networkeurope.radio.cz/feature/poles-not-pleased-with-decion-to-send-1000-troops-to-afghanistan* (accessed on April 2, 2008).

Tak, Lieutenant Colonel Nicolaas (Netherlands Army). Based on interviews conducted January 11 2008 at Carlisle Barracks, PA, U.S. Army War College,.

Talent, Senator Jim. "New Wine in Old Bottles: Moving Towards a Post Cold War Policy." *Forward!* (The Heritage Foundation, November 28, 2007). Available from *www.heritage.org/press/commentary/112807a.cfm* (accessed on December 31, 2008).

Thies, Wallace J., *Friendly Rivals: Bargaining and Burden-Shifting in NATO.* Armonk, NY: M. E. Sharpe, Inc., 2003.

_____. *Why NATO Endures.* Washington DC: Catholic University of America, 2009.

"Transatlantic Public Opinion Survey Shows Support for NATO Rising," *NATO News,* September 11, 2008. Available from *www.nato.int/docu/update/2008/09-september/e0911c.html* (accessed September 21, 2008).

Tyson, Ann Scott and Josh White. "Gates Hits NATO Allies' Role in Afghanistan." *Washington Post.com,* February 7, 2008. Available from *www.washingtonpost.com/wp-dyn/content/article/2008/02/06/AR2008020604690.html* (accessed on February 13, 2008).

Ujfalusi, Brigadier General Csaba (Hungarian National Military Representative). Based on interviews conducted January 28, 2008, at SHAPE Headquarters, Mons, Belgium.

United Nations, *United Nations Security Council Resolution 1776 (2007)*. New York: NATO, September 19, 2007. Available from *www.nato.int/isaf/topics/mandate/unscr/resolution_1776.pdf* (accessed October 22, 2008).

_____. *United Nations Security Council Resolution 1833 (2008)*. New York: NATO, September 22, 2008. Available from *www.nato.int/isaf/topics/mandate/unscr/resolution_1833.pdf* (accessed October 22, 2008).

U.S. Department of State. "Military Assistance." undated. Available from *www.state.gov/documents/organization/17783.pdf* (accessed November 21, 2006).

U.S. Department of State, Bureau of European and Eurasian Affairs. "Background Note: Czech Republic." Available from *www.state.gov/r/pa/ei/bgn/3237.htm* (accessed April 2, 2008).

_____. "Foreign Operations Appropriated Assistance: Estonia." Fact sheet, April 28, 2008 Available from *www.state. gov/p/eur/rls/fs/104123.htm* (accessed November 5, 2008).

_____. "Foreign Operations Appropriated Assistance: Estonia," Fact sheet, April 28, 2008. Available from *www.state. gov/p/eur/rls/fs/104123.htm* (accessed November 5, 2008).

_____. "U.S. Government Assistance to and Cooperative Activities with Central and Eastern Europe." January 2007. Available from *www.state.gov/p/eur/rls/rpt/92682.htm* (accessed November 11, 2007).

_____. "U.S. Government Assistance to Eastern Europe under the Support of East European Democracy (SEED) Act." January 2006. Available from *www.state.gov/p/eur/rls/rpt/ c17488.htm*.

U.S. Department of State, Office of the Spokesman. "U.S. Response to Pakistan's Earthquake Disaster." November 9, 2005.

Available from *www.state.gov/r/pa/prs/ps/2005/56703.htm* (accessed September 21, 2008).

Velinger, Jan. "Czech Government to Send Troops to Counter Al-Qaeda in Afghanistan." *Radio Prague,* January 15, 2004. Available from *www.radio.cz/en/article/49458* (accessed November 12, 2008).

Wallander, Celeste A. "NATO's Price." *Foreign Affairs,* Vol. 81, No. 6, 2002.

Walt, Stephen M. "Alliance Formation and the Balance of World Power." *International Security,* Vol. 9, No. 4 (1985).

Weinrod, W. Bruce (Secretary of Defense Representative, U.S. Mission to NATO). Interviewed by author, January 31, 2008. NATO Headquarters, Brussels, Belgium.

Wendt, Alexander. *Social Theory of International Politics.* Cambridge, UK: Cambridge University Press, 1999.

Werkhäuser, Nina "Ten Years On, Germany Looks Back at Return to War in Kosovo," *Deutsche Welte,* March 24 2009. Available from *www.dw-world.de/dw/* (accessed March 24, 2009).

Williams,Cindy. "From Conscripts to Volunteers: NATO's Transitions to All-Volunteer Forces," *Naval War College Review,* 2005.

Williams, Michael J., Dr., *NATO, Security, and Risk Management: from Kosovo to Kandahar.* New York: Routledge, 2009.

Wlezien, Christopher. "Dynamics of Representation: The Case of U.S. Spending on Defense." *British Journal of Political Science,* Vol. 26, 1996.

Wojciechowski, Colonel Slawomir. Based on interviews conducted December 11, 2007, Carlisle Barracks, PA, U.S. Army War College.

Zaryn, Bogdan. "New Defense Minister Promises to Pull Out Polish Troops from Iraq in 2008." *Polish Radio*, November 19, 2007. Available from *www.polskieradio.pl/ zagranica/news/print.aspx?id=69776* (accessed November 20, 2007).